D1393949

PROCEEDINGS OF THE BATTLE CONFERENCE ON ANGLO-NORMAN STUDIES
II · 1979

Edited by R. Allen Brown

THE BOYDELL PRESS

SHL
WITHDRAWN
LONDIN.
UNIV.

© by contributors 1979, 1980

First published 1980 by The Boydell Press, an imprint of Boydell &
Brewer Ltd, PO Box 9, Woodbridge, Suffolk IP12 3DF

British Library Cataloguing in Publication Data

Battle Conference on Anglo-Norman Studies, *2nd, 1979*
Proceedings of the Battle Conference on Anglo-Norman Studies, 2, 1979.
1. Great Britain—History—Norman period, 1066–1154—Congresses
2. Great Britain—History—Angevin period, 1154–1216—Congresses
I. Brown, Reginald Allen
942.02   DA195

ISBN 0–85115–126–4

The cover illustration is from BL MS Cotton Domitian AII f. 21, and is
reproduced by kind permission of the Trustees of the British Library

Printed by St. Edmundsbury Press Bury St. Edmunds, Suffolk.

PROCEEDINGS OF THE BATTLE CONFERENCE ON ANGLO-NORMAN STUDIES

II · 1979

Preface

The second Battle Conference in Anglo-Norman Studies took place between 20 and 25 July 1979. Like its predecessor, it was centred upon Pyke House whose hospitality (and that of the neighbouring 'Chequers') makes no small contribution to the success of a now established annual event. This second volume of our *Proceedings* contains the papers then read, with the exception of the communication of Ifor W. Rowlands, MA, which has to be held over until next year. The volume also contains a record of the formal discussion which was held, in one of our working sessions, upon the *Carmen de Hastingae Proelio*. A summary of Professor R. H. C. Davis's opening remarks and of the subsequent discussion is printed from the tape recordings taken, while Professor L. J. Engels's formal paper following Professor Davis's opening is printed in full, substantially as delivered, and in the position which it occupied within the whole discussion.

Our thanks are due to the East Sussex County Council as the sponsors of the Conference, and especially to Mrs Gillian Murton and Mr David Thornton who carry most of the burden of its organization; to the Warden and staff of Pyke House; and to the British Academy for a generous grant towards the expenses of distinguished speakers from overseas. They are also due to the Headmistress of Battle Abbey School, who kindly made available for our opening reception the splendidly appropriate Abbot's Hall, and the rest of the abbey buildings for a visit by the conference upon another day; to Mr Jonathan Coad who conducted that visit and Dr Richard Gem our excursion to Rochester and West Malling; and also to Dr John Hare who showed us over the excavations then current at Battle Abbey. As in the previous year, a visit was also made to the battlefield, chiefly conducted by Mr Ian Peirce and after an introduction by Nicholas Hooper, MA, and David Cook, MA. I, especially, am particularly indebted to Mr Richard Barber of the Boydell Press for his labours, greater than mine, in seeing this volume through the press.

Thelnetham, Suffolk. 24 December, 1979   R.A.B.

Contents

Abbreviations

ASC	*Anglo-Saxon Chronicle*
BIHR	*Bulletin of the Institute of Historical Research*
BL	British Library
BN	Bibliothèque Nationale
BT	*The Bayeux Tapestry* ed. F. M. Stenton, 2nd ed. London 1965.
Carmen	*The Carmen de Hastingae Proelio of Guy bishop of Amiens* ed. Catherine Morton and Hope Muntz, Oxford Medieval Texts, Oxford 1972.
De gestis regum	William of Malmesbury, *De gestis regum Anglorum libri quinque*, ed. W. Stubbs, RS 1887.
Domesday Book	*Domesday Book, seu liber censualis . . .* , ed. A. Farley, 2 vols, Record Comm., 1783.
Eadmer	*Historia novorum in Anglia* ed. M. Rule, RS, 1884.
EHD	*English Historical Documents* i ed. & tr. D. Whitelock, London 1955; ii ed. & tr. D. C. Douglas, London 1953.
EHR	*English Historical Review*
Gesta Guillelmi	Guillaume de Poitiers, *Gesta Guillelmi . . .* , ed. R. Foreville, Paris 1952.
Historia Novella	William of Malmesbury, *Historia Novella,* ed. K. R. Potter, Nelson's Medieval Texts, Edinburgh 1955.
Hollister	C. W. Hollister, *Anglo-Saxon military institutions on the eve of the Conquest*, Oxford 1962.
Huntingdon	Henry of Huntingdon, *Historia Anglorum*, ed. T. Arnold, RS 1879.
Jumièges	Guillaume de Jumièges, *Gesta Normannorum ducum*, ed. J. Marx, Société de l'histoire de Normandie, 1914.
MGH	*Monumenta Germaniae Historica*, Scriptores
ns	New Series
Orderic	Ordericus Vitalis, *Historia ecclesiastica*, ed. M. Chibnall, Oxford Medieval Texts, Oxford 1969–.
RS	Rolls Series, London
ser.	series
Trans.	Transactions
TRHS	*Transactions of the Royal Historical Society*

VCH	Victoria County History
Vita Eadwardi	*The Life of Edward the Confessor*, ed. and tr. F. Barlow, Nelson's Medieval Texts, London 1962.
Wace	Wace, *Le Roman de Rou*, ed. A. J. Holden, 3 vols, Société des anciens textes français, Paris 1970–3.
Worcester	Florence of Worcester, *Chronicon ex Chronicis*, ed. B. Thorpe, English Historical Society, London 1848–9.

List of Illustrations

Some developments in military architecture c. 1200:
Le Coudray-Salbart

List of Figures

Some developments in military architecture c. 1200:
Le Coudray-Salbart

Bishop's Lynn: the first century of a new town?

The Carmen de Hastingae Proelio

1. Editor's Note

Shortly before the first Battle Conference in 1978, Professor R. H. C. Davis published his paper on the *Carmen de Hastingae Proelio* (*EHR*, xciii, April 1978, 241–61), with its conclusion that 'the *Carmen* is neither an original source nor the poem by Guy of Amiens which was used by Orderic Vitalis . . . it seems to have been composed as a literary exercise in one of the schools of northern France or southern Flanders between 1125 and 1135 or 1125 and 1140. As a literary curiosity it was worth the attention of an anthologist at Trier, but as a source for the history of the Norman Conquest it is simply ridiculous.' Since this is clean contrary to what had more or less become received opinion that the poem (recently and at last made available in a modern critical edition by Catherine Morton and Hope Muntz, *The Carmen de Hastingae Proelio of Guy Bishop of Amiens*, Oxford Medieval Texts 1972) is indeed that mentioned by Orderic as written by Guy and finished before 1068, it was obvious from private conversations at the Conference, and in informal discussion after papers read, that much interest and, indeed, excitement had been aroused among those present and in the world of Anglo-Norman studies at large. It therefore seemed appropriate and most desirable that this year, 1979, some more formal discussion should be arranged as a part of our proceedings. R. H. C. Davis, while for obvious reasons not wishing to read a full paper so soon after the publication of his *EHR* article, readily agreed to open such a discussion, and Professor L. J. Engels very kindly accepted an invitation to follow with a communication setting out his views and his reactions to Professor Davis's original article. Amongst other scholars directly concerned with the *Carmen*, Catherine Morton and Hope Muntz were unwilling to attend and Professor Frank Barlow was unable to attend, but the presence in particular, amongst a distinguished gathering of Anglo-Norman historians all deeply interested, of Professor Raymonde Foreville (the editor of William of Poitiers) and Dr Marjorie Chibnall (the editor of Ordericus Vitalis), ensured that a lively and enlightening debate would follow.

It was also decided at the Conference that an attempt should be made to print a record of the occasion in these Proceedings even though, with the exception of Professor Engels' communication, all the contributions made were informal in the sense of not being prepared and written papers. Accordingly tape recorders were set up, and the chairman-editor entrusted with the task of producing such a record. As it turned out, the tapes proved

1

most difficult to edit and even to interpret, but it is hoped that (with the aid of much consultation with those chiefly concerned, for which I thank them) what follows is indeed a faithful record. Again with the exception of Professor Engels' paper, which is printed in full below substantially as read, no attempt has been made, or was intended, to print a verbatim transcript of all that was said, but the various contributions to the discussion are edited and summarized in the order in which they occurred.

2. Professor R. H. C. Davis said that he had always found the *Carmen* implausible. He had appreciated, however, that if the manuscript in which it was found was really no later than 1100, the poem would have had to be composed very near to the time of the Norman Conquest. Consequently he had not questioned the attribution to Guy of Amiens seriously until he had examined the manuscript and found that it was later than had been supposed. Professor Engels had subsequently examined the manuscript thoroughly and had made further discoveries about it, but it was pleasant to learn that there was no real disagreement about the date of the quire containing the *Carmen*. It could not be as early as 1100; and though Professor Engels would prefer to place it in the first quarter of the twelfth century, he admitted that at the present state of research a date as late as 1150 could not be excluded.

In Professor Davis's view the basic question was one of historical criticism, how to ascertain whether a story which *seemed* implausible was really false or true. It was a common problem. In the years before 1939, for example, many people had been unwilling to believe the stories they heard about Nazi concentration camps. What had been needed to convince them was a demonstration that particular stories came from an impeccable source, and that they were confirmed by other sources which were independent. So also with the *Carmen*; it was necessary to show that the author was in a position to know the facts (which in practice might amount to proving that he was Guy, bishop of Amiens), and to find confirmation of his most striking stories in other sources.

Professor Davis did not wish to repeat what he had written about these stories in his article, but he pointed out that some critics, such as Barlow, accepted the early date and the attribution to Guy of Amiens, but nonetheless viewed some of the more important stories with scepticism, claiming that they were examples of poetic license. Professor Davis submitted that there was a limit to the license which any poet could exercise when writing about important contemporary events, especially when the poem was intended for people who played an important part in those events. This was particularly true of the story of the death of Harold. The killing of a king was a serious matter and could not lightly be attributed to people who had had nothing to do with it. No other source had the story found in the *Carmen*, and no other source pretended to know by whom King Harold had been killed, so it looked as if the story was untrue. If one wanted to claim it as true, it would have to be assumed that it had subsequently been censored and suppressed. But even if such suppression had been possible in England and Normandy, it was hard to see how Bishop Guy of Amiens, if he had been the author, could have been prevented from repeating the story at the court of the French king, who would have delighted in anything which discomfited the Normans.

Professor Davis accepted that poets and literateurs had always used a good deal of convention to put their narratives into 'proper form', but he submitted that the sort of 'poetic license' found in the *Carmen* went beyond the bounds of convention, and could not have been exercised until the events described were past history and the main participants dead and buried.

3. *Professor L. J. Engels* replied with a paper entitled 'Once more: the *Carmen de Hastingae Proelio*', which is next printed here as read with the addition of an initial survey of the research on the *Carmen* since its discovery, some further data illustrating his arguments, and notes.

ONCE MORE: THE *CARMEN DE HASTINGAE PROELIO*

Since Georg H. Pertz discovered in 1826 the so-called *Carmen de Hastingae proelio* (transmitted without title), the poem has confronted scholars with a still controversial and sometimes hotly debated question which embraces two distinct problems, one regarding authorship and date (the author's name being merely indicated by an initial in the second part of v. 2: *L W salutat*) and the other concerning the value of the *Carmen* as a historical source (in v. 555, for instance, we are told that the Conqueror himself slew 2000 men). Naturally these two problems are closely tied up with each other, and in the discussion on the *Carmen* they often interlock.

In the course of time two opposite views on the *Carmen* have crystallized. On the one hand, Pertz[1] already advanced the hypothesis that in v. 2 we should read *Lanfrancum Wido salutat* and that the *Carmen* is the poem in which, according to Orderic Vitalis,[2] Guy of Ponthieu (bishop of Amiens, † 1074 or 1075[3]) *Senlacium bellum descripsit* before escorting the Conqueror's wife on her journey to England where she was anointed as queen consort on 11 May 1068. Consequently, the *Carmen* would be our oldest source dealing with the Conquest, written by a man in a position to know the facts, although it is obvious that the information given is not always reliable. In the nineteenth and the first half of the twentieth century, Pertz's hypothesis was taken for granted, without any further proof, by a majority of scholars. On the other hand, there have been, from the outset, doubts about the attribution of the *Carmen* to Guy of Amiens, and after many years cautious reserve (as shown by

Henry Petrie,[4] before 1833, and Sir Thomas Duffus Hardy[5]) was followed by confident rejection. After questioning, in 1944, the reliability of the story of Taillefer (the *histrio* or *mimus* who, according to the *Carmen*, vv. 389 seqq., rode before the Norman army and struck the first blow) and having looked in vain for a person to be identified as the *Pontivi nobilis heres* (mentioned in v. 537), G. H. White[6] concluded, in 1950, from corresponding passages in both the *Carmen* and the *Gesta Guillelmi* of William of Poitiers (written c. 1077) that the author of the *Carmen* copied from the *Gesta Guillelmi* and that, consequently, the *Carmen* cannot be Guy's poem mentioned by Orderic Vitalis. Basing himself on the moment at which the Taillefer story emerges in other sources, White proposed to date the *Carmen* some 60 years after the Conquest, between 1125 and 1129, and to eliminate it from the list of original sources for the battle of Hastings.

Without querying the priority of the *Carmen* (White's paper was printed only in 1953), Raymonde Foreville[7] described William of Poitiers' technique of borrowing from the *Carmen* in her edition of the *Gesta Guillelmi* (1952). After that, however, the prevailing opinion on the *Carmen* was repeatedly subjected to critical reconsideration, and up to 1978 research, covering an ever increasing number and variety of aspects of the problem, has led to, roughly speaking, the same conclusion, though there are, of course, some nuances. Sten Körner,[8] Frank Barlow[9] and Kurt-Ulrich Jäschke[10] consider the attribution to Guy of Amiens as very likely but not conclusively proved, and they consider the *Carmen* as a historical source, although they do not accept almost every detail in the *Carmen* as reliable evidence. Catherine Morton and Hope Muntz[11] defend Guy's authorship as a case 'too strong to be rejected without clear proof to the contrary',[12] and they also argue for an unequalled importance of the *Carmen* as a historical source.

In 1944 White expressed some fear that his comments on Taillefer and the heir of Ponthieu would lead historians to 'hold that genealogists have unduly suspicious minds'.[13] He obviously could not have dreamt of what happened in 1978, when R. H. C. Davis[14] published a remarkable and persuasive article ending with the statement 'the *Carmen* is neither an original source nor the poem by Guy of Amiens', the suggestion 'it seems to have been composed as a literary exercise in one of the schools of northern France or southern Flanders between 1125 and 1135, or 1125 and 1140', and the verdict 'as a literary curiosity it was worth the attention of an anthologist at Trier, but as a source for the history of the Norman Conquest it is simply ridiculous'.[15]

In my Inaugural Lecture,[16] I dealt with the Latin poetry on William the Conqueror, including, of course, the *Carmen*, and I rejected White's view on the *Carmen*. Since even plain Dutch is less accessible for the international world of learning, I shall translate my opinion on the date and the authorship of the *Carmen* as summarized at the end of the lecture: 'Restored to its place of honour, the *Carmen* fits perfectly well into the sketch I have given of the evolution of the poetry on William the Conqueror. . . . There are a number of reasons that speak for an attribution to Guy of Amiens. . . . The counter-arguments advanced . . . are outweighed by the pleas for Guy. . . . Yet there remain queries . . . which prevent me from identifying with absolutely settled conviction Guy of Amiens as the author of the *Carmen* and from unfolding the idea, however seductive on this occasion,[17] that the poem was written about 21 February 1067, when the Conqueror, *adveniente quadragesima*, returned from England to Normandy'.

Professor Davis's article has not brought about a fundamental change in my opinion on the *Carmen*. Nevertheless, I appreciate his study very much indeed. It gives an almost complete survey of the objections that can be raised against the attribution of the *Carmen* to Guy of Amiens, and on several points of the issue Davis goes further into the matter than anybody did before, thus forcing us to reconsider very seriously our views on the *Carmen*. Furthermore, the article is very stimulating, for it induces one to give thought to some general problems concerning our sources. But, as far as I can see, the arguments put forward do not justify the confidence with which the identification of the *Carmen* with Guy's poem is rejected and its value as a historical source nullified. In order to make this clear I shall comment on some of Professor Davis's arguments. As both my competence and the space allotted to me are limited, I cannot be exhaustive; moreover, completeness would require a tedious listing of subjects discussed time and again.[18] I shall therefore concentrate on the main points and on the new arguments; for the moment the proposal for a later date of the *Carmen* will be passed over.

First, then, there admittedly is no conclusive proof for the identification of the *Carmen* with Guy's poem mentioned by Orderic Vitalis.[19] There are also some other names than *Lanfrancus* and *Wido* which fit both the initials and the hexameter, and Guy of Amiens is not even the only *Wido* one could put on the stage (as a matter of fact, two other *Widones* can be found in the entourage of Lanfranc[20]). But very much indeed speaks for Guy of Amiens, whose provenance and circumstances in life fit in with certain characteristics of the *Carmen*, and for Lanfranc, who was anything but just an ecclesiastic[21] and who, according to Sigebert of Gembloux, himself wrote *laudes, triumphos et res gestas Guillelmi Northmannorum comitis*.[22] The new objections raised by Professor Davis are far from convincing. As for the spelling of Guy's name with *W-* and not *Gu-*, it is very much open to question whether (as Professor Davis alleges) in the eleventh century *Guido* is more usual than *Wido*; anyhow, in 1867 Corblet[23] published an eleventh-century inscription in which, as the facsimile clearly shows, we find *Wido praesul Ambianensium* spelt with *W-*. A *salutatio* (perhaps we should not call it a dedication) to Lanfranc can be queried in some respects, but is, I think, less difficult to understand, if one bears in mind that Dudo of Saint-Quentin presented his *De moribus et actis primorum Normanniae ducum*, written at the request of Richard I and

Richard II, to Bishop Adalbero of Laon,[24] and that Hugh of Fleury sent the *Ecclesiastical History* he wrote for Adela of Blois also to Ivo of Chartres.[25]

The arguments for the assertion that the facts told by Orderic Vitalis about Guy's poem are not in the *Carmen* and for the suggestion that there might have been two poems about the Conquest—one of them (Guy's) known to Orderic and the other (the *Carmen*) to us—do not hold. In the words *In clero qui ad diuina ei* (sc. *Mathildi transfretanti*, in 1068) *ministrabat: celebris Guido Ambianorum praesul eminebat, qui iam certamen Heraldi et Guillelmi uersifice ediderat* (*Hist. eccl.* 4.9: ed. Chibnall II, p. 214), I cannot find any clue for the assumption that they have been taken from the prologue or dedication of Guy's poem. Only by overstraining the interpretation can one derive from this sentence that Guy's poem was dedicated to the queen. The same goes for the toponym *Senlac* which, like a dedication to Mathilda, does not appear in the *Carmen* but might be, according to Professor Davis, the one detail Orderic took from the poem of Guy. A passage in which Orderic claims *expressis verbis* that he used the poem of Guy of Amiens cannot be found in the *Historia Ecclesiastica*. Moreover, a source mentioned by Orderic is not necessarily used by him (as is, for instance, the case with Fulcher of Chartres[26]), and possibly Orderic is even unlikely to use a poem as a historical source— anyhow, I could not find a single example. As to *Senlac(ius)*, which is, moreover, by no means the only fact in Orderic that cannot be traced to any authority we know,[27] it seems rather arbitrary to assume that Orderic borrowed precisely this toponym from Guy of Amiens. It occurs fairly often in the *Historia* (*Senlac* four times at least; *Senlacius* eight times, always with *bellum*, five times, *certamen*, twice, or *proelium*, once[28]). The use of *Senlacium bellum* in only one of the two statements of Orderic on Guy of Amiens seems as insignificant as the fact that *certamen Senlacium* is found in a reference to William of Jumièges,[29] from whose *Gesta Normannorum ducum Senlac(ius)* is absent, as it is from the *Carmen*.

Next comes the relationship between the *Carmen* and the *Gesta Guillelmi* of William of Poitiers,[30] perhaps the most vexing point at issue. This problem has been tackled on two distinct levels, On the one side that of the similarities in the contents of both works, and on the other that of the resemblances in their wording.

As to the first, Frank Barlow especially has made a very careful and cautious comparison of the two stories (and not only of the flattery they contain) and he has shown by flawless reasoning that very probably the *Carmen* was a source for the *Gesta Guillelmi*.[31] In my lecture I drew attention to a phenomenon which confirms Barlow's conclusion: there is a sort of dialogue between the *Carmen* and the *Gesta Guillelmi*, perceptible in what seem to be reactions of William of Poitiers to passages in the *Carmen*. The story of Harold's death (vv. 531 seqq.) corresponds with the asseveration *Cum Heraldo, tali qualem poemata dicunt Hectorem vel Turnum, non minus auderet*

Guillelmus congredi singulari certamine, quam Achilles cum Hectore, vel Aeneas cum Turno (2, 22: ed. Foreville, p. 198). In the *Carmen* (vv. 571 seqq.) we are told that the Conqueror left the corpses of the English unburied, but William of Poitiers says: *Par fuisset Anglorum, qui sese per injuriam tantam pessundederunt in mortem, carnes gula vulturis lupique devorari, ossibus insepultis campos fore sepultos. Caeterum, illi (sc. Guillelmo) crudele visum est tale supplicium. Volentibus ad humandum eos colligere liberam concessit potestatem* (2, 26: p. 210). In the *Carmen* (v. 595) William the Conqueror assumes the title *rex* the day after the battle, immediately after the burial of Harold, and according to Jäschke[32] the poem thus gives evidence for a very important act in the Conqueror's strategy which moves in a straight line towards kingship. At the same point in the story there is in the *Gesta Guillelmi* the phrase *posset illico victor . . . imponere sibi diadema* (2, 26: p. 208), and later on the duke is even depicted as being anything but eager to be crowned as early as on Christmas Day (2, 28: p. 216–18). It is noteworthy that in all these passages William of Poitiers uses the subjunctive; thus his words read as if, whilst praising the Conqueror's deeds, he is denying the reality of what another source tells.

Professor Davis's argument against Barlow's conclusion consists in the suggestion that the author of the *Carmen* 'if he was writing after the Conqueror's death . . . might well have thought it both safe and desirable to tone down the flattery which William of Poitiers had provided in such copious supply',[33] but an example of such a specific situation is not given, and in literary history I have not found any clue for it: after 1087 poets continued praising the Conqueror to the skies, and after 1114 Hugh of Fleury wrote in the prologue of his *Modernorum regum Francorum actus* (Migne, PL 163, c. 873C): *Nullus rex nostrorum temporum hoc Guillelmo fuit felicior ac moderatior. Eius magnanimitatem et magnificentiam nemo laudare sufficit, quibus ille usque ad terminos terrae super omnes aevi nostri reges ac principes apparuit gloriosus. Pauci posthac reges, sicut reor, illum imitabuntur. . . .* Anyhow, the supposition that after 1087 the admiration for the Conqueror might have diminished for some reason in certain circles is not the only point in the argumentation that needs further proof. When arguing that the *Carmen* was composed long after the death of the Conqueror, one should also offer a plausible explanation for facts suggesting that the *Carmen* was written shortly after the events described and when the Conqueror was alive, for instance, the poet's intention of recording for posterity (v. 22), his addressing William as a living person (vv. 26 seqq.) and the remarkable, if from a literary point of view anything but successful,[34] form of the first part of the story (up to v. 148 at least) which is phrased as an address to the Conqueror.

As to the verbal similarities between the *Carmen* and the *Gesta Guillelmi*, in my lecture I advanced some linguistic evidence for the priority of the *Carmen* by showing that words which both texts have in common in obviously related passages fit better into the whole of the vocabulary of the *Carmen* than into that of the *Gesta Guillelmi*. I shall give three examples. In the story of Harold's mother offering to ransom her son's corpse for its weight in gold, both texts contain the word *corpus*:

> Si placet, aut corpus puro praeponderet auro (v. 581)
> matri pro corpore . . . auri par pondus offerenti (2, 25: p. 204).

Elsewhere in the *Gesta Guillelmi* we find *interemptus, mortuus* (each three times), *peremptus, ossa, cadaver* and *carnes* (each once),[35] whereas *corpus* is used only once to indicate the bones of a saint (1, 6: p. 160). In the *Carmen*, however, *corpus* is the most frequent term: apart from vv. 138 (parallel with *Gesta Guillelmi* 1, 6) and 581, it is found no less than ten times.[36] In the passages describing how Duke William tries to stop his fleeing men, the word *hasta* occurs:

> Dux, ubi perspexit quod gens sua uicta recedit,
> Occurrens illi, signa ferendo manu,
> Increpat et cedit; retinet, constringit et hasta.
> Iratus galea nudat et ipse caput.
> Vultum Normannis dat, uerba precantia Gallis
> Dixit: 'Quo fugitis? Quo iuuat ire mori? (vv. 445 seqq.)

> Princeps namque prospiciens . . . fugientibus occurrit et obstitit, verberans aut minans hasta. Nudato insuper capite detractaque galea exclamans: 'Me, inquit, circumspicite . . .' (2, 18: p. 190)

In the *Gesta Guillelmi* this is the first occurrence of *hasta* (in the preceding part of the *Gesta* William of Poitiers uses *lancea*),[37] but in the *Carmen hasta* is found twice before,[38] and in one of these passages it is used in a very similar way (*Et faciles hasta conglomerare facit*, v. 310). Thirdly, I call attention to the words for 'sea'. In both texts *mare* is the usual word.[39] For the rest the authors show distinct preferences. The *Gesta Guillelmi* has *pontus* three times, which does not occur in the *Carmen*, and the *Carmen* stands alone in using *aequor* (five times) and *fretum* (twice).[40] In addition to these words we find *pelagus*. In the *Carmen* it appears four times, and it seems part of the poet's *copia verborum* allowing of *variatio* (in v. 79 after *aequor* in vv. 69 and 72, in v. 101 before *aequor* in v. 103, in v. 117 after *mare* in v. 113). But in the *Gesta Guillelmi pelagus* occurs only twice, and in both passages its use seems suggested by a model or a source. In 2, 7: p. 164 it is found in a chapter which shows the influence of Virgil's *Aeneid*, and in 2, 25: p. 204 it appears in a passage clearly parallel with the *Carmen* (in which, as we have seen, *pelagus* is a common term):

Dictum est illudendo, oportere situm esse custodem littoris et pelagi, quae cum armis ante vesanus insedit.

> Per mandata ducis rex hic Heralde quiescis,
>   Vt custos maneas littoris et pelagi (vv. 591 seqq.)

A student of medieval Latin literature is perhaps not optimally qualified for joining in a discussion on the information given in the *Carmen* which is questioned as more or less implausible. I shall not, therefore, comment on Taillefer, Stigand, the *Siculi*, the death of Harold, the list of people mentioned in eleventh-century sources and so on.[41] But I really must dwell upon some general problems at issue in the discussion on each of these details.

There are gaps in our information. All sorts of sources taken together, we have no full account of what happened in 1066. Moreover, the narrative sources often diverge, even those coming from the same (mostly the Norman) side. Thus historians are left with controversy and doubt. In such a situation, the appraisal of a source's value is both extremely important and terribly difficult, and, as the discussion on the *Carmen* shows, special difficulties may arise from the literary character of a source.

The *Carmen* is a work of literary art. There is, of course, some disagreement on its literary value too,[42] but this does not alter the fact that its author was subject to certain literary conventions which, even if (or in so far as) the poem was intended as an account of the events of 1066, have left their mark on the presentation and the form of his story as well as on the measure of respect paid to truth and reality. The historian, when looking for factual information in a literary text, should interrogate his source with an appreciation of its specific character which conditions its range of possibilities as a source. As for the *Carmen*, one cannot reasonably hope to find a historical fact in every element of a poem. Apart from the medieval concept of truth, the margin for fiction is, in the Middle Ages and before, much larger in poetry than in prose[43] (as one should also bear in mind when comparing the *Carmen* and the *Gesta Guillelmi*). William of Poitiers for instance tells us that poets, unlike historiographers, may invent battles to be fought with the pen, and amplify roaming the fields of fiction: *parturire suo pectore bella quae calamo ederentur, poetis licebat, atque amplificare utcumque cognita per campos figmentorum divagando. Nos ducem sive regem ... pure laudabimus; nusquam a veritatis limite passu uno delirantes* (1, 20: p. 44)—words which sound somewhat regretful, and perhaps William is alluding to what poets have already done in the case of the Conquest. To give one example taken from the *Carmen*: as far as I know, no historian has taken for *literatim* true what we are told about Harold killing Tostig with his own hands at Stamford Bridge (vv. 129 seqq.). And rightly so, for it might well be poetic invention providing the author with a self-evident reason for decrying Harold as a Cain (v. 137). Thus I come to a first point: the argument that contemporary poets will refrain from fiction because their readers are able to check the story, and that therefore all that is implausible in a poem suggests that it was not written shortly after the events dealt with, is in my opinion not cogent. The poet who describes Charlemagne as the *summus in orbe sophista* who eclipses all masters in the liberal arts, Cicero and Homer included (*Karolus Magnus et Leo papa*, vv. 67 seqq.[44]), wrote in 799, whereas Einhart's more reliable appraisal of Charlemagne's learning dates from c. 830/836 (*Vita Karoli* 25). In short, literary invention and fiction cannot be a conclusive argument for dating a poem to a rather long distance from the events described, and, as far as poetic art is concerned, the description of the siege of London (*Carmen* vv. 673 seqq. and 697 seqq.) is neither an argument against an early date nor an argument for a late date of the *Carmen*.

Next, poetry has its literary technique and convention. When the author of the *Carmen* uses the ship metaphor (vv. 5 seqq.) or when he gives his reasons for *Normannica bella reponi* (vv. 15 seqq.), he is possibly just taking themes from the stock of commonplaces for the preface.[45] Likewise, the invocations (of Mars when the battle is about to start, vv. 345 seqq., and of God when fierce fighting is described, vv. 495 seqq.) belong to the technique of the *apostrophe*,[46] and there is no question of a carefully calculated use of a rhetorical device in order to conceal a failure of the Conqueror or a critical situation for the Normans (as Morton and Muntz argue[47]). We are not justified in taking all details in the *Carmen* to be inspired by historiographical (in this context including propagandistic) motives.

On the other hand, if an author dealing with historical events shows a command of poetic engineering by inserting speeches, fighting scenes, a learned description of jewels, comparisons and so on, this is not a compelling reason for concluding that he has little or even no knowledge of the facts. The presence of literary contrivances—which, I observe in passing, are not only found in the twelfth century—does not prove the absence of factual knowledge. Literary expertise and factual knowledge are compatible with each other, and it is quite possible that this is the case with our poet. It is, for instance, beyond doubt that the *Carmen* (vv. 537 seqq.) mentions Hugh, heir of Ponthieu (this was noticed as early as in the *editio princeps* by Petrie, but it was forgotten, perhaps as a result of indirect consultation of the source[48]). Now, the name Hugh appears regularly in the house of Ponthieu,[49] and Morton and Muntz drew attention to a charter dated 1084 and subscribed by a Hugh, Count of Ponthieu who seems to be otherwise unknown.[50] Even if one is not inclined to accept the *Carmen*'s version of Harold's death (vv. 531 seqq.), there is, as far as I can see, no reason for ignoring (as Professor Davis does) that the *Carmen* and the charter confirm each other's evidence for the existence of a hitherto unknown Hugh of Ponthieu.

I am aware that I am defending generally accepted principles which, for lack of tools, cannot always be put into practice in such a way that doubt and controversy are completely excluded. There is, indeed, no infallible instrument for separating mere artistry from reliable historiography in a literary text. This, however, is not an excuse for losing sight of the principles. Moreover, we should try to avoid a situation in which students of literature deal with the *Carmen* as if there were no doubts about its historical value, and in which historians reduce their problems at the cost of misunderstanding the implications of the poem's literary character. Historical and literary scholarship should join forces in order to avert the imminent danger of one-sided conceptions which are mutually found unacceptable.

Finally, there is the question of the date of the manuscript in which the text of the *Carmen* so far as we know it is preserved, ms. Brussels Bibliothèque Royale 10615–729 (henceforward ms. A), and of the conclusions to be drawn from that terminus ad quem with regard to the date of the *Carmen*.[51] Professor Davis makes an extremely good point when he questions the opinion (held, among others, by Barlow and Morton and Muntz) that ms. A was written c. 1100 and that it provides us with evidence for dating the composition of the *Carmen* to some decades before 1100. He rightly confronts the results of a palaeographical analysis leading to c. 1100[52] with the findings of scholars who have studied the provenance of a group of manuscripts to which ms. A belongs (together with ms. B, Brussels Bibliothèque Royale 9799–809, which contains only the first 66 lines of the *Carmen*). From data of various kinds (handwriting, general style, contents, marginal notes and so on) Horst Schlechte (1934) and Karl Manitius (1955)[53] have concluded that ms. A was written at St Eucharius-Matthias in Trier about the middle or even at the end of the twelfth century. But even a rather cursory look at the problem makes it clear that the manuscript has not yet been studied with the thoroughness appropriate to its complicated character, and that the date of ms. A seems to remain open to question. Besides, I must level some criticism against a few details in the argument built up in this section of Professor Davis's article.

Ms. A is a very valuable codex, because it contains a vast amount of miscellaneous texts, and it is for a considerable proportion of these our only or at least an outstanding witness. Nevertheless, there is no adequate description of the manuscript available in print, despite the fact that it has been dealt with in numerous publications. Editors of texts contained in ms. A concentrate on parts of the manuscript, and at best they offer a superficial description of the whole codex. On the other hand, scholars who have studied the provenance of ms. A have confined themselves to the general characteristics and to details relevant to their object of inquiry. The catalogues give neither a full account of the contents of the manuscript nor a reliable survey of its codicological peculiarities. Moreover, when going through this immense mass of literature one is harassed by contradictions, obscurities and errors, and I am sorry to say that (even with regard to the quire containing the *Carmen*) this is also the case with recent publications on our poem. As I have not yet been able to find the opportunity to study the manuscript thoroughly *in situ*, I have made provisional descriptions of mss. A and B in which important and sufficiently documented data have been put together for the moment (see Appendix). In what follows here, I restrict myself to a few remarks justified at this stage and relevant to the discussion on the *Carmen*.

A first question of consequence is whether ms. A is one coherent unit or not. As to ms. B, it is almost self-evident from the different dates of the hands and from the differences in lay-out that the codex is composed of three parts (the *codicilli* indicated by Roman numerals) which were bound together at a later stage of their existence. On the other hand, ms. A has up to now been considered as a single unit.

The manuscript contains a hotchpotch of texts: classical poetry, patristic texts, works dealing with the liberal arts, but also with geography and land surveying, hagiography and hymns, satirical and moralizing poems, epigrams and aenigmata, poetry on medieval topics (for instance, the Investiture Controversy and the First Crusade) and so on. In the first few *codicilli* prose dominates, but from V onwards poetry prevails and after XII prose is found only incidentally. The criterion for the selection of the texts is for the volume as a whole anything but transparent, whereas most *codicilli*, taken by themselves, form units or at least sufficiently coherent collections.

The variety of quire signatures suggests that not all the *codicilli* were intended to be combined into one single manuscript. Furthermore, there are obvious mutilations and errors of binding. The marginal note on fol. 73v (*hic aliquid desideratur*), written by a hand later than the twelfth century, is an indication that possibly V is incomplete; anyhow, it apparently provoked the binding of some loose folia or bifolia after V. Of these fol. 74 belongs after fol. 65 (thus confirming that IV is mutilated), fols. 75–76 are related to XI (a *codicillus* composed of two regular quaternions and three leaves glued together), and fols. 77–78 belong to X. Perhaps ms. B gives a clue for one more gap in A. In the second part of ms. B all texts but one have been copied from ms. A (but from three different *codicilli*, a fact which is illustrative for the manner of selecting from an older manuscript). Given the fact that several parts of the present ms. A are damaged, I have a strong feeling that the only text in B II which at the moment is not found in A (parts of the *Epigrams* of Martialis, B ff. 125r–129v) also comes from A, where it afterwards got lost.

These provisional findings provide, I think, a sufficiently solid base for the conclusion that codex A is in its present state not so much the result of a deliberate process of manuscript production as the outcome of certain unforeseen circumstances. Consequently, the problem of its date has to be reconsidered, and this will require further study. Perhaps it will turn out that all *codicilli* date from roughly the same period, but for the time being this is as open to question as the moment at which, and the reason why, these were put together.

As to the *Carmen*, one can of course attempt to establish a terminus ad quem for its composition by ascertaining the terminus post quem for the copying of the texts it is associated with. In that case one should concentrate on *codicillus* XVII, which contains the *Carmen* and was written by one single scribe. Apart from the fragments of the *Noctes Atticae* of Gellius, this part of ms. A contains only one text which can be dated independently from the manuscript, namely the *Satira in Mettenses* (the *Novus Avianus* of the poet from Asti has been dated on stylistic grounds; but before doing so, Hervieux wrote as follows: 'Quant à l'époque à laquelle l'auteur vécut, nous n'avons pour nous fixer que l'âge du manuscrit'[54]). According to internal evidence the *Satira in Mettenses* was composed between 1097 and 1103 in the neighbourhood of Trier, so that it seems reasonable to suppose that it was available for copying in St Eucharius-Matthias in the first quarter of the twelfth century. But this does not prove that the text on fols. 224–31 was actually written at that time.

Moreover, supposing that our text of the *Carmen* was copied c. 1125, or even about the middle or at the end of the twelfth century, what would this prove for the date of its composition? Professor Davis understandably has focused on the more recent works in ms. A, but I wish to stress the fact that, as ms. A clearly shows, texts dating from very different periods can be associated with each other in a codex and even in one single gathering.

A final word about the time elapsing between the composition of the *Carmen* and its inclusion in ms. A. Possibly we must reconsider the opinion advanced by Morton and Muntz and accepted by for instance Davis and Jäschke that the text of ms. A has been copied from a codex in which the *Carmen* was contained together with an already dislocated *Novus Avianus* and the *Satira in Mettenses*.[55] It is not implausible that, as Hervieux already supposed,[56] the scribe of A XVII himself (who skipped more than one verse in the *Carmen*[57]) jumped over 140 lines of the Novus Avianus (one page or one leaf) and corrected this omission afterwards. If this is what happened, we can dispose of one link in the chain of transmission as reconstructed up to now. Furthermore, Morton and Muntz seem to be right in assuming that most errors in the text of the *Carmen* as given in ms. A have been introduced by the scribe of A himself,[58] and although it is conceivable that they have underrated the number of corruptions in the text,[59] the nature of these corruptions seems to allow of the supposition that there have been only a few phases in the transmission of the text. All that, however, does not give us the certainty that the text in ms. A was written shortly after the composition of the *Carmen*. If

the phases in the transmission of the text have been few in number, they did
not necessarily take a short time.

L. J. ENGELS

APPENDIX: PROVISIONAL DESCRIPTIONS
OF THE MANUSCRIPTS

Select Bibliography: F. J. F. Marchal, *Catalogue des manuscrits de la Bibliothèque Royale des Ducs de Bourgogne*, I: *Inventaire*, Bruxelles 1839, nos. 10615–729 and 9799–809; Baron de Reiffenberg, 'Manuscrit de Kues', *Annuaire de la Bibliothèque Royale de Belgique* 4, 1843, 51–79 (ms. A); L. Traube, *MGH, Poet.* III (edition of Sedulius Scottus), Berolini 1896, 152 sq.; id., 'Zu Notkers Rhetorik und der Ecbasis Captivi', *Zeitschrift für deutsches Altertum* 32, 1888, 388 seq.; L. Hervieux, *Les fabulistes latins*, III, Paris 1894, 194–205; J. van den Gheyn, *Catalogue des manuscrits de la Bibliothèque Royale de Belgique*, II, Bruxelles 1902, no. 1327 (ms. B); M. Manitius, 'Zur poetischen Literatur aus Bruxell. 10615–729', *Neues Archiv* 39, 1914, 155–75; R. Ehwald, *MGH, Auct. Ant.* XV (edition of Aldhelm), Berolini 1919, 44 seq.; H. Schlechte, *Erzbischof Bruno von Trier. Ein Beitrag zur Geschichte der geistigen Strömungen im Investiturstreit*, Leipzig 1934, 71–8 (ms. A); K. Strecker, *Ecbasis cuiusdam captivi per tropologiam*, Hannoverae 1935, viii seq.; K. Manitius, 'Eine Gruppe von Handschriften des 12. Jahrhunderts aus dem Trierer Kloster St. Eucharius-Matthias', *Forschungen und Fortschritte* 29, 1955, 317–19; L. M. de Rijk, 'On the Curriculum of the Arts of the Trivium at St. Gall from c. 850–c. 1000', *Vivarium* 1, 1963, 35–86 (64–81: An analysis of the Brussels MS. 10.615–10.729, fols. 58r–65v and 74r + v); R. Düchting, *Sedulius Scottus. Seine Dichtungen*, München 1968, 15–21 (Verzeichnis von fol. 214–223v des cod. Bruxell. 10615–729); J. and M. Götte, *Virgil, Landleben*, München 1970, 542–6 (ms. A).

A. Bruxelles, Bibliothèque Royale, ms. 10615–729 (olim Bolland. 120a), s. XII, St Eucharius-Matthias, Trier.
Vellum, 233 ff. (the foliation suggests 231 ff., but the numerals 51 and 213 have been used twice), c. 28 × 19 cm (written space c. 23 × 15 cm), 2 col., 70 (to 72) lines, composite (17 codicilli), gatherings (mostly quaternions) often incomplete and showing various prickings and quire signatures (regularly pared off), some isolated (bi)folia (incidentally transposed in binding), texts in Carolingian minuscule written by several roughly contemporary hands, corrections, miscellaneous content.

I (fols. 1–21)	1ra–12vb	AUG. serm. 65, 150, 5, 6, 45, 97, 277, 130, epist. 60; NICET. REMES. de vigiliis, de psalmodiae bono; AUG. serm. 53, 1; exc. NIL. ANCYR. (trsl. Rufin.); AUG. serm. 254; GREG. NAZ. tractatus decimus (trsl. Rufin.)
	13ra–21rb	THIOFR. EPTERN. flores epitaphii sanctorum
	21v	*blank*
II (fols. 22–35)	22ra–35ra	SALV. gub.
	35vb	*blank*

III (fols. 36–57)	36ra–55va	GROMATICI (e.g. FRONTIN. ad Celsum *and* HYGIN. de limitibus constituendis)
	56r–57v	*blank*
IV (fols. 58–65)	58ra	NOTKER LABEO epist. ad Hugonem episc. Sedunensem
	58ra–60rb	Excerptum Rethorice Notkeri magistri
	60rb–62vb	Incipit quomodo VII circumstantie rerum in legendo ordinande sint
	62vb	De natura quid sit; 'Omne quod simplex est caret numero . . .'; Quomodo quid sit; 'Omnes res significant substantiam aut accidens . . .'
	62vb–63rb	L(IUTBERTUS archiepisc. Mogunt.?)epist. ad I(sonem Sangall.?)
	63rb–64va	Incipid (*sic!*) Dialectica
	64va	Quomodo septem circumstantie (*the same treatise as 60–2, but not copied from the same manuscript; the text breaks off abruptly*)
	64va–b	De partibus logicae
	65ra–vb	Incipit distributio omnium specierum nominum inter cathegorias Aristotelis (*the text breaks off*)
V (fols. 66–73)	66ra–69rb	exc. SEN. controv.; ISID. de natura angelorum; LANFRANC. contra Berengar.
	69va	*blank, as is the first part of 69vb*
	69vb	'Anulus et baculus duo sunt insignia' (Walther no. 1347b)
	70ra	'Anulus et baculus sunt pontificalia sacra'
	70ra–vb	HUGO METELL. certamen regis cum papa
	70vb–71ra	'Gens Romanorum subdola' (Walther no. 7159)
	71ra–b	HUNALD. de anulo et baculo
	71rb	'Fert genitrix natum Stephano testante beatum' (Walther no. 6440)
	71va–73vb	APPENDIX VERGILIANA (Ciris 454–541; Catalepton; 'Quid hoc novi est'; Elegiae in Maecenatem); exc. FLOR. Verg. orator an poeta (71va *by a hand s.XII*^{ex}: quod in Virgilio sancti Eucherii deest in libro Ciris, hic est; 73v *by a later hand*: hic aliquid desideratur)
fol. 74 (transposed folium)	74ra–vb	*continuation of the text breaking off on fol. 65v*
fols. 75–6 (separate bifolium)	75ra–vb	PAUL. NOL. epist. 17 (*lacking its first part*), 27 (*see* XI)
	76	*blank*
fols. 77–8 (separate bifolium)	77ra–78va	SIDON. epist. 5, 5–5, 11 (*see* X)
	78vb	*blank*
VI (fols. 79–92)	79ra–90vb	WANDALB. martyr.; HEITO Wett.; Visio pauperculae mulieris; WALAHFR. Wett.

	90vb–91rb	FULG. RUSP. serm. 250
	91v	'Speciales Francorum protectores sunt Dionysius martyr . . .' (*one column only*)
	92	*blank*
VII (fols. 93–8, a ternion including a bifolium inserted by the Bollandists)	93ra–96rb	POLEM. SILV. (*on 94rv a Bollandist transcript of the text of 93rv*)
	96v–98v	*blank*
VIII (fols. 99–106)	99ra–105ra	ARATUS de signis caelestibus (trsl. Germanic.)
	105v–106	*blank*
IX (fols. 107–22)	107ra–122rb	MANIL. astron.
	122v	*blank*
X (fols. 123–37)	123ra–136ra	SIDON. carmina omnia, epist. selectae 129vb *blank*
	136v–137	*blank*
XI (fols. 138–56)	138ra–156ra	PAUL. NOL. carm.
	156v	*blank*
XII (fols. 157–64)	157ra–163rb	CASSIOD. inst. div.
	163v–164	*blank*
XIII (fols. 165–72)	165ra–172	GILO de crucesignatis
fols. 173–4 (two separate folia)	173–174	MAGISTER PAULINUS carmen Winrici
fols. 175–8 (four separate folia)	175r–178v	Carmen Mettense; Duo hymni de sancto Gorgonio
XIV (fols. 179–86)	179ra–186vb	THEODER. TRUDON. Solinus metricus, de cane mortuo, de ventorum turri; exc. VITRUV.; exc. AUG. civ.; GREG. ad Constantium Augustum; LACT. Phoen.; Carmina de nummo; Epitaphium Iuliani Apostatae
XV (fols. 187–200)	187ra–191va	ECBASIS CAPTIVI
	191vb–194rb	ALDHELM. aenigm.
	194rb	'Linea Christe tuos prima est que continet annos' (Walther no. 10329)
	194rb–va	AUSON. epigr. 24 Peiper
	194va	AVIANI VIRI CLARI ad amicos
	194va–b	Versus cuiusdam Scoti de alphabeto
	194vb–199ra	HILDEB. CENOMANN. de nummo
	199ra	'Deposcat requiem cum nox breviata diurnam' (Walther no. 4265)
	199ra–b	'Si te nosse potes felix nil amplius optes' (Walther no. 17990)
	199v–200	*blank*
XVI (fols. 201–23)	201ra–204ra	ARNULF. deliciae cleri; Versus de duodecim ventis; exc. SUET.
	204va–212va	Carmen quod dicitur Sanctus Augustinus de laudibus dei
	212vb–214ra	Carmen de sancta Lucia
	214ra–223vb	SEDUL. SCOT. carmina
	223vb	exc. PAULIN. NOL. carm. 15, 16, 18, 28

XVII (fols. 224–31)   224ra–227va   ASTENSIS POETA novus Avianus (*the text jumps from 1, 5 (De asino pelle leonis texto), 5 on 224rb70 to 1, 10 (De milite et lituo), 3 on 224va1; the scribe has marked the omission by a letter A at the bottom of 224rb and a B at the top of 224va*)

       227va–b   Satira in Mettenses 'Nulla salus aut pax veniat tibi gens tenebrosa' (Walther no. 12369) (*the scribe has left a blank for line 97 in which a corrector has written the last two words of this verse*)

written in one hand

      227vb–230vb   Carmen quod dicitur de Hastingae proelio

      230vb   exc. GELL. (14, 5, 1–4; 15, 2, 7; 15, 4, 3)

      231ra–b   ASTENSIS POETA novus Avianus 1, 5, 6–1, 10, 2 (*marked by an A at the top of 231ra and by a B at the end of 231rb*)

      231v   *blank*

B. Bruxelles, Bibliothèque Royale, ms. 9799–9809 (olim Bolland. 105), s.XI and XII, St Eucharius-Matthias, Trier

Vellum, 201 ff., c. 29.5 × 20 cm, composite (3 codicilli: I s.XI, 1 col.; II–III s.XII, 2 col., 65 to 69 lines), miscellaneous contents (the texts of II, written by one hand, have all except one been copied from ms. A, codicilli V, XV and XVII), f 1r and 122r fifteenth-century *ex libris* of the Hospitale s. Nicolai prope Cusam (perhaps a terminus post quem for the composition of the present volume):

  I (fols. 1–121)   1r–121v   ISID. mysticorum expositiones sacramentorum

  II (fols. 122–43)   122ra   'Anulus et baculus duo sunt insignia' (*see* A, fol. 69v)

      122ra–b   'Anulus et baculus sunt pontificalia signa' (*see* A, fol. 70r)

      122rb–vb   HUGO METELL. certamen regis cum papa (*see* A, fol. 70r)

      122vb–123ra   'Gens Romanorum subdola' (*see* A, fol. 70v)

      123ra–b   HUNALD. de anulo et baculo (*see* A, fol. 71r)

      123va–124ra   HILDEB. CENOMANN. de nummo *breaking off at vs. 198* (*see* A, fol. 194v)

      124rb–v   *blank*

      125ra–129vb   exc. MARTIAL.

      130ra–134va   ECBASIS CAPTIVI (*see* A, fol. 187r)

      134va–137va   ALDHELM. aenigm. (*see* A fol. 191v)

      137va   'Linea Christe tuos prima est que continet annos' (*see* A, fol. 194r)

         AUSON. epigr. 24 Peiper (*see* A, fol. 194r)

         AVIANI VIRI CLARI ad amicos (*see* A, fol. 194v)

      137va–b   Versus cuiusdam Scoti de alphabeto (*see* A, fol. 194v)

      138ra–142rb   ASTENSIS POETA novus Avianus (*see* A, fols. 224r and 231r)

	142rb–va	Satira in Mettenses 'Nulla salus aut pax veniat tibi gens tenebrosa' *v. 50 has been skipped and the scribe has left a blank for v. 97* (*see* A, fol. 227v)
	142vb	Carmen quod dicitur de Hastingae proelio vv. 1–66 (*see* A, fol. 227v)
	143	*blank*
III (fols. 144–201)	144–201	LACT. inst.

4. At the conclusion of the above paper by Professor Engels, the chairman, thanking him warmly, observed that the situation seemed almost one in which the historical evidence pointed in one direction and the literary evidence in another, and called for general discussion.

Professor Raymonde Foreville spoke first and expressed the thanks of the Conference to R. H. C. Davis for reopening the whole question of the *Carmen*, which for her involved in particular a re-examination of its relationship with William of Poitiers. On that matter she wished, as noted last year (*ante*, i.57–8 and N.34), to confirm her conclusions published in 1952 in her edition of the *Gesta Guillelmi*, i.e. that William of Poitiers had used the *Carmen* which was thus the earlier of the two sources. Without wishing to repeat the arguments in detail, she stressed the weight of the internal literary evidence for that relationship. On this occasion she preferred to say a few words first about the dedication of the *Carmen* to Lanfranc, which, albeit before 1070, would be neither odd nor inappropriate if one recalled Lanfranc's pre-eminence in juridical studies and his arguable position as the principal exponent of duke William's legal right to the English succession. Next, her recent work upon the coronation rite (*ante*, i) made it certain, in her view, that the *Carmen* with its valuable information on that subject was the work of an ecclesiastic. As for the difficult questions of the *Carmen's* account of the battle of Hastings, the siege of London and the death of Harold, judgement should be reserved until we have a new and definitive edition of the poem, for, in spite of the merits of the recent edition of Morton and Muntz, there are still corruptions in the printed text (as well as infelicities of translation) and further work is still required upon the manuscript from which it is derived.

Dr Marjorie Chibnall, called upon next, said that her main point must be the negative one that the mention of a source by Orderic Vitalis did not necessarily mean that he had used it, and in this case, she can find no positive evidence that he had (or had not). Orderic could well have heard of the poem by Guy, Bishop of Amiens and chaplain to the queen in 1068, through a monk at St Evroult called Samson, who had previously been the queen's messenger. (Having acted as an intermediary between Mathilda and the rebellious Robert, he had fled to the cloister to avoid the king's wrath on that account.) This unfortunately does not solve the main problems presented by the poem as we have it, and she, also welcomed the re-opening of the whole question of the

Carmen by Professor Davis, because of the extreme difficulty of interpreting some of the passages in the poem as emanating from a contemporary source, not least the apostrophe of the monk addressing William in terms more applicable to his son Prince Henry (his father conquering the English, *etc.* vv. 329–33). Part of the answer may well be, as Professor Foreville has suggested, corruption in the text, combined with the overenthusiastic editing of Morton and Muntz. The question remains how far we can accept this poem; but it cannot be accepted in their interpretation.

Professor Engels intervened at this point to say that in his own opinion the recent review by Orlandi of Morton and Muntz's edition of the *Carmen* (*Studi medievali*, xiii, 1972) had overestimated the number of points at which their text required emendation or further research. His own estimate was of some ten or fifteen. Such corrections would, of course, provide some room for manoeuvre in the interpretation (and translation) of difficult passages. Asked by the chairman if he thought necessary textual emendations could sufficiently alter those whole passages which at present historians found themselves unable to accept, he declined to promise any such escape. The chairman ignoring his request for an escape to tea (the tea bell was then ringing), Professor Engels proposed that textual matters should for the moment be put on one side, and that the historians present should tell him if they would accept the *Carmen's* versions of the death of Harold, the siege of London, *et al.* if it were in fact proved to be an early and contemporary account from the late 1060s.

Professor Foreville thereupon sought leave to add two points relative to the date of the poem. The monk's apostrophe to the duke before the battle represented, in her view, no great obstacle to an early date, for it was addressed 'great duke', which could only be Duke William, while that duke's father, Robert the Magnificent, had in fact been involved with expeditions to England though scarcely to the point of conquest. Further, and more important as positive evidence of an early date, the statement in the *Carmen* (vv. 803–4) that two metropolitans 'of equal rank' supported William at his coronation could scarcely have been made after 1070 and 1072.

Professor Davis re-entered the discussion at this point to observe that it would be a pity if the literary evidence continued to pull in one direction (for an early date) and the historical evidence in another. What was necessary to resolve the dilemma was to find out what literary sources were available to contemporaries and thus to the authors both of the *Carmen* and the *Gesta Guillelmi*. He had often thought when both used the same language that they might be using a common text-book. And so, for example, what other king or hero in literature died like Harold in the *Carmen*? Who else but William had a banquet on the open sea? What other mother offered his weight in gold for the body of her slain son?

Professor Engels agreed that this was important, but put again his problem and his question noted above. If it were certain that the *Carmen* was written in, say, 1070, what would historians say about its version of the death of Harold? Would they change their minds about what could and could not be said and the limits of poetic licence?

Dr Chibnall intervened to say that she had met this problem with Orderic Vitalis, where there were several passages in which he was quite plainly using literary sources (possibly conveyed to him orally). The speed with which legend could gather round known and verifiable events is most strikingly shown with the battle of Fraga, of which Orderic's account, though written within five years of the event, is in part a true account of what happened, but in places takes off into pure *chanson de geste*. The double moral is (a) the inclusion of such elements does not prove a late date for one's source, and (b) they can nevertheless make an early source unreliable.

Miss Cecily Clark usefully drew attention to the controversy currently building up about the credibility of the *Song of Maldon* as very similar to that now surrounding the *Carmen*.

Professor Eleanor Searle said that her own agnosticism to the *Carmen* had been strengthened by Professor Davis's assault upon it. The one thing that worried her in his paper was his attribution of the monk's curious apostrophe to Henry I in 1125, which date, she felt, it did not fit at all.

Professor Davis agreed, and the session ended with a further discussion of this particularly difficult passage, principally by *Professor Engels* and *Dr Elizabeth von Houts* but including the suggestion from *Dr G. A. Loud* that the reference to the duke's father subduing the English might stem from the lost *chanson de geste* concerning Duke Robert the Magnificent.

R.A.B.

Battle c. 1110
An Anthroponymist Looks at an Anglo-Norman New Town

CECILY CLARK

When, in her recent book on *English Medieval Towns*, Susan Reynolds raised the question of medieval townspeople, their origins, and their outlooks, she remarked that 'Medieval records are more or less inadequate to answer such questions. . . .'[1] She did not leave the matter there; neither should we. How can we learn more about our earliest burgesses? At least we know some of their names, from such twelfth-century records as list the holders of individual burgess-plots. Of these the most imposing are the *Winton Domesday*, with its two surveys of c. 1115 and of 1148, and the great series of Canterbury rentals published a dozen years ago; hardly less valuable is the 1177 taxation-list from Newark.[2] Less impressive perhaps, but with special claims on our attention, is the list, dating from c. 1110, which records the names of nearly all the householders in Battle: some 110 names, arranged, as in the larger surveys, according to the lay-out of the town.[3] What can such lists be made to tell us?

The personal names alone will concern us here, not the lay-out of the town, still less the rents. To a limited extent such names already form an accepted source of historical evidence, occupational terms being scrutinized for light on economic activity and *noms d'origine* for population-shifts. Over the last half-dozen years, however, experience has suggested that, when evidence on social and cultural history is sparse, these domains too can be illuminated by analysing the whole bodies of personal names used by the groups in question (merely comparing, for instance, the lists of personal names figuring in the place-name surveys of Wiltshire, of Nottinghamshire and of Westmorland gives a certain insight into cultural patterns). For twelfth-century England in particular this technique seems to bring out social patterns hardly perceptible by any other light.[4]

Before looking at the Battle document itself, we must consider the principles and methodology of personal-name study.[5] For the implicit purpose here, ultimately the more important one, is not so much to throw light on the early history of an Anglo-Norman new town but, even more, to invite discussion of an investigative technique so far still experimental.

With place-names, their use as historical clues—as evidence of migrations and settlements, of land-holding customs and of cultivation-patterns, even of prehistoric religions—is something with which we have all been familiar (corporately if not individually) for well over half a century. Often the most significant elements in the place-names thus exploited have been the personal names of early lords and land-holders, as Geoffrey Barrow showed last year in his fascinating paper on alien settlement in south-western Scotland.[6] On their own, however, personal names have far less often been treated as a source of historical evidence. Indeed, for all the striking use which certain scholars have made of them—most notably, each in his own way, David Douglas, Eilert Ekwall, and Sir Frank Stenton—their testimony seems widely under-estimated. Necessarily, personal names present different problems from place-names; but, equally, they offer distinct advantages. Instead of remaining current for centuries, no individual personal name lasts for more than a single human life (hereditary family-names being for the moment left aside); so that a chronological succession of personal names can mirror changing patterns of cultural allegiance. Not being tied to specific locations, personal names may reflect, more promptly and more closely than place-names can, demographic shifts and other causes of cross-cultural influence. Above all, personal names are hundreds of times, often tens of thousands of times more numerous than the corresponding place-names, so that they can give a shaded, nuanced impression both of settlement-patterns and of cultural ones, representing minorities and repressed elements as well as the dominant ones stamping the place-names.

This numerousness invites analytical and comparative techniques of study. A pioneering work in this field has been Veronica Smart's paper on moneyers' names from late Anglo-Saxon England.[7] Mrs Smart has shown that analysing separately the names representing each locality and then comparing the analyses offers valuable pointers to cultural variations. Her own survey shows the frequencies of Scandinavian forms, among moneyers' names at least, to vary in close relationship with the presumable densities of the different Viking settlements. Such an approach I have been trying to apply more widely, taking less specialized samples of personal names and, until now, considering the Norman settlement in England rather than the Scandinavian one.

Unfortunately, study of personal names proves beset by problems grave enough to have persuaded some medieval anthroponymists, among them the great Karl Michaëlsson, that neither statistical analysis nor, *a fortiori*, comparison is at all feasible.[8] A major stumbling-block is the non-comparability of the extant materials. It might, indeed, be wise to compare only like with like—manorial extent with manorial extent, Assize Roll with Assize Roll, Feet of Fines with Feet of Fines. On the other hand, as work has proceeded, so often have similar patterns emerged from materials which, although of disparate types, roughly represent the same place, date and milieu, that faith in the representative value of all the types of record becomes partly restored. One precaution is, however, essential: to disregard the smaller apparent discrepancies— for instance, those of 5% or less. Any name-analysis citing percentages to several decimal places gives a misleading view of the precision even theoretically obtainable by even the best investigator. All the extant records contain random elements, none offering anything approaching a complete or systematic census-return: the Battle list, for instance, names rather less than one individual per holding, omitting all juvenile or otherwise subordinate members of households, showing less than 10% of women, and remaining silent about possible sub-tenants. Often, too, unsystematic rep-etitions make it impossible to calculate the exact total of individuals involved: does the Battle list contain two *Emmas* (46, 72), or one holding two burgage plots; three *Sevugels* (24, 56, 95), two of whom (24 and 56) each held two plots, or only two, one a sub-landlord exploiting four plots?[9] Moreover, not even the most learned investigator possible will ever succeed in definitively classifying every name-form under one category and one only, for ambiguities are rife.

The personal names of twelfth-century England fall into manifold cate-gories.[10] Most obviously, they are divided into baptismal names and by-names; but even here an overlap occurs, because a by-name, instead of qualifying a baptismal name, might sometimes replace it, as here with 80 *Brembel* and 101 *Cocard*, and then perhaps be adopted by subsequent generations as a baptismal name in its own right.[11] The baptismal names proper stem either from the pre-Conquest or 'insular' stock or from the post-Conquest, 'continental' forms introduced by the Norman settlers. In turn, the insular stock falls into Old English names and the Scandinavian ones introduced by the Viking settlers in the Danelaw. The continental names likewise fall into several groups: those stemming from Continental Germanic but mostly brought to England in Gallicized forms— the conventional written forms being sometimes ambiguous, owing to the close links between Continental Germanic and Old English; the specifically 'Christian' names taken from saints and from Biblical characters—a category which, although available to the pre-Conquest English, had been little favoured by them; the Scandinavian names brought to Normandy by the Vikings—in written form often hard to tell from the corresponding Anglo-Scandinavian forms; and, lastly, certain minor categories, such as Breton names, and the Irish ones which the Dublin-based Vikings had brought to Normandy. By-names too fall into several categories, this time semantic as well as etymological. Necessarily, patronymics and metronymics belong to the same classes as baptismal names in general, although often differing in kind from the par-ticular ones they qualify. Residential names may involve either place-names proper, whether English or continental, or farm-names, again either English or continental, such as may not survive on the modern map, or simple topographical forms of the 'Atwood' type. Terms of rank and occupation may occur in either of the two vernaculars or, more commonly, in Latin. As for the most fascinating and most perplexing category, personal and characteristic nicknames, most of those recorded in twelfth-century England are either English or French, although a few fossilized Scandinavian survivals also occur and a few stray specimens that look Flemish; especially when forms are obscure, it is wise to confirm them as far as possible by parallels and analogues—a process emphasizing that most French by-names seen in England echo forms current on the continent, in Normandy and Picardy especially.

Some of the ambiguities dogging name-classification have just been noted; and how rife these are can hardly be overstated. The criteria are of two kinds: distributional and linguistic. The latter are by far the safer: thus, all names beginning with $\bar{E}ad$- (by the twelfth century usually spelt $\mathcal{E}d$-) must be English in origin, because in Continental-Germanic dialects the corresponding element is Aud-, Od-. Too often, however, evidence comes from distribution alone, as for classing the specifically 'Christian' names as (for the present purpose) 'continental'. With many Germanic name-elements and name-compounds too their apparent distributions form the main grounds for labelling them as either 'English' or 'continental'; and, as not all the extant documents have yet been excerpted and as, even though they had, they could still not have been trusted to have recorded every name-form ever used, labelling based solely on distribution can never be certain, now or in the future. Sometimes distributional and phonological evidence converge, as with 11 *Legarda*: as no feminine second element corresponding to Continental-Germanic *-garda/-gardis* is certainly found in Old English names and as it would in any case have had an initial [j] such as would not have absorbed the final consonant of a preceding *Lēof-* (or the much rarer *Lēod-*), therefore *Legarda* cannot be other than continental. Sometimes the two kinds of evidence clash, as with 52 *Maðelgar*, 3 *Malgar*, and the patronymic 76 *Hunger*, showing different reflexes of the same second element, OE *-gār*/CG *-ger*. For *Hunger* the continental origin the form suggests is likely: the existence of an OE *$H\bar{u}ng\bar{a}r$ is little more than conjectural, and the third possible etymon, Scandinavian *Hungeirr*, is very rare.[12] *Maðelgar/Malgar* presents, however, greater problems: Continental-Germanic *Madalger* and the OFr *Malger* > *Maugier* derived from it are common, whereas in Old English the element *Mæðel-* is one of the rarest and the compound *$Mæðelg\bar{a}r$ hardly occurs, being no more than tentatively identified in a place-name or two (the reduction to *Mal-*, although not impossible, would be anomalous); on the other hand, the second element of continental *Ma(da)lger* would not normally appear as *-gar*—perhaps it has here been remodelled by analogy with Old

English names such as *Ordgār*.[13] Even a name seemingly as archetypically Old English as *Godwine* had its continental counterpart, often spelt *Godoinus*; and it may be the latter that appears here beside a possibly continental patronymic in 112 *Goduinus Gisard*.[14]

These difficulties inherent in the material are at present exacerbated by the inadequacy of the reference-books available. A comprehensive *Old English Onomasticon* had been planned by the late Olof von Feilitzen, but since his death in 1976 the project has lain fallow.[15] Meanwhile, Searle's *Onomasticon Anglo-Saxonicum* is so obsolete that every investigator must compile a personal working-list of pre-Conquest English names from a myriad miscellaneous sources, not least by casting a properly critical eye over every survey so far published by the English Place-Name Society.[16] At present a *Middle English Onomasticon* is hardly conceivable, so vast and so disorganized is the corpus of relevant material. As for Reaney's *Dictionary of British Surnames*, this remains, even in its second edition revised by Professor R. M. Wilson, an heroic but wholly premature essay, valuable mainly for its citations.[17] Likewise, the essential continental sources and analogues are only partly available in usable form; as most studies available happen to concern Picardy rather than Normandy, the continental parallels cited for forms found in England are probably unrepresentative. Thus the would-be anthroponymist must choose between devoting a lifetime merely to laying the foundations of adequate reference-books, in the hope that later generations may complete and then exploit them, or else making amateurish and approximate attempts to show how the discipline might develop if only circumstances were more propitious.

If the second choice is made, then the inevitability of being, in some respects, 'amateurish and approximate' must not entail any further abrogation of scholarly standards. The technique adopted must take full account of dialectal and orthographical problems. Spelling, fundamental to all studies in the vernaculars, is the thorniest aspect of all twelfth-century English documents. With name-material uncertainties are at their worst, because names lack the grammatical and semantic contexts usually allowing identification of words, however oddly spelt, used in connected verse or prose; moreover, the Latin contexts so common afford few clues to the writer's vernacular spelling-systems. Certainly twelfth-century England knew a plurality of such systems. As Old English literature, and the homiletic works especially, continued to be recopied well into the twelfth century, the 'standard' Anglo-Saxon orthographic patterns remained familiar, although now sometimes garbled and always presumably interpreted in terms of current pronunciation.[18] An example of specifically Old English spelling relevant to our present study concerns *c*, which in the vicinity of [i] and [e] usually indicated the assibilated [tʃ], as in *cild* [tʃiːld], modern *child*, so that for [k] before [i] or [e], whether in a foreign word or a native one, some other symbol was desirable. Even more, perhaps, all scribes of this time would have been familiar with the Latin, or rather Franco-Latin, 'powers of the letters'— best deduced not from the highly conventionalized Latin itself, but from some of the earliest Anglo-Norman manuscripts, such as the text of the *Vie de saint Alexis* preserved in the so-called 'St. Albans' Psalter. A relevant spelling here is *ch*, which had several values, including [k], for which a number of other spellings also occurred.[19] So the first step in analysing any name-list must be to decode its spellings into conventional 'dictionary' forms; then dialectology takes over. For Sussex the spelling- and sound-systems of the medieval dialects have already been studied, mainly through the personal names and place-names found in documents such as the Lay Subsidy Rolls.[20] A dialect boundary, probably responding to the pattern of medieval woodland as well as to that of the original settlement, approximately coincides with the modern administrative boundary between East and West Sussex.[21] Not surprisingly, the East-Sussex dialect of the Rape of Hastings agreed in certain features, though by no means in all, with Kentish. As Battle itself, like the other Wealden settlements new in the eleventh century, could have had no native dialect of its own, the forms found here may throw light on the settlers' origins.

With all these caveats in mind, we may now turn to the document itself, the rental of c. 1110 incorporated into the late-twelfth-century *Chronicle* of Battle Abbey, to see whether the personal names there may reveal anything of value. This is not the first time such an exercise has been tried. In 1967 Maurice Beresford glanced briefly at the occupational terms there.[22] Then, in 1974, Dr Searle, using criteria slightly different from mine, suggested that, whereas those holding outlying plots mostly bore names of insular types and pursued agricultural occupations, those living close beside the Abbey bore names of continental types or else by-names marking them as administrators or skilled craftsmen—a distribution squaring with the general impression that in early-twelfth-century England those enjoying high status either were of immigrant origin or at least followed continental fashions.[23] So far, then, the omens seem modestly favourable for further investigation along similar lines.

Historians complain of knowing too little about medieval townspeople, and especially about the first burgesses of new towns. For origin and status, the most obvious clues lie in by-names, such as some three-quarters of the subjects here display, of one kind or another. Not quite half the by-names are occupational: that is, we know the trades of only some third of the burgesses here (the rest need not all be supposed unskilled, for a man with another sort of by-name or a distinctive baptismal name would be adequately identified without mention of his trade). Mostly the terms are Latinized (*aurifaber, bovarius, bubulcus*, 95 *cannarius, carpentarius* 2x, *clericus, cocus* 3x, 6 *corduanarius, dapifer, dispensator, faber* 2x, *molendinarius, ortolanus*, probably 10 *pionius, pistor* 3x, *porcarius* 2x, *presbiter*, 16 *purgator, textor, secretarius* 2x, *sutor* 3x), but one or two occur in English (1 *Bedel*, and perhaps 77 *Cniht*) and two, towards the end, in French (109 *braceur*, 106 *corueiser*).[24] Incomplete though it is, this list shows Battle to have already been a true 'town', not only in its enjoyment of a quasi-burgage tenure, but also in living by craft and trade.[25] Mostly commonplace, the crafts include a few, such as 'goldsmith', 'bursar' and 'butler', and 'bell-founder' (38 *Ædric qui signa fundebat*), which recall that the town served the Abbey as well as boosting its revenues; and a few presage the importance the leather industry was later to have here.[26] As for the languages in which the terms are set down, these reflect the usages of the scribes rather than that of the townsfolk themselves.[27] For determining the geographical origins of the settlers, *noms d'origine* might have been hoped to provide useful clues, in spite of the suspicion with which some historians regard them; but they prove rare, unexpectedly so, by contrast with their profusion in such documents as the two Winchester surveys.[28] Three link their bearers with places in southern England, two within the *leuga* itself (2 *de Bece*, 104 *de Bodeherstegate*) and one on Battle's Kentish estates (35 *de Dengemar'*); and one remains unidentified (18 *de Hauena*).[29] Only one links its bearer with the continent: 51 *de Cirisi*, which, ambiguous though it is, must refer to one of the several French places called Cerisy or Cérisy.[30] Such paucity of *noms d'origine* contrasts with their plentifulness among the overseas settlers here in the thirteenth century.[31] Another by-name, 34 *Gilebertus extraneus*, vaguely labelling its bearer as 'foreign', seems at the same time to imply that neither of the other Gilberts (9, 63) was such. Indeed, almost all by-names, if rightly examined, will throw some light on social background. Of the probable patronymics and metronymics, up to ten may be insular (5 *Dot*, 7 *Gotcild*—if not a nickname, 12 *Trewæ*—if not a nickname, 14 *filius Colsuein*, 28 *filius Siflet*, 31 *Hert*—if not a nickname, 62 *filius Fareman*, if not a nickname, 83 *Tipæ*, 103 *Hecæ*), whereas only two at most seem continental (108 *Ælfwine Turpin*, and probably 112 *Godwine Gisard*), and they qualify what look like insular baptismal names.[32] A somewhat different cultural balance seems implied by the characteristic nicknames; for, beside the many English ones (7 *Gotcild*—if not a patronymic, 12 *Trewæ*—if not a patronymic, 27 *Grei*, perhaps 29 *Gris*, 31 *Hert*—if not a patronymic, 41 *Cild*, 53 *Stigerop*, 70 *Gest*—if not a patronymic, 77 *Cniht*—if not occupational, 80 *Brembel*, 93 *Abbat*, 94 *Crul*, 107 *Barhc*), there occur nearly as many French ones, mostly well paralleled in continental records (21 *Pinel*, 24 *Coche*[*t*], perhaps 29 *Gris*, 43 *Franc enfant*, 81 *Barate*, 90 & 100 *Peche*(*t*, 101 *Cocard*, 105 & 111 *Genester*) and, again, as with the patronymics, sometimes qualifying insular-looking baptismal names. In so far as this evidence allows of any conclusion at all, it suggests a community predominantly English, yet with a tinge of bilingual cosmopolitanism.

Can the baptismal names help to clear the view? Notorious for capricious relationships with the nationalities of their bearers, they might be feared to offer the social historian testimony even less reliable than that of by-names. Yet, misleading as an isolated name often is about its bearer's 'race' or nationality, in the mass names cannot but reflect the cultural influences at work in the group concerned. Here, analysis of the just under a hundred men's names shows the dominant elements to be Old English and Continental Germanic; Scandinavian forms appear only in a patronymic or two (14 *Colsuein*, 62 *Fareman*—both among the most widespread of such forms, seen both at Winchester and in Devon place-names—and perhaps 70 *Gest*), forms identifiable as Normanno-Scandinavian being notably absent; the specifically 'Christian' names are only a little less sparsely represented.[33] The paucity of Scandinavian forms not only contrasts with the name-patterns of the old Danelaw, whether at Newark or even at Colchester, but even undercuts the 4% seen in the *TRE* tenants at Winchester; it agrees, however, with Mrs Smart's findings about Sussex moneyers' names of the pre-Cnutian period.[34] About Sussex this says little new; but about the English settlers at Battle it confirms the tentative deduction from the few *noms d'origine* that most of them were local men, southerners, rather than from the East Midlands or further afield. Dialect also bears on this question: an abbey founded in a district previously uninhabited would have needed models for its vernacular usage, whether its own English recruits or its new burgesses; the dialect here, south-eastern without being specifically Kentish, confirms the local origin of most settlers.[35] That the immigrants' own versions of their names were respected is implied by western 40 *Burnulf* alongside the commoner south-eastern forms such as 67 *Chebel* and 98 *Cheneward*; and this gives the latter's predominance added force. The paucity of 'Christian' forms, amounting to no more than some 7% of the 'continental' names here, agrees with the 6% or so in the earlier Winchester survey (perhaps a shade later than our Battle list).[36] As the twelfth century saw the ratio of 'Christian' forms steadily increasing, both on the Continent and in England (by 1148 the Winchester figure has risen to over 16%), the low figure at Battle confirms the early date which Dr Searle assigns to the rental.[37] The main interest must, however, lie in the balance between the two main categories, insular and continental. As far as the ambiguities allow us to judge, continental forms here account for almost 40% of men's names, whether reckoned by stock or by frequency of use—a figure whose significance can be gauged only by comparison. The earlier Winchester survey shows such forms constituting nearly 60% of the name-stock and accounting for between 65% and 70% of occurrences: great as the discrepancy seems between this distribution and the Battle one, it proves easily explicable, because the Battle list deals mainly with actual householders (the persistence of certain surnames among later burgesses modestly confirms that the names belong to residents, not to property middlemen), whereas many Winchester entries concern Norman magnates renting plots for investment.[38] Another survey approximately contemporaneous is 'Burton B', where continental forms constitute less than 20% of the men's names: this opposite discrepancy too may be at least partly explained by the status of those listed—at Burton peasants, not burgesses.[39] A like explanation may be proffered for the discrepancy between the almost 40% at Battle and the mere 5% found in the Bury St Edmunds survey datable no more than a dozen years earlier, if that.[40] The question needs pursuing, however; and so, as no other contemporaneous lists of names seem available, comparison will have to be risked with material from nearly two generations later, from the 1160s, that is. A Canterbury rental of that date shows continental forms accounting for some 75% of the occurrences of men's names, beside some 65% in the roughly contemporaneous list of Canterbury 'votaries of St. Anselm'—the latter being perhaps on average older than the Christ Church tenants, or of more modest condition.[41] As all our mid-twelfth-century records show an accelerating shift from insular names to continental ones, does the almost 40% at Battle c. 1110 seem high beside this average of some 70% at Canterbury about fifty years later, and that in one of the most cosmopolitan of cities? The question is more insistently raised by the 1166 Pipe Roll and its list of citizens of King's Lynn, amongst whose names continental forms amount to little more than 50% and whose patronymics and metronymics are predominantly insular.[42] Even though the men of Lynn were (as is suggested elsewhere) the senior merchants of the day, born in the 1120s or earlier, even then a difference of hardly more than 10% between the incidence of continental forms in their names and that two whole generations earlier at Battle seems puzzling, and all the more so because the Lynn patronymics and metronymics imply fashions of the 1120s notably less advanced than those of Battle c. 1110. These discrepancies might be lightly dismissed by supposing each district to have had its own rate of change; but that seems facile. Perhaps the discrepancy between Battle and Lynn was, paradoxically, due to what the two had in common; for, as both were, in their different ways, late-eleventh-century new towns, with 'artificial' populations, the different name-patterns might reflect different sources of recruitment, Battle's settlers being more strongly tinged with continental influences.[43] Thus, the baptismal names, albeit so much more indirectly and indeed uncertainly, are pointing the same way as the by-names did: to a modest cosmopolitanism about the early days of Battle.

All the figures, it must be reiterated, refer to names, and all the deductions to cultural influences; neither refer to individual men or to their nationalities. And what such material can ever tell us is limited—perhaps no more than the stamps on incoming mail could tell about the professional, social, and familial relationships of a household. Of its nature, name-evidence cannot, except by some happy accident, answer the central question historians ask about recruits to medieval towns: what manner of men they were, whether craftsmen, or minor gentry, yeomen, or the younger sons of burgesses elsewhere, itinerant traders, or fugitive villeins. As with the stamps, all it can illuminate, and that dimly, are geographical origins. The Battle householders' names show most of them as English, native to East Sussex and speakers of its dialect. But there is also that admixture of continental forms: not only the common baptismal names, such as *William* and *Robert*, which in post-Conquest England spread so rapidly through all regions and classes, but also French sobriquets such as 43 *Franc enfant* and 101 *Cocard*. Continental baptismal names were, as the example of 28 *Rotbert filius Siflet* makes clear, already being adopted by English people; and Englishmen might equally have picked up and copied the sobriquets of French immigrants they met. Yet, whether or not borne here by Englishmen, such names imply some French presence, either in Battle itself or in the places from which the settlers had come; for, among populations in the main illiterate, names can have travelled only on people's backs. And, to judge by comparison with name-patterns elsewhere, for Battle the French presence in the background seems to have been substantial. Moreover, the occasional pairings of insular forms with continental ones, such as 10 *Dering pionius* and 108 *Ælfuine Turpin*, imply some eagerness to merge the two cultures.

A side issue remains for comment. So far only men's names have been studied, the eight or nine women's names being disregarded because observation elsewhere in twelfth-century England has shown that women's names follow fashions of their own.[44] In any case, the sample is not only too small to represent a female population of some three hundred individuals or more, but also too small for safe expression in percentages (thus, the solitary Scandinavian name—39 *Gunnild*, one of the commonest—represents over 15% of the insular forms recorded, out of all keeping with the findings elsewhere of lower ratios of Scandinavian forms among women's names).[45] For what it is worth, the ratio of continental forms to insular ones amounts at most—that is, if the two *Emma*s are taken as separate individuals—to between 30% and 35%, against nearly 40% for the men's names. Some discrepancy between the names of the sexes is regular in twelfth-century England; the one here might, however, be slighter than usual and, moreover, the tiny stock of names includes not only the common *Emma* but the rarer 11 *Legarda*. Without dwelling too much on the dubious statistics, we may ask whether name-patterns at Battle might have shown some idiosyncrasy. Then as now, new towns must have begun with abnormal population-structures, for the settlers must have arrived in the early prime of their lives, unencumbered by elderly relatives. Even by 1110 Battle may still not have had a normal age-stratification, because the growth from a score of households in 1086 to over five score some twenty years later implies continuing new settlement. There is no foolproof way to investigate age-stratification through the names recorded, but the high proportion of continental names would be in keeping with a population young as well as subject to fair French influence. Furthermore, the original settlers must have arrived mainly as couples, for, in a community so new, lone men would have found few potential wives. In so far as the regular discrepancy between the names of the sexes in twelfth-century England is attributable to a large surplus of men among the Norman incomers, settlement of a new town by couples might have warped the name-pattern by reducing that discrepancy. The sample is, however, inadequate to confirm whether such was the case here.

One metronym occurs: 28 *Rotbert filius Siflet*. At first sight unremarkable, this begins to raise a demographic question when set beside the profusion of such forms in the Pipe Roll list of Lynn burgesses (obvious metronyms there are *Alfled*, *Alfware* 2x, *Alswed*, *Ælveve*, *Edilde*, to which may be added the less clear short-forms, *Biffæ*, *Duvæ*, *Givæ*, *Godæ*, *Munnæ*, *Tettæ*, *Tittæ*). To suppose all bearers of metronyms to have been illegitimate would be naïve; yet some of them may have been so, especially if post-Conquest English society were somewhat unstable. The question these forms therefore raise is whether new towns may have attracted the illegitimate, who at home might have had to be content with inferior positions and prospects.

Speculation grows apace—can its validity be checked? The suggestion that at Battle most settlers had come from elsewhere in East Sussex chimes both with the general observation that recruits to medieval English towns often came from near at hand and with the specific one that Wealden assarters chiefly hailed from the coastal towns and villages of Sussex.[46] Indeed, 'burgess' stock for Battle might have come from the towns already existing on the coast, Pevensey, Hastings, and Rye.[47] Likewise, a French presence here would agree with the well-recorded pattern of post-Conquest French immigration into so many other English towns.[48]

Indeed, even though full background documentation will remain impossible until more of the surviving archives have been published, the tentative findings from our name-evidence are amply confirmed by the very *Chronicle* into which the rental was copied. Two contingents of founding monks, nine in all, had been brought from Marmoutier, near Tours; and even three-quarters of a century later the continental connections of the house were well enough remembered to be urged in an admittedly tendentious political speech.[49] During the building of the abbey cross-Channel commerce had been constant. Because at first the locality seemed to offer no suitable stone, the Conqueror himself gave funds for bringing supplies from Normandy and ships 'quibus a Cadomensi vico lapidum copia ad opus propositum transveheretur'.[50] For overseeing the work 'peritissimi . . . artifices' were assembled from far and wide and, although exactly whence is nowhere specified, Normandy and France might have been laid under contribution.[51] Given this background, it seems natural that the *Chronicle* notes 'overseas' (presumably, that is,

French) elements both among the first farm-tenants and among the first burgesses:

> In villa vero de Bello et per totam leugam . . . quamplurimi ex comprovincialibus, et nonnulli etiam ex transmarinis partibus asciti, . . . sibi mansiones jam parabant . . .[52]
>
> Igitur leuga circumjacente in prædicti loci proprietatem hoc modo redacta, et jam ecclesiæ etiam proficiente fabrica, accitis hominibus quampluribus ex comprovincialibus quidem multis, ex transmarinis etiam partibus nonnullis, coeperunt fratres qui fabricæ operam dabant circa ambitum ejusdem loci certis dimensionibus mansiones singulis distribuere . . .[53]

Exactly whence on the Continent the new burgesses 'from overseas' may have hailed is never stated, and the paucity of *noms d'origine* does nothing to assuage our curiosity.[54] The crucial point is that the *Chronicle* confirms our main deductions from the name-evidence: that there might have been a fair French presence here; and that the English majority had come mainly from districts near-by, 'ex comprovincialibus . . . partibus'. In the long run, for all the superficial eagerness to pick up fashionable French names, the latter strain proved dominant: in the later twelfth century, so the *Chronicle* notes, the accomplished Abbot Odo preached 'ad edificationem audientium nunc Latine, nunc Gallico sermone, frequenter vero ad edificacionem rudis vulgi lingua materna publice pronuntiabat'—and in this context the 'mother-tongue' Odo shared with the uncultivated mob can only have been English.[55]

Nevertheless, our evidence, both from the personal names of all kinds and from the *Chronicle*, all points the same way: to a substantial, even influential French minority in Battle, among the burgesses as well as among the monks. What then of the local place-names? Do they show any unusual French element? If not, that will hardly undermine our argument, because place-names are so much less ready than personal names to reflect minor or short-lived influences; that very inflexibility will, of course, enhance the significance of any French place-names that may occur. The name *Battle* is itself purely French, recalling how a Norman king settled monks from Touraine here in thanksgiving for his victory over the English. Did French influence leave any further marks? Unfortunately, the English Place-Name Society's Sussex volumes, compiled though they were by two of its most distinguished scholars, date from its pioneering days, before the analytic schemes had been fully worked out, when prehistoric elements attracted more attention than medieval accretions, and when farm- and field-names were treated less thoroughly than they are nowadays. Nonetheless, names collected from around Battle include some significant forms. From the mid-thirteenth century at least there has been a *Caldbec* Hill close by.[56] Apparently a Scandinavian form for 'cold stream' and as such inexplicable in Sussex except as an implantation from Normandy, where several such forms occur, this might have arisen in either of two ways: from the *nom d'origine* of some immigrant land-holder (the unpublished archives may one day show whether or not this is likely); or as a Normanno-Scandinavian name for the cold spring said to rise there. Not noted at all by the Place-Name Society is the field poetically named from the *Malfossed, Malfossé, Maufossé*.[57] Above all, there is the name *Mountjoy, Montjoie*, given to the little township's new suburb developed during the thirteenth century—even when its etymological complications are disregarded, a name of manifold evocations.[58] As a French war-cry, it seems to recall how a battle inspired the town's foundation. The site on which it was bestowed is hilly, and, whatever the true etymology, some contemporaries certainly understood the term as 'hill of rejoicing', 'Mons Gaudii', 'Mons Gaudia'. Moreover, the name reappears elsewhere among medieval new towns, for instance, in Gascony.[59] Although by no means the only place-names in Sussex to show Norman-French influence, these forms may nonetheless confirm the cultural influence we have surmised from the external history of town and abbey as well as from the personal names.

'Confirmation' has indeed been the key-note of this study, which cannot pretend to have brought to light much not deducible from other sources. At the outset, however, it was made clear that the underlying purpose was not so much to illuminate the early history of Battle as to test the technique; and with that in mind it was essential to take a topic on which ample independent evidence survived. In the event, findings from the purely onomastic study have proved wholly in keeping with those from the narrative sources; and to that extent the technique may be claimed to have vindicated itself. Whether or not it will ever be deemed reliable enough to use in contexts where such cross-checks from other evidence are not available remains to be seen. Meanwhile, testing it has for a while concentrated attention on one of the less-studied facets of the community at Battle: its cultural affiliations.

APPENDIX: HOUSEHOLDERS AT BATTLE c. 1110

The list is transcribed as closely as possible from BL Cotton ms. Domitian A II, fols. 16r–18r, but without note of erasures or of apparent changes of hand. Expansions are italicized. Emendations are kept for the commentary. Letter-variants other than *u/v* are not, however, reproduced; tagged *ę* is transcribed as *æ*, for which the lower-case form does not otherwise appear (of the OE letters only capital *Æ* is regularly used here; although *ð* occurs, often it is replaced by *d*).

To keep the commentary within bounds, the commoner OE and CG names are not annotated and the following special abbreviations are used:

Amiens   Morlet, M.-Th., 'Les noms de personne à Amiens au XIVe siècle', *Bulletin philologique et historique 1960*, Paris 1961, 527–52.

5. Ælurici [OE *Ælfrīc*] Dot [p.; OE *Dodd*—see *PNDB* 224–5, cf. *DBS s.n. Dod*; but *PNDB* 226 suggests a genuine form *Dot*]

Dot: for -*t* instead of -*d*, see *Winchester* 225, and cf. 28 *Siflet*, 82 *Lefflet* < OE -*flǣd*.

6. Willelmi [CG] corduanarii [o.; see *OEB* 248, *Winchester* 201, and *MED s.v. cordewaner*]

cordoanarii: the surname *Cordewaner* found here later (*BAB* 118 n. 37) need not belong to the same family, because leather-workers abounded in Battle (*BAB* 268, 299–303).

7. Æduardi [OE *Ēadweard*] Gotcild [n. or p.; OE *Gŏdcild*—cf. *DBS s.n. Goodchild*]

8. Radulfi [CG] Dvcgi

Dvcgi: perhaps miscopied from a Latinization of ME *dwergh* 'dwarf' (*MED s.v.*) as *Duergus, **Du^{l}gus*. Cf., however, *DBS s.n. Dodge*.

9. Gileberti [CG] textoris

textoris: the surname *Webbe* occurs in 1296 (*SSR* 17).

10. Deringi [OE *Dēoring*] pionii [o.; OFr/L]

pionii: Latinization of the OFr by-name *Pion* (*Haute Picardie* 140, cf. *France II* 486; cf. TL *s.v. pëon* 'foot-soldier').

11. Legardæ [CG *Liutgard* f.—*Gaule* 159, *Winchester* 164; see above 24]

12. Ælfuini [OE *Ælfwine*] Trewæ [n. or, more probably, p.; OE *Trēowa*—*UCPN* 79, *Winchester* 174, cf. *DBS s.n. True*]

Trewæ: the surname persists (*BAB* 114 n. 25, 141 n. 29).

13. Godieue [OE *Gōdg(i)efu* f.]

14. Goduini [OE *Gōdwine*] filii Colsuein [p.; S *Kolsveinn*—*SPLY* 179–80, see also *London* 79 and above 28 and below 170 n. 33]

15. Goduini [OE] coci

16. Ædvardi [OE] purgatoris

purgatoris: sense uncertain, see *CBA* 53 n. 5.

17. Rotberti [CG] Molendinarii

18. Rotberti [CG] de Hauena [t.; see above 27 and below 170 n. 29]

19. Selaf [OE *Sǣlāf*] bovarii

20. Wulurici [OE *Wulfrīc*] Aurifabri

Aurifabri: the surname *Goldsmyth* appears here later (*SSR* 205, 317).

21. Willelmi [CG] Pinel [n. or t.; OFr *pinel* 'small pine-tree']

Pinel: an OFr by-name very common in England (see *OEB* 369); opinion seems divided as to whether it refers to residence (*Haute Picardie* 69) or stature (*DBS s.n. Pinnell*).

22. Lamberti [CG] sutoris

23. Ordrici [OE *Ordrīc*] porcarii

24. Sevugel [OE *Sǣfugol*—*Winchester* 171] cochec

cochec: probably a mistake for *cochet* (TL *s.v.*), a diminutive of *coq* and a common OFr by-name (*Amiens* 551, *Eu* xii 216, *Haute Picardie*

215, cf. *France I* 198–9 and *France II* 145). As Sevugel held at least two plots (24 and 25), possibly four (also 56 and 57), the sense 'coq de village' might fit. (The suggestions in *DBS s.n. Cockin* are to be disregarded.)

fol. 16v
26. Blachem*anni* [OE *Blæcmann*] bubulci
27. Wille*lm*i [CG] grei [n.; OE *grǣg* 'grey-coloured']
> *grei*: the exact sense is uncertain, as OE *grǣg* has two secondary senses: a) 'badger', a possible nickname, as with OFr *taisson*; and b) 'grey fur', applicable either to a furrier or to an ostentatious dresser (see *MED s.vv. grei* adj., n. (1), and n. (2)).
28. Rotb*erti* [CG] filii Siflet [m.; OE *Sigeflǣd* f.]
29. Sewardi [OE *Sǣweard*] Gris [n.; ?]
> *Gris*: ambiguous (see *DBS s.n. Grice*), involving either: a) the ME loan from S *gris* 'pig(let)' (see *MED s.v. grĩs* n. (1)); or b) OFr *gris* 'grey' (see *France I* 186, *France II* 308).
30. Ælurici [OE] dispensatoris
31. Wulfuini [OE *Wulfwine*] hert [n. or, more probably, p.; OE *Heort—SN* 8, cf. *PNSussex* 555]
33. Lefui [OE *Lēofwīg*] Nvc
> *Nvc*: so far unexplained; perhaps for *Not* < OE *hnott* 'bald' (see *NOB* 83), or for *nute* < OE *hnutu* 'nut' (cf. *DBS s.n. Nutt*).
34. Gileb*erti* [CG] extr*anei*
35. Ælvrici [OE] de Dengemar*l*
> *Dengemar*[l]: Dengemarsh, Kent, in Battle's manor of Wye (*BAB* 23 &c.)
36. Benedicti [L] Dapiferi
37. Mauricii [L]
38. Ædrici [OE *Eadric*] qui signa fundebat
> *fundebat*: on the tense, see *CBA* 55 n. 6.
39. Gunnild [S *Gunnildr* f.—*SPLY* 114–16, see also below 171 n. 45]
40. Burnulfi [OE *Beornwulf*] carpentarii
> *Burn-*: a rare example, for this list, of western *u* for 'standard' OE *eo* by Breaking (see *Dialect*, 192, 198–204).
41. Æilrici [OE *Æðelrīc*] cild [n.; OE *cild*—see *London* 144–5, *Winchester* 209, and *DBS s.n. Child*]
42. Æilnodi [OE *Æðelnōð*] sutoris
43. Francenfant [n.; OFr *franc* + *enfant*]
> Although no exact continental parallel has yet been noted, cf. *Franc homme* (*Eu* xii 214, *Haute Picardie* 192, cf. *France II* 266) and *Bo(i)n enfant* (*Arras* 1347, cf. 1276); also the English *Freebairn* (*DBS s.n.*)
44. Ælduini [OE *Ealdwine*] coci
46. Emmæ [CG *Emma* f.]

47. Ælstrildis [OE *Ēastorhild* f.—*NOB* 78–9] nonnæ

    Ælstr-: read *Æstr-*, the *-l-* being either repeated from 44 *Æl-* or anticipated from the next syllable.

    nonnæ: n. rather than o. (in spite of *DBS* s.n. *Nunn*), or perhaps more probably a mistaken Latinization of a p. *Nunne* < OE *Nunna* masc. (*UCPN* 68; common in place-names, e.g., *PNSussex* 556).

48. Pet*ri* [L] pistoris

fol. 17r

49. Sewini [OE *Sæwine*]
51. Rotb*erti* [CG] de Cirisi [t.; see above 27 and below 170 n. 30]
52. Maðelgari [? OE/CG; see above 24 and below 169 n. 13] Ruffi
53. Siwardi [OE *Sigeweard*] Stigerop [n.; OE *stigrāp* 'stirrup']
54. Golduini [OE *Goldwine*]
55. Æduini [OE *Ēadwine*] fabri
56. Sevugel [OE]

    Cf. 24.

58. Gotselmi [CG—*Gaule* 105, cf. *France II* 299, s.n. *Gossart*, and 346, s.n. *Josse*]
59. Russelli [n.; OFr *Roussel*—*Winchester* 215]

    In C13 *Russel* occurs here as a surname (*BAB* 125 n. 21).

60. La*mberti* [CG]

    Cf. 22.

61. Ailrici [OE] pistoris
62. Æilnodi [OE] filii fareman [p.; S *Farmaðr*—*SPLY* 79–80, see also above 28 and below 170 n. 33]
63. Gileb*erti* [CG] clerici
64. Lefuini [OE *Lēofwine*] pistoris
65. Herod*l* [? L]

    As the Biblical name is hardly suitable for baptismal use, this and similar forms from elsewhere in C12 England (e.g., Davis, R. H. C., ed., *Kalendar of Abbot Samson*, London 1954, 37) and from France (*Haute Picardie*, 223, cf. Michaëlsson, K., *Etudes sur les noms de personne français*, i, Uppsala 1927, 89, 97) may be nicknames, possibly so-called 'pageant names'. Perhaps (in spite of *DBS* s.n. *Harold*) the origin of modern *Harrod*.

66. Orgari [OE *Ordgār*]
67. Chebel [OE **Cybbel*—see *Winchester* 209 n. 5, and cf. *DBS* s.n. *Keeble*]

    Commonish in place-names, including a C14 Sussex field-name (*PNSussex* 563). This example shows Kentish and ESussex *e* < [y] (cf. 1 *Bedel*) and the Anglo-Norman spelling *ch* for [k] (cf. 98 *Chene-* < *Cyne-*, and see above 26 and below 169 n. 19)

68. Deringi [OE]
     Cf. 10.
69. Leffelmi [OE *Lēofhelm*]
70. Benwoldi [OE *Beornweald*] Gest [n. or p.; OE *gæst* 'stranger'—*OEB*
     219, *DBS* s.n. *Guest*, cf. *MED* s.n. *gest*; or S *Gestr*—*PNDB* 260]
     Ben-: as there is no such name-element, read *Bern-* < *Beorn-* (but cf.
     40 *Burnulfi*).
71. Wulfrici [OE] porcarii
72. Emmæ [CG]
     Cf. 46.
73. Slote [?]
     DBS refers *Slot(t* to ME *s(c)lott* 'mire', so this may be a topographical
     nickname; less probably a characteristic one.
74. Gosfridi [CG] coci
75. Godefridi [CG]
76. Lefuini [OE] hunger [p.; ? CG—see above 24]
77. Ædvini [OE] Cniht [n. or o.; OE *cniht*—cf. *DBS* s.n. *Knight*]
     Cniht: the surname *Knyst = Knight* occurs in 1296 (*SSR* 17).
78. Goldstani [OE *Goldstān*]
79. Wulbaldi [OE *Wulfbeald*] Winnoc [p.; OE *Winuc*— *UCPN* 152]
80. Brembel [n. or t.; OE *brǣmel, brēmel* 'bramble']
     The surname *Brembel* occurs here later (*BAB* 364, *SSR* 317). Note
     also the place-names *Bremblegh* (*BAB* 72 n. 10, 73—apparently for the
     district where *Brembel* lived), *Bremlisferd, -fricht* in late C12, and
     Brembelshulle c. 1240 (*PNSussex* 496).
81. Rotberti [CG] Barate [n.; OFr *barat, barate*—*Winchester* 207,
     Canterbury 303]
82. Lefflct [OE *Lēofflǣd* f.] loungæ [n.; ? OE Latinized]
83. Edildæ [OE *Ēadhild* f.] tipæ [p.; OE *Tippa* masc.]
     tipæ: the masc. OE *Tippa* here assumed is well evidenced in place-
     names, including one in Sussex (*PNSussex* 214–15, also *PNDevon* 606,
     PNEssex 66, 307, and *PNHerts* 149). Ignore the comments in *DBS* s.n.
     Tipp, but cf. s.n. *Tipping*.
84. Goldingi [OE *Golding*]
86. Ælurici [OE] Curlebasse [? n.; so far unexplained]

fol. 17v
87. Wulfuini [OE] Scot [p.; OE *Scot*—*Winchester* 171 n. 8]
88. Hvgonis [CG] Secretarii
89. Hunfridi [CG] presbiteri
          Cf. 111.
90. Pagani [L] Peche [n.; ? OFr]
     See 100 *Pechet*.

91. Durand*i* [L/CG—*Winchester* 155]
92. Jvliot [OFr dimin < L *Julianus*] lupi [n.; cf. OFr *le Leu*—e.g., *Amiens* 551; see also *Winchester* 213]
93. Ælfuini [OE] abbat [n.; ME *abbot*—*London* 177, also *DBS s.n. Abbatt*]
94. Siwardi [OE] Crulli [n.; ME *crul* 'curly-haired' Latinized—*Winchester* 210, *DBS s.n. Curl*]
95. Sevugel [OE] cannarii
    cannarii 'reed-cutter', according to Latham; but, as the surname *le Cannere* appears here later (*BAB* 125), perhaps a Latinization of ME *cannere* 'potter' (see *Canterbury* 297, *DBS s.n. Canner*, and *MED s.v.*).
96. Brictr*i*ci [OE *Beorhtrīc*] ortolani
    ortolani: the surname *Gardener* occurs in 1296 (*SSR* 17).
97. Ælwini [OE *Ælfwine*] secretarii
98. Chenewardi [OE *Cyneweard*]
    Cf. 67 *Chebel*.
99. Balduini [CG] svtoris
100. Osb*erti* [CG] pechet [n.; ? OFr]
    pechet: possibly identical with the name, Latinized as *Peccatum*, borne by the well-known *Peachey* family, including an early C12 bishop of Coventry (see *OEB* 353, also *Complete Peerage s.n.*); TL classes this spelling under *pechié* 'sin'. The question remains open whether 90 *Peche* represents the same name with loss of *-t* (in which case it would be dissyllabic) or OFr *pesche* 'fishing'. *DBS s. nn. Peckett, Petch* &c., fails to go into the matter deeply enough.
101. Cocardi [n.; OFr *cocart*, pej. < *coq*—*Eu* xii 216, *Haute Picardie* 215, cf. *Lynn* 59]
102. Ælfuini [OE] Hachet
    Hachet: current on the Continent (e.g., Fauroux, *Recueil des actes*, 366, and Gysseling, M., and Bougard, P., *L'Onomastique calaisienne*, Louvain 1963, 41) as well as in C12 England (see *SPLY* 123–4); needs fuller study.
103. Æilnoð [OE] Hecæ [p.; OE *Heca* masc.—*UCPN* 97]
    Hecæ: the bearers of OE *Heca* included a mid C11 bishop of Selsey.
104. Blachemann*i* [OE] de Bodeherstegate
    Bodeherste-: Bathurst, within the *leuga* (*PNSussex* 496). This surname appears in 1296 (*SSR* 17). Note the ESussex *herst* < OE *hyrst* (= WSussex *hurst*).
105. Rei*n*berti [CG] Genestær [n. or t.; OFr *genestier* 'broom-bush'—*France II* 286]
106. Ælurici [OE] Corueiser [o.; OFr—*Winchester* 201, also *MED s.v.*]
107. Brictr*i*ci [OE] barhc [n.; OE *bearg* 'pig'—see *MED s.v. barow*]
108. Ælfuini [OE] Tvrpin [p.; OFr *Turpin*—e.g., *Beauvais* 298, cf. *Winchester* 175]

109. Rogeri [CG] braceur [o.; OFr]
110. Walt*eri* [CG] ruffi
111. Hunfr*idi* [CG] Genester
    See 105.
    Either this man or 89 *Hunfridus presbiter* might be the ancestor of the
    Umfray family found here later (*SSR* 17, 317).
112. Goduini [? OE/CG] Gisard [p.; ? OFr]
    See below 169 n. 14.
113. Siwardi Crulli
    See 94.
114. Brunieve [OE *Brūng(i)efu* f.]

fol. 18r
115. Wulfuini [OE] Carpentarii
    Carpentarii: cf. 40; the surname *Carpentar'* occurs in 1296 (*SSR* 17).

Some Developments in Military Architecture
c. 1200: Le Coudray-Salbart

I would like to discuss certain traits exhibited by military architecture c. 1200 which seem to me to be of some interest in the development of castle design, a development which does not always follow a consistent line and where variations may appear and are then sometimes discarded. Whilst there are certain broad characteristics which are common to medieval military architecture (the evolution of the mural tower and, in the west, the progressive disappearance of the donjon are examples), it would be appropriate here to limit my observations largely to the areas open to Franco-Angevin influence. Even within these admittedly wide areas there are local variations, or perhaps specialities.

I am not even sure whether my comments will be found to be strikingly original—all I can say is that I have arrived at them independently and after some thought. Certain features whilst they have been noted, in some instances many times, have not in my view always received an adequate explanation of their evolution or incidence. Derek Renn's discussion of the Avranches Tower at Dover and its relationship with the Bell Tower at the Tower of London[1] is an excellent example of how fresh light may be shed on quite well-known buildings by a detailed examination and comparison of plan and fabric. Dennis Cathcart King's discussion of the Horseshoe Gate at Pembroke[2] is another case where attention is drawn to a particular development—one with which I shall be concerned.

Increasingly the study of castles is being directed on the one hand to the consideration of the mechanism of defence by detailed studies such as those mentioned above and on the other to a further understanding of the domestic buildings—their planning and function in relation to the status and household organization of the lord.

It is however to the former aspect that I would now like to refer. The latter part of the twelfth century and the beginning of the thirteenth century has always been accepted as a period of major change and much has been written, for example, on the transitional keep and the burgeoning of the keepless towered enceinte castle, exemplified by Framlingham c. 1190 and in its more regular and developed form by Boulogne 1228–1234.[3]

Certain developments of these decades remain fundamental even if many of the older techniques stayed in use and indeed were sometimes apparently revived—the great tower and rectangular gatehouses for instance.

I have here chosen one or two castles to highlight certain of these changes— some fundamental and some relatively ephemeral. For the most important of these I must thank Dr Arnold Taylor—who first mentioned it to me in 1965. It is the castle of Le Coudray-Salbart in Poitou; I visited it in the same year and was so far moved by it that I attempted a rough sketch plan of it—something of which I am normally incapable. Subsequently in 1967 an excellent article by Henri Paul Eydoux—there had been earlier comments—appeared in the *Bulletin Monumental*,[4] together with sketch plans which clearly placed on record the importance of this relatively neglected castle and corroborated the conclusions which had been derived from the examination of it.

Le Coudray-Salbart stands on a low and level spur flanked by the Sevre Niortaise on the south—a common type of site of only limited natural strength (pl. 1). The plan consists of a roughly rectangular inner bailey with a bailey to the west and a broad terre-plain to the east.

The defences of the lower bailey are fragmentary although excavation

1. Le Coudray-Salbart: aerial view from the south-west

would undoubtedly reveal a great deal. The inner bailey, upon which interest centres, is bounded by impressive ditches, especially notable on the east, which is the weakest approach, and on which the defences are concentrated. Although the site is described by M. Eydoux as being an early one of strategic importance in relation to Niort and routes over the marshy areas of Poitou (Fig. 1) he states that nothing in the present castle can be dated earlier than the early thirteenth century and the fabric generally confirms this. On the other hand indirect documentary evidence suggests that the latest period represented can hardly be later than c. 1227.

I realize that this latter date hardly coincides with the period of Anglo-Norman studies but the works represent a culmination of developments taking place at the end of that era. Poitou, as one of the frontiers of Angevin Aquitaine after the loss of Normandy and the death of King John, remained something of a cockpit for many years, the legacy of the earlier fall of such Angevin strongholds as Chinon and Loches; further, the interplay of Anglo-French warfare during the late twelfth and early thirteenth centuries undoubtedly led to rapid development and perhaps experiment in military architecture under Henry II and his sons on one side and Philippe Auguste on the other. This rapid change of design is strikingly portrayed here.

M. Eydoux notes that the lordship was in the hands of the pro-Angevin party and that evidence for English subsidies to strengthen the castle exists for

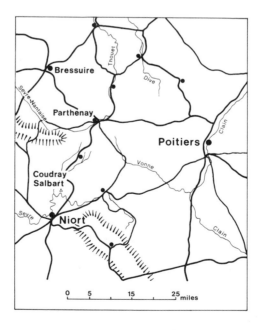

Figure 1. General map of area

the years 1202 and 1227 and that it was used as a base for an expedition in 1219 and 1220.

The rôle of Coudray-Salbart is thus established as an important border castle developed by a powerful vassal with the aid of English subsidies as a bulwark against French southward expansion. This rôle, which lasted only some 40 years, was effectively terminated by the triumph of the French in 1242. Although occupied subsequently its value was much reduced and, unlike many French as opposed to English castles, it was ruinous at least by 1460.

It is against this background and within this narrow date bracket that the castle can be examined.

What then are the principal characteristics of the castle?

1. A regular plan for the upper bailey with 4 flanking angle towers and intermediate towers on the longer transverse curtains east and west.
2. The angle towers project well beyond the curtain and are of large size with extremely thick walls.
3. The two towers facing the only easy approach are of exceptional size and of beaked form.
4. Of these two towers one, the south-east tower, performs the function of the donjon with first-floor entry and a chamber of hall-like proportions.
5. A central gateway leads from the lower bailey, otherwise there are only small posterns at low level opening to the field. This gateway consists of a substantial round tower with a straight-through gate-passage of quite small size.
6. The curtain is provided with an internal gallery equipped with loops.
7. This gallery either by-passes the towers or stops against them.
8. The upper wall head is less isolated from the towers but its most interesting feature is to be found in the provision of internal access stairs from the lower gallery.
9. Finally the castle exhibits evidence of substantial strengthening of the defences, probably carried out before the initial build was even completed.

In considering the basic polygonal plan Boulogne has already been noted[5] (Fig. 2). Simple polygonal plans with strong angle towers commanding straight intermediate curtains represent the hallmark of the early thirteenth-century castle. Earlier plans are frequently irregular with many angles or even curves to the curtain which were often originally undefended by flanking towers; Arques was an example of this, Warwick and indeed Windsor in this country betray their early origins as motte and bailey castles—admittedly as befits their status with large baileys.

The newer castles frequently depended for their strength on their fortifications rather than the natural strength of their sites combined with vast earthworks; this in turn allowed greater freedom for their siting. Thus of the

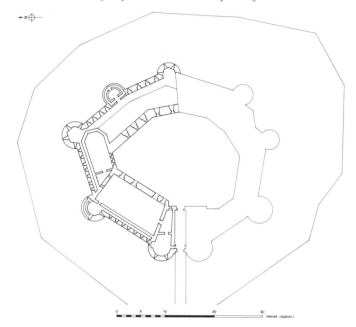

Figure 2. Boulogne-sur-Mer

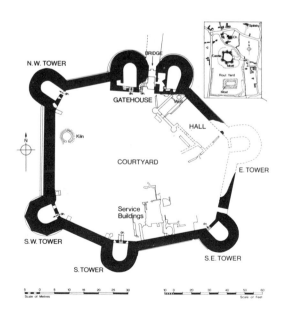

Figure 3. Bolingbroke, Lincolnshire

three Blundeville castles built or rebuilt in the 1220s; one, Beeston,[6] occupies a site of enormous natural strength—but the inner ward is built on a simple, virtually quadrilateral, plan with a powerful towered gatehouse as its strongest feature in the forefront of defence. Another, Chartley,[7] boasts an early motte but otherwise its plan conforms closely to the new style. The third, Bolingbroke,[8] descends from the hill to the flat marsh and was planned as a regular pentagon from the beginning (Fig. 3). These developments may be paralleled—e.g. at the trilateral of Welsh border castles—Skenfrith, Grosmont and White Castle.

Determining when and where the supremacy of the keepless geometrically planned tower and curtain castle occurred does not seem to be answerable with precision although often discussed. Regular forms may be found from the Conquest onward in Britain, some using Roman Walls like Portchester, and the Tower of London, Exeter and the like. Ludlow early had a moderately regular towered enceinte but with variable and limited projection of the towers beyond the curtain. Trim in Ireland was also so provided.

By the reign of Henry II, although keeps were still almost a *sine qua non*, closely spaced rectangular towers with straight intervening curtains were almost always the hallmarks of major new royal works, for example, the inner bailey of Dover, Orford (a totally new castle), Chinon (fort St Georges) and Gisors. The military planning of a new castle at this stage of development was clearly based on the need for higher walls, flanking towers and powerful gatehouses, all with good intercommunication and with one tower commanding another; further, the inadequacy of purely passive defence seems to have been increasingly strongly felt. Thus the development of loops at all levels in both towers and curtains was rapid.

The domestic planning requirements were also better met by the regular plan: thus chambers in the major towers—no longer open backed as at Gisors and Framlingham—provided superior lodgings, private and appointed with garderobes and fireplaces. The straight curtains between towers often seem to have been designed specifically to accommodate the great hall, chamber blocks, chapels, etc.; this can be clearly seen, for example, at Boulogne, Ainey le Vieil, also thirteenth century, and in the fourteenth century at Caldicot.

Certain factors clearly militated against the ideal solution in many instances; the pre-existence of the substantial earthworks of an early motte and bailey, the bank often crowned with an early or mid-twelfth-century curtain of equally demodé plan, for example, Berkhamstead and Castle Rising, as well as examples already cited. Again, as already stated, the naturally strong site would often preclude a regular plan if it was placed on a volcanic plug or a pinnacle of rock, e.g. Murol, although Najac achieved a quite early regular plan on its limited summit.

The evolution of the classic polygonal castle does not seem to have been realized in all its implications in the examples of Henry II's works although the form is present at Dover and Orford. It is to the period immediately after 1200 that one must look for the true realization of form and content. Ritter[9] considers the Château at Carcassonne to be a prototype, and it is certainly early but not, I think, as early as he states, and hardly before the last two decades of the twelfth century. Yèvre-le-Châtel[10] (Fig. 4), a simple rectangle, must be little later; it has no need of a strong gatehouse, being elevated above the outer bailey which is, however, provided with a twin towered gatehouse.

The fortresses of the later years of Philippe Auguste notably the Louvre, Lillebonne and perhaps above all Dourdan[11] are regarded by Ritter, and more reliably by Héliot,[12] as examples of the uniquely French castle of the period, and at Dourdan one can see the fully developed quadrangular enceinte with powerful gatehouse and angle towers.

One aberrant survives in these later castles of Philippe Auguste—that is the isolation of the circular donjon, placed at Lillebonne and Dourdan at one of the corners. Of the numerous Philippe Auguste round donjons it is worth noting that two of the earlier ones are beaked; Issoudun and Roche Guyon.[13] From the above it may be concluded that the components of the classic thirteenth-century castle, whether in its polygonal or rectangular form, existed by c. 1200 to reach complete achievement in the 1220s and '30s under Henry III in England and Louis IX in France.

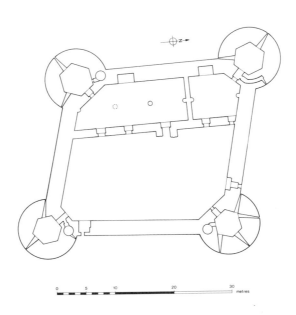

Figure 4. Yèvre-le-Châtel

2. Le Coudray-Salbart: east curtain from the east

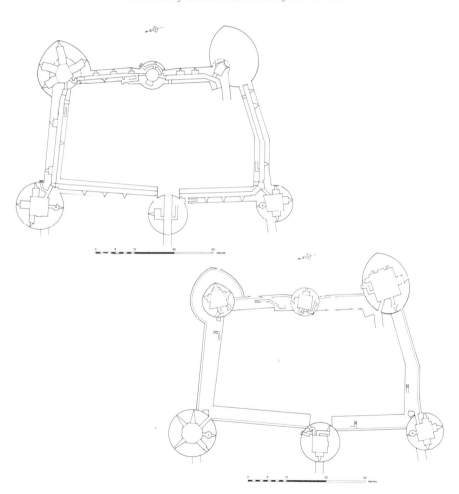

Figures 5 and 6. Le Coudray-Salbart, ground floor; Le Coudray-Salbart, first floor

SH'L
WITHDRAWN

Le Coudray Salbart may be said to exhibit all the characteristics noted above.

The angle towers can be seen to be of great strength and enormous projection (pl. 2 and Figs. 5, 6), and are integrated with the defences of the curtain—if integrated is the right word—for in four of the towers both upper and lower chambers are carefully isolated from the curtain defences.

The two great eastern angle-towers present massive prows to the field. These are among the most striking examples of this type of tower to be found. Beaked towers are found sporadically both as regards time and area in France and, to a lesser extent, elsewhere on the Continent and occasionally in England.

The height of their flowering must be placed in and close to the frontiers of the Angevin Empire in the period just before the loss of Normandy, and for some quarter century following, i.e. c. 1200–1230.

Richard I's donjon at Château Gaillard although containing unique constructional features and Philippe's Roche Guyon are almost the earliest of the true almond-shaped *tours à bec*—both on the Norman frontiers. Issoudun in Berry follows just after 1200. The superb trio of beaked mural towers at Loches[14] may follow its fall in 1205—but could they be slightly earlier than stated by M. Valery Radot? Coudray-Salbart and no doubt Parthenay (pl. 3), the seigneury of William l'Archévèque, must be placed shortly after this; perhaps in the second decade of the thirteenth century. Structural evidence indicates that at both Loches and Salbart they are without doubt secondary recladdings of existing *tourelles*. The refortification of the main northern and the Fitzwilliam Gates at Dover follows the siege of 1216 and must date to the 1220s.[15] However, beaked towers of angular form may be found both earlier and later, thus—the small twelfth-century donjon-like tower at Chalusset[16] in the Limousin, at Gisors forming part of Henry II's work, at Provins, e.g. one of the town gates, and a mural tower at Vendome. At La Ferté Milon c. 1400 there are superb *tours à bec* adorning the massive front of this palace-castle of Louis d'Orleans (pl. 4) but although powerful, they must be regarded as isolated architectural 'tours de force' unrelated to the search for defensive power taking place c. 1200.

Of the two great beaked towers at Coudray-Salbart the south eastern became the donjon. Before enlargement, however, the original 'Tour Double' was the larger of the two.

Of great size and like the rest of the castle built in fine ashlar, the donjon has only two floors—much of the external face is below courtyard level and like the rest of the east face represents a revetment of the ditch. The scale of this great tower may be gauged from the illustrations (pls. 5, 6).

It is isolated from mural passages and wall walks and the entry to the lower floor is in fact at first-floor level. Within there is a single dark but spacious vaulted chamber with a hooded fireplace (pl. 7). A garderobe opens from it

3. *Parthenay: inner gate showing* tours à bec

4. *La Ferté Milon: entrance front of château*

5. *Le Coudray-Salbart: donjon and small intermediate tower from the north-east*

6. *Le Coudray-Salbart: donjon from the courtyard* (*west*)

7. *Le Coudray-Salbart: donjon, fireplace
and vault in lower chamber*

and discharges in the angle with the east curtain and a staircase rises within the
thickness of the wall on the west. The vault corbels here and elsewhere confirm
the date suggested. Indeed they would be at home in the second half of the
twelfth century. The great tower at Coudray-Salbart fulfils all the requirements of a donjon except that of structural isolation and in this it is paralleled
by the Tour des Prisonniers at Gisors and at Bothwell with its own partial
ditch.

The increasing subordination of the great tower to the general scheme of
defence is characteristic of this period although the independent design has a
long life, Edward I still using it at Flint at the end of the thirteenth century.

The gatehouse of Coudray-Salbart (pl. 8) is of a type which was not to
become generally acceptable, unsurprisingly in view of its relative weakness,
and indeed the form seems to be something of a regional variety although
sometimes found elsewhere. The outer gate may well have been of a different
type but has not been identified. The single round tower with a straight-
through gate-passage may be found at Arques, Dourdan, Ludlow, all
thirteenth-century, and a variation of c. 1200 at Caldicot, but its most striking
manifestation occurs at Bressuire (Deux Sèvres) where not less than three such
gate towers existed. One is a postern, which should be noted for the evidence
of a thickening comparable to that shown at Coudray-Salbart (pl. 9), but two
were principal gates housed in massive round towers rising more than fifty feet

8. Le Coudray-Salbart: gatehouse and north-west tower from the west

from profound ditches. The main entry to the outer ward can be seen to have a round-headed gate arch (pl. 10). A further blocked gate invisible from the outside occurs between the outer gate and the entry to the inner ward. The simple impost and rough semicircular arch strongly suggests a date not far from 1200, and it may well have been blocked when the tower was strengthened and powerful additions provided to the inner bailey gate.

At Coudray-Salbart the small central gate arch has a square-headed recess for the drawbridge, the stone pivot holes of which survive (pl. 11). There is a small guard-room on the left and a staircase on the right. The first floor contains a single room with a forward loop and a rear passage giving onto the north curtain only and containing a garderobe.

On a small point of architectural detail, the forms of the gate-arch and drawbridge recess are remarkably akin to the entry to the keep at Lillebonne.

The single round or D-shaped gatehouse tower with a straight passage is a short-lived and obviously unsatisfactory development. It is not impossible, however, that the development of the right-angled entry in a round tower as at the Horseshoe Gate at Pembroke and at Caldicot, and the development of the idea in the form of the large and relatively low barbican to the same design, originate from a common source. The original single-storey barbican at Tenby—before its heightening—is much earlier than the fourteenth century, perhaps close to 1200. In the thirteenth century such barbicans are common—

9. Bressuire: postern angle tower showing core of original tower above

10. Bressuire: round tower with one of principal gateways to outer bailey

11. Le Coudray-Salbart: detail of gateway

Pembroke, Montreuil Bellay, Tower of London, Carcassonne, Goodrich, etc.

A more important development exhibited to a remarkable degree at Coudray-Salbart is the complete system of wall passages. Derek Renn has shown in his comparison of the late twelfth-century Avranches Traverse at Dover and the Bell Tower at the Tower of London that one of the newer features is the provision of partial mural galleries related to these towers. Access to mural loops, when these were provided, seems heretofore to have normally been by means of a timber platform cantilevered from the wall. The putlog holes for such may be seen in London Wall c. 1200 and must have been provided for access to the loops at, for example, Framlingham. The provision of a mural gallery giving protection from the rear and providing excellent covered communication between various curtains and towers remained something of a rarity in castle design although the provision of ranges of mural loops—often multiple—are a feature of Edward I's Welsh castles, e.g. Caernarvon, and are increasingly provided in the thirteenth century. A partial mural gallery with loops is, however, provided at Beaumaris, in the wall north of the Beauchamp Tower and in St Thomas' Tower at the Tower of London, all by Edward I.

The complete gallery at Coudray-Salbart is a remarkable and precocious example of this provision. In addition, the lower gallery is provided with internal staircases on each curtain giving covered access to the upper wall walk. The careful isolation of the towers from the gallery should be noted, together with the different means of doing so. The donjon is of course completely cut off, as on the lower level is the gatetower; in the case of the west angle-towers, a short diagonal passage leads off the gallery; the entry to the Tour Double is less protected and must be accounted for by the fact that in its original form it differed greatly in size and function. Only in the case of the small intermediate tower does the gallery pass through the tower—but there is a carefully devised meurtrière/loop commanding the passage from the staircase (pl. 12).

At wall walk level the back of the entrance tower is traversed by a mural passage, and the Tour Double is again treated differently—was it ever completely finished?

The last point I would like to touch upon briefly is the ever-present need to keep at least those castles in the 'shooting line', as it were, in an up-to-date state of defence. In a period of rapid development in defence which equates to a period famous for great sieges—Kerak, Acre, Château Gaillard, Chinon, Dover and Bedford—it should not be surprising to find rapid changes in defensive techniques.

An intermediate or perhaps experimental phase in the development of mature mural towers seems to me represented by the provision of small solid or largely solid towers, a number of which can be dated to c. 1200. Castle Acre, outer and middle gates,[17] and Corfe, outer gate,[18] amongst gatehouses; together with Conisborough, Loches, already noted, and, a long way away, Sayun[19] all look remarkably similar. Allied to these are the very small mural towers found at Bressuire and Coudray-Salbart which have already been mentioned.

It would seem that such towers had a short life, being either interspersed or replaced by much larger towers at a date only shortly after their initial erection. This relationship is clear at Loches, at Bressuire, where the inner bailey wall and at least some of the towers were doubled in thickness shortly after building, and at Coudray-Salbart; at the outer gate at Corfe strengthening almost amounting to rebuilding appears to have happened somewhat later.

Small round towers of the type described do seem to be a distinctive class and not just an intermediate development between the normal rectangular and round-fronted mural tower. In the twelfth century a number of Poitevin keeps boasted large rounded projections half-way between buttresses and turrets both at the angles and intermediate on the faces, for example, Tiffauges and Pouzauges, although these may perhaps derive from the earlier habit of providing rounded pilaster buttresses at such keeps as Loches and Montbazon—a further characteristic of the area.

The small round tower, partly solid, may be found in the near east, however, and several Umayad fortified enclosures are so provided, e.g. Quasr

12. Le Coudray-Salbart: east front mural passage looking north to doorway through small intermediate tower; note small horizontal loop above trefoil-headed door which commands the passage from the stair

13. Loches: tourelles *and one of later* tours à bec

14. Le Coudray-Salbart: interior of small tower embodied in the donjon

al Hair Ash Sharqui and Ukhaidir, both eighth century. Cresswell[20] suggests that early Umayad fortifications derived from Roman and Byzantine models and certainly their basic rectangular form indicates this, as does the fact that Imperial forts were re-utilized, e.g. Hallabat, where substantial and palatial buildings were built. Indeed the round towers, solid up to the parapet level of the curtain, and with a single chamber formed at this level, may also have a Roman precedent and can perhaps be compared with the solid-based Roman bastions which were designed as ballista platforms, and may be derived from them, but their proportions differ appreciably.

The tourelles, as they may be called, at Loches and Bressuire also have small rectangular chambers on their upper levels—much of the lower part of which is solid being below courtyard level and revetting the profound ditches. The family likeness between these and the examples at Coudray-Salbart (the original S.E. tower), Conisborough, and indeed the crusader castle of Sayun, is I think too great to be ignored even if their derivation and relationship may be difficult to establish.

The comparative inadequacy of the smaller type of tower does, however, seem to have been recognized quite quickly especially when it was at the forefront of defence. The rapid change in defensive techniques whereby mural towers of ample projection and provided with plentiful loops replaced lesser towers is nowhere better illustrated than at Loches where three great beaked towers superseded the small late twelfth-century tourelles to the extent of engulfing at least one of them (pl. 13).

The alternative to replacing the smaller towers by repositioning or rebuilding new and more powerful ones was to reinforce existing towers. Three remarkable examples of this may be cited of which the most telling is Coudray-Salbart where it is quite clear that the transformation of the Tour Double and donjon (N.E. and S.E. towers) from small angle tower to massive beaked tower took place before the castle was completed. The two periods of the Tour Double are clear from the plan and from the way the smaller early tower survives above the beaked lower part. In the case of the donjon tower its predecessor can be seen to be of extremely small size, being virtually embedded in the thickness of the wall of the later construction (pl. 14). Three round-headed loop recesses within the small tower contain loops of a developed design, the cross-slits being pierced independently of the vertical slot. It was and still is entered from the mural passage which bends at this point. The plan suggests that the construction of the donjon tower involved the replanning of the curtain in this the S.E. corner of the defences by pushing the south curtain further south to cover the vastly increased size of the tower, the remains of the older curtains being utilized to provide access to the first-floor level entry to the donjon. The actual constructional chronology has not hitherto been dealt with and needs much further examination. It could be tentatively suggested that building operations may perhaps have begun with

15. Le Coudray-Salbart: Tour St Michel, upper vault

16. Le Coudray-Salbart: interior of inner bailey, looking east

the most vulnerable east fort and proceeded in a clockwise direction. The gatehouse to the inner bailey could have been built in advance of its flanking curtains with which it is not well integrated. The construction of the outer bailey cannot easily be related in view of its fragmentary and largely buried condition. The large round towers of the west front are clearly more powerful than the small eastern ones, and it may be that the decision dramatically to increase the strength of the Tour Double and donjon was reached by the time the north curtain was built, since the former relates to a single curtain in both its phases whereas the donjon engulfed the small tower asymmetrically as noted above.

The general strengthening of mural towers must be seen as part of a general acknowledgement of their importance in providing more than the passive defence of high walls. The means employed at Coudray-Salbart and Bressuire to achieve this end, i.e. by greatly increasing the thickness and projection of existing towers, is only one way of doing this, but a very clearly demonstrable one. A striking parallel may be found in the strengthening of the angle-towers of the citadel of Cairo built by Saladin 1176–1184. These were vastly increased in size by al Adil only some 25 years later in 1207–1208.[21] It is worth noting that already in Saladin's work the curtains are provided with the looped wall passages. It is not necessary to show a direct architectural relationship between these buildings to explain the similarities in developments in areas where the common circumstances of warfare and indeed personalities obtained, for example, Richard I, Philippe Auguste, Saladin and al Adil were, after all, all present at the siege of Acre in 1189–1190. The potential for 'offensive' defence offered by the increased number of loops in these great towers shows a great and precocious improvement in defensive technique.

In the absence of clear documentary dating evidence it is all too often difficult to assign dates to military architecture since identifiable architectural detail is scarce. Coudray-Salbart, however, is unusual in that it provides examples of most of the types of vaults in use c. 1200: these are enumerated by M. Eydoux,[22] who describes them as 'un veritable catalogue des voûtes en usage à l'époque'. Further, the corbels for these and for the fireplace in the donjon possess foliated capitals almost equally. The volute corbels in the north-west tower (Tour du Moulin) (Fig. 7, I) and the small intermediate east tower (Tour St Michel) (pl. 15) are basically similar, but the former is more conservative and would be acceptable in the middle of the second half of the twelfth century, whereas both ought to be the same date unless the vault in the latter is a slightly later insertion. The capital of the engaged vaulting shaft in the donjon is of a more developed type but should not be later than c. 1220. The architectural evidence can thus be seen to support the dating proposed by M. Eydoux rather than that of Ritter. In this respect it is instructive to compare the capital from the Tour du Moulin already mentioned with the capital from Yèvre-le-Châtel (Fig. 7, I, II).

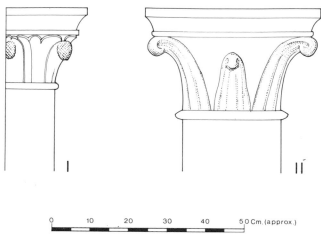

| 0 | 10 | 20 | 30 | 40 | 50 Cm.(approx.) |

Figure 7. Volute Capitals

I. Le Coudray-Salbart, Tour Double.   *II. Yèvre-le-Châtel, central arcade*
                                                  of ground floor of Hall range

The features described above, architectural, defensive and of planning, make Le Coudray-Salbart something of an exemplar in early thirteenth-century military architecture. The extent, quality and condition of the visible remains combined with the potential for recovering the plan of the domestic buildings within the inner bailey (pl. 16) as well as the outer bailey defences—all either buried or overgrown—would make the meticulous excavation, recording and consolidation of this castle a most rewarding task. Because of the quality of its evidence as existing it certainly should not be a candidate for the extensive *dégagement* and reconstruction which occasionally mars the otherwise admirable works carried out on such monuments.

The location of Coudray-Salbart in Poitou, one of the principal counties of the Angevin Empire which for a time survived the losses of Normandy and the Angevin heartlands on the Loire, make the study of this and neighbouring castles just as relevant to the general development of Anglo-French military architecture as examples from the French royal domains, England or Normandy.

Despite some characteristics not frequently found elsewhere, the Angevin castles of the Loire and northern Aquitaine are therefore a proper study for the student of the Anglo-Norman kingdom, and a rewarding one especially in the seminal period c. 1200, when the Angevins were fighting for their patrimony.

The Piety of the Anglo-Norman Knightly Class

C. HARPER-BILL

Orderic Vitalis, like most historians who have followed him, found it difficult to reconcile the predatory and pious instincts of the upper echelons of Norman society. Many aristocratic estates of the eleventh century were founded upon the pillage and appropriation of ecclesiastical lands. The Montgomery family, for example, even before the troubled years of William's minority, had annexed certain revenues of Bernay, Fécamp and Jumièges.[1] To the fortunes of such great men were hitched those of a far larger number of knightly families. Orderic woefully recounts numerous acts of aggression by such men against his own community, and the picture which he paints of the *milites* is realistic. The attitude even of the benefactors of St Evroul was ambiguous. Ascelin Goel, despite his gifts to the abbey, was condemned as a vicious bandit.[2] Foucher de Chaudry was a brave knight, but he was always eager to seize the property of others in order to dispense it in generous gestures, and he alternated between oppression and patronage of the monks.[3] Peter, the founder of the priory of Maule, was munificent in almsgiving, and yet abhorred austerity in himself; lavish in his promises and prodigal with his goods, he was grasping and generous at the same time, and was little concerned whether his possessions were acquired by lawful acquisition or by plunder.[4] After 1066, the patrimonies of the English saints were not immune from violent misappropriation, and the great land pleas of the Conqueror's reign testify to the numerous 'invasions' of the lands of Christ Church Canterbury and Ely by Norman knights who were commemorated as benefactors by Norman houses.[5]

If during William's minority and again during the Conquest the judicious use of violence could often bring spectacular worldly success, the prospects of eternal salvation for the knightly class were slender. The torments of hell, portrayed so vividly in the mid-twelfth century in the Winchester Bible and on the west front of Lincoln cathedral, were a reality to which the minds of the laity were constantly directed. When Orderic recounted the encounter of a young priest with Hellequin's Hunt, the legendary procession of the damned, he was anxious to emphasize the particularly unpleasant fate which awaited the generality of knights. Their bodies were coal-black and flickered with fire, the weapons which they bore were red-hot. One carried in his mouth a burning mill shaft, heavier than Rouen castle; another was tortured by a ball of fire around his ankles, because in his life he had used sharp spurs in his eagerness to shed blood.[6]

The legislation of the church constantly reminded the warrior how precarious were his hopes of eternal bliss. The peace movement in Normandy was used by the duke as an instrument of governmental policy, but the preaching of bishops and monks across the French principalities consistently contrasted the avarice and violence of the knightly class with the beatitude of the *pauperes* whom the church sought to protect.[7] The penitential ordinance imposed after the Hastings campaign emphasized that no violence was exempt from spiritual punishment, even if committed in a public war at the command of a lawfully constituted prince.[8] In the eyes of St Anselm, even holy war against the infidel was to be deprecated; far preferable was the quest for peace in the monastic Jerusalem.[9]

Mere survival in the highly competitive Norman world of the late eleventh century was dependent upon acts condemned by the church as sinful. The military activity for which the knight had been trained from a tender age, and the discharge of the obligations upon which tenure of his fief depended, had as a corollary the desperate need for divine forgiveness. Every evil act must be balanced by some visible manifestation of atonement. Despite the novel ideas expressed in *Cur Deus Homo*, even St Anselm was far from the theology of contrition and confession formulated in the twelfth century.[10] The obligations owed to God were equated with those due to the greatest of feudal lords, and for every transgression of the divine law an amercement must be paid. To achieve salvation it was essential to secure the *benevolentia* of the Almighty. Salvation was a matter of negotiation with God, represented by His ministers on earth.

Such negotiation is well illustrated by an early twelfth century agreement between Mont St Michel and Thomas de St Jean, who had devastated three of the abbey's woods to obtain material for his new castle. The monks prayed to God to avenge this wrong, and on hearing this Thomas 'in horror hastened like a madman to the Mount ... and enquired of the monks why they were clamouring against him and his brethren.' He threw himself at the abbot's feet and begged for reconciliation; in return for his quitclaim he received the confraternity of the house.[11] Consciousness of guilt in specific matters was a frequent motivation for grants. Roger de Conches, son of Roger de Tosny, before he set out for Spain came to the chapter house at St Evroul and sought pardon for his participation in the burning of the town, promising many gifts to the monks if he returned safely.[12] Roger de Vitot, mortally wounded in the English campaign, had temporarily lost his estates for his part in the murder of Gilbert de Brionne; on his deathbed he confirmed, for the salvation of his soul, the gifts made by others from his lands.[13] In England Nigel d'Aubigny restored two manors to St Cuthbert when he begged for his intercession as he lay severely ill and terrified of what would befall him.[14] Remorse might even be felt for a political miscalculation. Eustace fitz John founded four monastic houses in penance for his participation in the Battle of the Standard on the Scots side.[15]

St Anselm did not encourage the religious to aid the laity in their quest for salvation. Employing military analogies, he saw the Christian laity as townspeople who would easily succumb to the assaults of their enemy, the Devil, while the monks were the garrison of the castle, safe from attack so long as they were not tempted by the slaughter of their kinsfolk to look out of the windows, and thus expose themselves to danger.[16] Most monastic communities, however, regarded it as their duty to provide spiritual succour and intercession for their fellow believers, providing that they made some tangible gesture of repentance. St Hugh, indeed, set out to make Cluny the *asylum poenitentium*, a refuge and means of deliverance for the faithful, and the Norman monasteries, strongly influenced by Cluniac tradition, followed suit.[17]

As an example of this relationship may be taken the family of Ralph de Montpinçon. Ralph, steward of Duke William, gave St Evroul the tithe of five mills, in return for which the monks agreed to accept into their community John of Rheims, hitherto a secular clerk, who undertook to pray for the salvation of Ralph and his wife. Ralph's son Hugh was received into the fraternity of the abbey, and when thirty years later he returned to St Evroul to renew his ties with the community, he requested their prayers for his brother who had died on a pilgrimage to Jerusalem, and obtained confraternity for his own son, Ralph II. Three generations were eventually buried within the abbey. For a small outlay, the family had acquired a share in a prestigious mausoleum, together with continuous intercession and liturgical commemoration.[18]

To illustrate the relationship between monks and their benefactors, Orderic employed the scriptural model of Abraham and Lot, the former representing the monastic order, the latter the generality of mankind ensnared by the sinful delights of Sodom and in consequence rejecting God. Yet Abraham did not achieve the deliverance of the people unaided, and by the biblical 'companions of Abraham' are signified those of the laity who furthered the spiritual endeavours of the monks. 'Many laymen,' Orderic believed, 'are graced with gentle and seemly manners and are joined by faith and goodwill to the dedicated soldiers of Christ, bringing them succour in their valiant battle against the demons. Nevertheless, they do not abandon the transient world and are unwilling to renounce worldly things completely; and so they accept lawful wedlock and give offence to God by many transgressions of His law, but yet redeem their sins with their alms, as Daniel counsels.'[19]

Monastic theologians and chroniclers were in agreement that the ideal remedy for sin was the complete emendation of life in conversion to the Rule of St Benedict, but if for certain worldly reasons this was not feasible, reparation might be made by the lavish donation of alms. At the highest level of society, the most effective display of charity was the foundation of a religious community, and in a famous passage Orderic described the proliferation of such foundations in the middle years of the eleventh century.[20] Such lavish benefactions were, of course, acts of conspicuous expenditure, bringing in their wake social, economic and even political advantage, but it would surely be incautious to ignore the religious sentiments expressed in numerous foundation charters. The words placed in the mouth of Richard count of Evreux when, between 1055 and 1066, he founded the Benedictine nunnery of Saint-Sauveur have the ring of truth: 'considering that this miserable life is worth naught, and in terror of the pains of hell, I have founded a house of nuns within the city of Evreux ... I Richard, unworthy count and sinner, believing that I may share with the nuns in the heavenly mansions, do upon my oath make the following donations to them.'[21]

Few, however, were capable of such expansive largesse, and if the endowment by the founder was normally the determinant of the economic condition of the house for all time, the greatest monasteries did not hesitate to encourage the lesser members of the knightly class to acts of charity. The biblical phrases attributed to donors by monastic scribes who composed their charters doubtless reflect the exhortations of the religious which had prompted the gifts, and were the basis of a popular theology of almsgiving. A charter of Gilbert Crispin for Jumièges, for example, cites three such texts, including 'Blessed are the merciful, for they shall obtain mercy'—merciful was glossed as those giving alms.[22] Most reassuring, perhaps, was the text used in a sermon by a monastic bishop, Herbert de Losinga: 'Alms extinguisheth sin, as water doth fire.'[23] Occasionally more intimate sentiments are expressed in a charter. A document from St Martin at Séez describes how in 1087 Robert, son of Tetbald, sheriff of the honour of Arundel, on his deathbed and in fear of the pains of hell, received good counsel from his faithful friends, and for the salvation of his soul and for the help of his kindred past and future granted to the monks the manor of Tottington.[24] A year later Ralph son of Ansered explained that he had considered well the foolishness of leaving his goods to others after his death when he could profit so greatly from their pious distribution during his lifetime.[25] The prospect of death on a dangerous expedition prompted many to take precautions for the welfare of their souls. In 1066 Roger, son of Turold gave three yokes of land to Holy Trinity at Rouen before his departure on the English campaign during which he died.[26] On the eve of the Maine expedition of 1073 William de Braose made several grants to his canons of Bramber.[27] His son Philip, about to depart for Jerusalem at the time of the First Crusade, confirmed all the gifts of his family to St Florent at Saumur, donations which he had previously resisted.[28]

While emphasizing the spiritual motivation for benefactions and the central rôle of almsgiving in the popularized theology transmitted to the laity, it would be facile to deny that there were practical incentives for the bestowal of gifts. The support of a particular religious house was frequently the expression of corporate solidarity within a feudal grouping. The tenants of the Giroie family had joined with their lords in the endowment of St Evroul, but when Robert de Grandmesnil was expelled from Normandy, the knights were suddenly transformed from benefactors into predators, each seizing what he could in retribution for the monks' enforced reception of a new abbot.[29] The Bigod tenants in Norfolk joined their lord both in the harassment of the Anglo-Saxon community of St Benet Holme and in the endowment of the new Cluniac foundation at Thetford.[30] The majority of monastic houses in Normandy and England were similarly linked with the fortunes of one great family. The priory of Stoke-by-Clare, for example, was the spiritual centre of the entire honour, attracting benefactions in the early twelfth century from most of the families who in 1166 can be identified as tenants of the Clare earl of Hertford.[31] A large proportion of these gifts were in the form of advowsons or tithes, the lay ownership of which had from the late eleventh century become a matter of reproach, while their transfer to a religious house represented a spiritual investment.

Many grants, indeed, were in reality commercial transactions. Orderic's list of the early acquisitions of St Evroul includes a considerable number of purchases.[32] There was, in fact, an inextricable confusion of worldly and spiritual profit, revealed by two Jumièges charters. Around 1128 Guidard de Farcis granted the abbey all his land in the parish of St Martin de Bouafle, for the redemption of himself and his kindred. In return the monks granted him the benefits of confraternity, with the promise of reception if he so wished, but in addition the abbot gave him sixty *solidi* and a palfrey, with a tunic worth seven *solidi* for his son.[33] Before the Conquest Gilbert Crispin had given to the same abbey his fief of Hauville, which he had won from Duke William by fighting. The land was considered by the local inhabitants to be of inestimable worth, but Gilbert had accepted from the abbey 200 l., a horse worth 20 l. and two ounces of gold. This, however, was of little account, for such material values are transitory, and of far greater value he considered the benefit which his grant conferred upon the souls of himself, his family and his lord.[34]

A similar fusion of practical and pious motivation may be seen in the numerous grants of children to religious houses, in which they would spend the remainder of their lives. In the late eleventh century oblation was certainly the most common form of entry to the religious life, and countless children were, like Orderic himself, taken weeping from their parents' arms. For the noble and knightly classes the practical wisdom of disposing of surplus children in this way was obvious. When Foucher de Chaudry placed two of his six sons in St Evroul, he was not only offering a living sacrifice to God, after the pattern of Abraham's sacrifice of Isaac, but he was making sensible provision to safeguard against the complete disintegration of the family estates.[35] In the 1060s Gerbert de Poterel admitted that it was the poverty of his estates, as well as the inspiration of God, which induced him to place his son Drogo as an oblate in Mont St Michel.[36] The importance of the institution is well illustrated by the relations of the Bohun family with Marmoutier. Humphrey de Bohun placed a younger son, Ingelram, in the abbey of St Martin. In 1092 his eldest son, Richard de Mereio, who was engaged in a violent property dispute with the monks, renounced his claim on condition that the convent should accept one of his little sons, Humphrey, and educate him until he reached the age when he could become a monk if he wished. If Humphrey died before this time, Richard should himself have the option of becoming a monk, but if he did not wish this, the community would take in another of his sons. The monks stipulated that they would only take one boy, and except in the case of Humphrey, his education should be the responsibility of his father until he was old enough to make his profession.[37] Yet, notwithstanding these examples, and despite the strictures of twelfth century reformers and modern historians, there is occasional evidence that considerations of secular policy were not always paramount. Around 1060 Ansfroi, a knight of William fitz Osbern, gave a substantial portion of his inheritance to Holy Trinity at Rouen, to which house he also offered Geoffrey, his only son.[38]

The prevalence of oblation produced a large class of monks schooled in the Benedictine observance from an early and impressionable age, but it had disadvantages, recognized by some contemporaries before the Cistercian onslaught on the practice. St Anselm described the rivalry which characterized the relationship between the *nutriti*, raised in the monastery, and the converts from secular life.[39] Guibert de Nogent described how the great majority of monks who had entered as oblates tended to believe that they were sinless, since they had always lived under the Rule, and hence their observance slackened through lack of commitment to personal atonement. Moreover, having no experience of the world beyond the cloister, they were generally incompetent in their administration of monastic temporalities.[40] St Evroul, like all contemporary houses, was largely staffed by *nutriti*. Reginald, youngest son of Arnold d'Echauffour, entered the community at the age of five, and although he lived an exemplary life for fifty two years, 'was stern and hard to the insolent and never stooped to flatter hypocrites,' in consequence suffering many difficulties.[41] William, son of Guy Bollein, entered in his tenth year, became a superb chanter and illuminator, but was constantly eager to reprove all those who broke the monastic rule.[42] Orderic, an oblate himself, had the highest praise for these men, but perhaps their spiritual arrogance, little in accord with the monastic ideal of humility and penitence, was a constant irritant to those who entered the cloister in their mature years. Indeed, the conflict between Abbot Thierry and Prior Robert de Grandmesnil at St Evroul is itself symptomatic of the tension between *nutriti* and *conversi*.

For practical and spiritual reasons, therefore, it was desirable that any monastic house should draw a proportion of its personnel from adults experienced in the world. A large percentage of the adult entrants, however, adopted the habit of religion only *in extremis*, or at least when broken down by illness or old age. On occasion such a conversion might be interpreted with cynicism, as in the case of Rodolf Pinellus, who replied to Abbot Herluin's criticism of his violent behaviour by promising that when he had had his fill of worldly pleasure and was tired of fighting, he would become a monk.[43] Yet the common conviction was that even long delayed entry would benefit the soul not only of the convert, but of his kindred, for whom he might pray as long as he lived. In a charter of 1110, for example, William de Tracy described how, on account of the magnitude of his misdeeds and for the salvation of his soul and the souls of his predecessors, he had assumed the Benedictine garb at Mont St Michel.[44] The scribe of St Wandrille in the mid-1040s placed in the mouth of Gerard Flagitellus an elaborate explanation of his decision to become a monk in extreme old age. Although he had hitherto been deaf and obstinate, he had at last heeded the call to sell what he had, give it to the poor and follow Christ; he had, like St Peter, been reduced to tears of lamentation for his previous denial, and now he proposed, as far as his faculties allowed, to answer the divine call and to cast off his worldly burden, finding in the tranquillity of the cloister a haven from the storms and tempests of the secular life.[45]

Monastic theologians did not disparage the prevalent custom of conversion *ad succurrendum*. Ralph of Canterbury, in a meditation devised in the form of a debate between a sinner and Reason, strongly emphasized the efficacy of deathbed conversion.[46] God does not desire the death of a sinner, but rather that he should repent and live. Because it was almost impossible to fulfil the promises made at baptism, He had instituted the monastic order, by the observation of whose Rule sinners might repair the ravages of the devil. Even if conversion was delayed to the very moment before death, the sinner could be assured that there was no more certain means of winning God's mercy. Ralph compared the man who died with the last rites of the church to one who died in the monastic habit; he was as the stars are to the sun, or as the man who, when he could have been king, chose only to be a count. Orderic showed no cynicism in his treatment of numerous such conversions, which he regarded either as the fitting culmination of a pious life, as in the case of Ansold de Maule, who for fifty-three years 'set an example even to monks living under a rule by the sober strictness of his abstinence', and then took the habit three days before his death, delivering a splendid exhortation to his son on the obligations of knighthood and lordship;[47] or as heavenly inspired repentance for a career of violence, as when Arnold d'Echauffour, who had burnt the town around the abbey, was inspired by a deathbed vision of St Nicholas to become a monk.[48] Orderic, indeed, regarded such conversion as the normal conclusion of a knightly career; writing of the knights of Maule, the cell of St Evroul, he observed that they not only made extensive benefactions, but discussed practical and speculative wisdom with the monks in the cloister, 'for the monastic order is honoured by them, and in the hour of death it is wholeheartedly sought by them for their souls' good.'[49]

At the highest level of Anglo-Norman society deathbed reception was common. In the first quarter of the eleventh century, Osbern and Anfredus, the two brothers-in-law of Duke Richard II, entered St Wandrille in extreme old age.[50] In England after the Conquest, Richard fitz Gilbert entered St Neot's a few years before his death, and Roger of Montgomery and Hugh of Chester became monks of their own foundations.[51] For the area of St Evroul, Orderic provides a wealth of detail about the conversion of knights both great and obscure. William son of Giroie, co-founder of the abbey, had lived a pious life, but only became a monk of Bec after he had been blinded and emasculated by William Talvas.[52] Robert, lord of Ivry, entered the same house in fear of death after being struck down by a disease in the genitals.[53] Odo son of Walo, a distinguished knight and a benefactor of St Evroul, fell ill and 'wishing to profit from his illness like a good son from his father's whip', he obtained confirmation of his grants from his kindred and took the habit ten days before his death.[54] A particularly dramatic instance of reception *ad succurrendum* is provided by Gilbert, son of Erchembald the *vicomte*, who was grievously wounded in the assassination of his lord, Osbern the seneschal, and was received as a monk at Holy Trinity Rouen, to which house his father had previously retired.[55] Such converts, of course, normally died within a few days of their reception. The communities received them out of Christian charity, and often enough in return for a substantial donation, but they did not provide any infusion of new blood, unless by chance they recovered, when their practical talents might be put to good effect, as in the case of Richard de Heudicourt, a vassal of Hugh de Grandmesnil, who was wounded in the back by a lance and on Hugh's advice 'determined from that time forward to fight under the monastic rule by the practice of virtue'. He survived and lived for seven years as a monk, despite his festering wound, and Abbot Osbern entrusted to him the management of finance and the supervision of the masons working on the new abbey church.[56] Norwich cathedral priory must have benefited similarly from the conversion of Peter Peverel, one of Henry I's knights who was frequently in the king's chamber.[57]

Reception into a monastic community in old age was rarely a sudden impulse, but rather a calm decision which involved long-term planning. Many charters granting lands or privileges to religious houses stipulate that in return for these gifts the donor may at some time in the future be clothed as a monk.[58] When Serlo de Lingèvres gave the church of Bucéels to St Stephen's Caen, for example, the abbot not only gave him money and a palfrey, but promised that in return for his donation he might be admitted as a monk whenever he wished.[59] A particularly elaborate arrangement was made in 1063 by Robert de Tosny with the abbey of Marmoutier, where his nephew John was a monk. In return for a grant of all his rights at Gournay, the community agreed to accept him if he should ever so wish, and if he did not take up this option, it was to be extended first to his brother Berengar, and then to any son whom Roger might beget, providing that he was at least six years old.[60] Roger de Monte Begonis made substantial donations in Normandy and England to St Martin at Séez on condition that he, his wife and his brother should be buried in the monastery if they died as laymen, and that if either of the brothers wished to become monks they should be accepted there.[61] Such arrangements frequently required some accommodation between the monastic community and the kindred of the *conversus*. A certain knight, Gilbert, gave all his inheritance to Préaux on condition that he might eventually become a monk, but in the meantime he had a daughter, whose husband, Roger de Crucemaris, eventually agreed to hold the land claimed as his wife's inheritance as a fief of the abbey.[62] Hugh Pain Crassalingua gave his vicecomital rights at Villegats to St Evroul before he became a monk, but the community had to pay his three sons to forestall their efforts to repossess them.[63] The pious prodigality of an old man might not be shared by his heirs, who had to survive in a harsh world.

It was, of course, more rare for a member of the Norman military élite to enter the cloister in the prime of life. Indeed, Gilbert Crispin, the biographer of Herluin, considered Normandy in the mid-eleventh century to be a land in which it was considered a marvel for a knight of unimpaired ability to lay down his arms and become a monk.[64] Certainly Herluin was exceptional, for not only did he adopt the religious habit, but himself founded a community, notable initially only for its poverty and simplicity in an area where ducal and aristocratic patronage combined with Cluniac influence to create a brand of monasticism particularly lavish in its observances. The *Vita Herluini*, moreover, provides a valuable picture of the crisis of conscience suffered by an active knight, and of the practice of private austerity which attracted the ridicule of fellow-soldiers.[65] Yet there is ample evidence to suggest that a 'Pauline' conversion during the most active phase of a military career was not an uncommon phenomenon.[66] In the early 1030s, while Herluin was passing through his spiritual crisis, a certain Peter, who held a fee of the Beaumonts and was known at the ducal court, became a monk at Fécamp. He withdrew as a recluse, with only one companion, to Bonneville-sur-Touque, where he found an ancient and disused chapel of St Martin, and with the authority of his abbot established the community of St Martin-du-Bosc, whose church was dedicated some time after 1059. Peter, however, persevered in his desire for the eremitical life and withdrew to the abbey of Préaux, where he was accepted as an anchorite attached to the house.[67] In other cases, the discovery of an ancient Christian site was probably of crucial spiritual significance. William son of Giroie, lord of Echauffour, discovered St Evroul's spring and the old church of St Peter on the banks of the Charentonne. He established there two priests, and it is possible that this contact with the roots of Gallic Christianity led him, after his mutilation, to become a monk at Bec; certainly he suggested this site to his nephews for their own foundation.[68] Half a century later the desolate ruins of St Hilda's abbey at Whitby made a profound impression on Reinfrid, a knight in the Conqueror's service, when he was engaged upon the harrying of the north. Within a few months he had made his profession at Evesham, and he soon returned north with two companions to reestablish a community at Jarrow. His desire for the hermit's cell was frustrated by a flood of recruits, and he soon moved to Whitby, but here too it proved difficult to avoid the burdens of ecclesiastical office.[69]

It is of course true that many recruits did not share Peter's and Reinfrid's revulsion from riches and desire for solitude. That conversion from the knightly life to the monastic vocation was not rare is indicated by the cynical and embittered satire of Serlo, canon of Bayeux, who around 1080 circulated a poem entitled 'Invective against a soldier, who because he was poor left the world and became a wealthy monk'.[70] The call of the cloister was by no means confined, however, to those who had been unable to make any impact upon the world. Guibert de Nogent listed with approval several examples of conversion from the highest echelons of northern French society. The most notable of these was Everard II, viscount of Chartres and lord of Le Puiset. The confused feudal politics of the region necessitated aggression merely as a means of survival, and the Puiset family acquired a singularly bad reputation among ecclesiastical chroniclers. Everard, who succeeded in 1070, rapidly tired of these conditions, and realizing that 'he was doing nothing else in the world than destroying and being destroyed, polluting and being polluted', he eventually fled to Jerusalem and a life of poverty, returning to become a monk of Marmoutier in 1075, whereafter he travelled widely at his abbot's command on the business of the house.[71]

An interesting connection can be established between pilgrimage and conversion. Penitential journeys were one of the most characteristic expressions of piety in the eleventh century, and Norman knights participated in large numbers in such exercises in the duchy, in France and in the Mediterranean.[72] Such expeditions had acquired a military character long before the First Crusade, and it was, traditionally, the sojourn of one hundred knights returning from Jerusalem which led to the initial Norman involvement in southern Italy.[73] There is other evidence to suggest that for some pilgrimage had already acquired the characteristics of a holiday promenade which became notorious in the fourteenth century,[74] and normally, no doubt, such a journey was a brief interval in a life devoted to aggression. Yet on occasion a visit to a holy shrine might result in a permanent emendation. A certain Ansgot, kinsman of Roger de Tosny, who had enjoyed a successful military career under Dukes Richard and Robert, forsook the delights of the world and devoted himself to a life of pilgrimage and voluntary poverty, eventually becoming prior of the great hospice at Melk in Austria.[75] William son of Giroie went to Jerusalem twice, once before and once after his terrible mutilation, and finally became a monk of Bec.[76] Osbert, viscount of Eu, took the road to the Holy Land and did not return, remaining there as a monk.[77] At the time of the First Crusade the knight Odardus, returning from Jerusalem, gave his allod at Longueville to Jumièges on becoming a monk,[78] and at St Ouen a layman, Gilbert, also became a monk on his return from the east, and devoted the estates of his wife, who had died there, to the completion of the fabric of the abbey church.[79]

Orderic Vitalis recounted the careers of many nobles and knights of the late eleventh century who deserted the world for the cloister. It is noteworthy that the learning of many of his recruits was in marked contrast to the rustic simplicity of Herluin. Most prominent among them was Robert de Grandmesnil, second abbot of St Evroul. As a boy he had received both an academic and a military training, he had become squire to Duke William and had been knighted by him. The turning point in his life came when Roger de Tosny and his two sons were killed fighting alongside his own father; 'deeply moved by this tragedy, Robert set his mind on fighting in better warfare.' He entered the family foundation and rapidly became prior, in which office he laboured ceaselessly to mitigate the poverty of the community, although his practical gifts were in such contrast to Abbot Thierry's prodigal spirituality that the convent polarized into two factions around them.[80] Robert's uncle Ralph, called 'ill-tonsured', the fifth son of Giroie, had been a passionate student of letters from his early days, had visited the schools of France and Italy and was skilled in all the liberal arts and in medicine; nevertheless, he had made his mark as a warrior and tactician, until he abandoned the world and became a monk of Marmoutier, subsequently after his contraction of leprosy returning to live in isolation at St Evroul.[81] Drogo of Neufmarché similarly terminated his military career, and after his profession his uncle founded the priory of Auffay as a dependency of St Evroul. Occasionally a charter provides similar evidence. A notification of 1055 by the monks of Marmoutier describes how John, son of Guy de Valle and nephew of Robert de Tosny, had reached the age of thirty and had served as a knight for many years when he felt compunction in his heart and began to shrink from the world, which he saw becoming worse every day. Despising temporal wealth that he might become rich in the poverty of Christ, he became a monk of Marmoutier, bringing his estate with him. Once more practical experience of the world proved an asset, and John was employed as the abbey's envoy to Duke William.[83]

The universal commitment to the Benedictine ideal is indicated by the acquiescence of lords in the alienation of military tenures by converts to the religious life. A typical reaction was probably that of Gilbert de Brionne to Herluin's change of heart; initially furious at the loss of a good knight, after long discussion and heart-searching he not only released his tenant from his oath of fealty, but allowed him to use land held of him for the foundation of Bec.[84] Often the lord received material or spiritual benefits for his confirmation. In the 1040s Roger of Montgomery, at the request of Goisfredus, one of his vassals who had become a monk of Jumièges, granted to the abbey the land at Fontaine which had been held of him, and in return received a horse and a hauberk, no doubt the military accoutrements for which the convert had no further use.[85] At the end of the century Hamelin de Baladone came to St Vincent's at Le Mans and begged the monks to receive Hubert, his knight, into the community; Hamelin himself received the confraternity of the house.[86] On occasion, indeed, a lord was prepared to release any prospective converts from their obligations. In 1094 Roger de Poitou conceded that if anyone should desire the prayers and benefits of the priory of Lancaster, he might give as much as half of his land, and that if anyone without an heir should wish to give all his land and to assume the monastic habit, he might do so with the blessing of his lord.[87]

Eadmer recounts the story of the knight Cadulus, whose piety led him to long nocturnal vigils, during one of which he was assaulted by the devil. He sought the spiritual guidance of Anselm of Bec, and subsequently made his profession as a monk of Marmoutier.[88] Despite his innovatory theology of the Atonement, St Anselm believed that in practice few men would be saved, and that for salvation conversion to the monastic life was little short of a necessity. Employing a potent analogy, he compared the Christian laity to mercenaries, who serve their paymaster while in receipt of wages, but quickly melt away in times of adversity. The angels, secure in their salvation, were comparable to those who held fiefs. Monks, however, were like those men who served a lord in the hope of recovering their lost patrimony, and the continual hope of recovering the kingdom of heaven, forfeited through the *diffidatio* of Adam, made them the most steadfast soldiers of God.[89] Anselm and his circle evolved a theology of monastic profession which was fully developed in the mid-twelfth century by Odo of Canterbury.[90] Profession was regarded as a second baptism, renewing that hope of salvation which had been sacrificed through the manifold sins committed by all men since their childhood. Odo used the analogy of David, who in his wars against the Philistines had considered it wiser to seek security in a fortified place than to expose himself to his enemies in the field. So it was more prudent to seek refuge in a monastery than to be buffeted by temptation in the world. The efficacy of monastic benediction was demonstrated, wrote Odo, by the fact that all sorts and conditions of men had recourse to the Rule. The tyrants who had persecuted the monastic order and the *iuvenes* who had delighted in worldly concupiscence, if they did not repent in their lifetime, ardently sought entry to the cloister as death approached, and rightly so, since by their profession they were purged.

Such theological treatises probably had little direct influence on the laity, but the doctrines of monastic theology might be presented in more palatable form for consumption by the knightly class. Orderic dwells at length on the preaching of Gerold, chaplain in the household of Hugh d'Avranches.[91] For the young men who accompanied Hugh in his hunting which resembled 'the daily devastation of his lands', Gerold composed a great collection of 'tales of the combats of holy knights, drawn from the Old Testament and more recent records of Christian achievement, for them to imitate.' He particularly told them of St William de Gellone, grandson of Charles Martel, who had abandoned a military career for the cloister. Gerold, it appears, presented the glories of monastic endeavour in a form akin to the great epic poems of the age, and as a result of his preaching three knights, an esquire and a chaplain followed the examples of his heroes and crossed the Channel to become monks of St Evroul, among them Roger, nephew of William de Warenne, who for forty-six years lived an exemplary life in the cloister. Orderic believed that their hopes of salvation were immeasurably improved: 'so Gerold, by preaching the word of God, roused men sunk in the darkness of spiritual blindness and caught in the deep pit of worldly temptation, to better things, as a cock crowing awakens sleepers in the dead of night.'

Despite the emphasis of monastic texts upon the penitential function of the monk and his death to the world, the cloister was not without attraction to members of the knightly class. The conventual church was the scene of 'liturgical ceremonies whose aristocratic glamour gave to this earthly community the allure of a heavenly court, resplendent with the music of angelic choirs, as if in foretaste of paradise.'[92] The adult convert from a military background would not feel a stranger in this environment, for if the cloister was a mirror image of heaven, it was surely the heaven of Mars. Monastic chronicles and *vitae*, although normally composed by *nutriti*, bear constant testimony to this militaristic interpretation of the religious life. Orderic saw the monastery as 'a citadel of God where the cowled champions may engage in ceaseless combat against Behemoth for your soul.'[93] Herluin after his conversion was 'the new esquire of Christ' who soon graduated to become 'a strong knight of Christ'.[94] Even the conversation of Anselm with his brethren was characterized by feudal analogies.[95] The description by Dr Rosenwein of the Cluniac liturgy may equally be applied to that of the Norman houses: 'it allowed aggression to be displaced from the real world to the supernatural. The monks fought the Devil instead of men and they freed souls from him in their war of liberation . . . the life of the Cluniac monk even inside the cloister was unconsciously a ritualized re-enactment of the life of the knight.'[96]

The popular theology of the eleventh century was permeated and dominated by the monastic ethos. The alms of nobles and knights were channelled to Benedictine houses, oblation provided both spiritual and economic benefits, and burial in the religious habit was a common aspiration. Yet the rôle of the active adult convert in this scheme has been minimized. This perhaps is a result of the Cistercian onslaught on oblation. The implication is that in the immediate past all monks had entered the cloister by this path, and that the conscious decision taken by St Bernard and his companions was a new phenomenon. The scattered evidence which has been cited may suggest that this is a misconception, and that if the *conversi* were far outnumbered by the *nutriti* and a knightly conversion was a matter of note to contemporaries, nevertheless the rôle of the adult convert in the eleventh century monastic community was of crucial importance. Certainly more knights entered the cloister in the twelfth century than in the eleventh; this was due in large part to the great expansion of the monastic order in the first half of the century, while the decline in oblation must have ensured that more young men were trained alongside their brothers as knights, to experience for themselves as young men the harsh economic realities which had hitherto recommended oblation, and which now might make the cloister appear as an attractive alternative to the endless search for a benefice. Many pious men might be attracted too by an environment in which personal communication with God had replaced the anonymous penitential function of an earlier age. Yet in the theology of salvation, conversion had ceased to be an urgent necessity. Towards the end of the eleventh century, and especially in the wake of the First Crusade, the profession of arms became respectable in the eyes of the church. Whereas by long usage the monk had been regarded as the 'soldier of Christ', 'in the letters of Gregory VII the traditional metaphor shades into literal actuality.'[97] Once knighthood was accepted as a respectable *ordo*, it was no longer essential to seek salvation within the cloister; the warrior might perform the work of God and the church in the rôle for which he had been trained. Ancient attitudes were transformed by 'the displacement of the boundary between sacred and secular'.[98] In his history of the First Crusade, Guibert de Nogent remarked that now knights were no longer obliged to leave the world and enter a monastery, as used to be the case, but might in some measure achieve the grace of God by exercising their own office.[99] Henceforth a knight might ask with some confidence, as did Arnulf of Montgomery at the turn of the century, that the monks should pray that he might be enabled to do the will of God in his earthly station.[100] The change of outlook is perhaps reflected in the attitude of Orderic Vitalis to Peter de Maule and to Ansold his son, the former eager to acquire wealth by any means and to dispense it in acts of flamboyant generosity, the latter a paragon of Christian virtue. Ansold succeeded his father around 1100, and the contrast in Orderic's evaluation of the two men is a reflection both of the dramatic transformation of the knight's view of his own vocation, and of a profound change in the attitude of the church to the institution of knighthood, which rendered obsolete the eleventh century emphasis on the absolute necessity for emendation and conversion.

The Byzantine View of the Normans—
Another Norman Myth?

JOS HERMANS

To speak on the Normans and their myth at this conference may seem rather superfluous, or even insulting to the author of the book on the same subject. In 1976 Professor Davis published his admirable study in which he discussed the Normans in the light of their myth.[1] He showed how they became Normans, how they changed their ideas of what a Norman was and how eventually they lost their identity. He gave us an impression of the Norman world as a whole: Scandinavia, Normandy, England and Southern Italy. Professor Davis's main emphasis was on truth and fiction in the views the Normans held about themselves.[2]

My purpose today is a different one: I would like to present to you some material for an additional chapter to Davis's book. I have chosen to treat the Byzantine view of the Normans, to give you an example of the ideas of outsiders and foreigners about the Normans.

The Byzantine Empire was, at the beginning of the period under consideration, i.e. the eleventh and twelfth centuries, the most civilized part of the Western world. Its emperor and inhabitants could be very proud of all those well-educated civil servants in, what Bréhier called, 'les grands services de l'état'.[3] One of these was the Ministry of Foreign Affairs. This must at all periods have served as a very well organized Intelligence Service for the Imperial Government.[4] They got their information not only from the official reports of ambassadors, but also from travellers, merchants and others traversing the countries that were as often as not hostile to the Empire, but always 'barbarian'—as a sincere Byzantine was calling every part of the world outside their own *oikoumenè*.

If we take this observation of Bréhier for granted, we may expect that there must have been quite a file on the Normans. Perhaps not on the Normans mainly to be discussed here at these Conferences on Anglo-Norman Studies, but most certainly on the Normans of the Italian branch. These were the conquerors of Southern Italy and Sicily, they ejected the last Byzantines from Bari in 1071, the same year as the disastrous battle in the East at Mantzikert, where even the emperor himself was captured by the Seljuk Turks. But this loss of Italy was not the only one, since Robert Guiscard tried, and at first with success, to establish a stronghold across the Adriatic in Dyrrhachium (Durazzo) and surroundings. The death of Guiscard in 1085 enabled the new emperor, Alexius Comnenus, to avert the Norman threat for a while.

A new danger appeared in the person of Roger II. In 1130 he was crowned as 'King of Sicily, the duchy of Apulia and the principality of Capua'. And again there was an attack on Durazzo which lies at the beginning of the Via Egnatia, the main road through Thessaly which leads to Thessalonica, the second city of the Empire, and from there straight to its capital, Constantinople. This time the attack was accompanied by a great raid in 1147 on Greece, where Thebes and Corinth were sacked. By defeating them heavily in 1149, however, the Byzantines for the moment put an end to any imperial ambition on the part of the Normans.

A third period of very dangerous menace from the Sicilian Normans started in the reign of William II during the 1180s, when they conquered and pillaged Thessalonica in 1185. This success nevertheless did not last very long, for in November of that same year they had to retreat; this time definitely out of the Byzantine history, unless we are to believe that the emperor Henry VI, son of Barbarossa and married to the Norman heiress Constance, truly wanted to conquer Constantinople.

Italo-Sicilian aggression was not the only contact. During the 1070s we meet Normans in the Byzantine mercenary troops. These Normans belong to a rather complicated group: often they had left their homelands because of quarrels with their local leaders, e.g. Robert Guiscard. Once in Byzantine service, however, they sometimes found themselves followers of an antagonist of the official emperor as e.g. Bryennius. Sometimes they deserted and tried to create small states of their own as was done by Crispin (Κρισπίνος) and Roussel de Bailleul (Οὐρσέλιος) in the north of Asia Minor. Another group of mercenaries was the Varangian Guard, a group I shall try to keep out of this paper because of the recent publication on the Varangians by Blöndal/Benedikz and of the paper read to this conference last year by the Reverend Godfrey.[5]

Knights of the first crusade formed a last cluster of Normans known to, if not feared by, the Byzantines. Among them Bohemund of Tarento certainly was the most impressive, at least to Anna Comnena the princess who wrote a history of her father's reign: the Alexiad. The crusaders went on and established small states to the north of the Holy Land, formally belonging to the Byzantine Empire. Now there were three groups of Normans: in Southern Italy, in the Byzantine Army—whether for or against the emperor—and in the Holy Land. Enough to keep a file on!

But how to find out what may have been in that file? Most of the imperial archives are now lost, so we must try to draw on other sources in order to find out what was known in Byzantium about the Normans. What was known of their origin, in Normandy or even earlier? Can we find a sound judgement on the relations between the several branches of Normans? The Anglo-Normans did keep in touch with their kinsmen in the South and they liked to boast of the victories of the latter in Apulia, Sicily, Greece and Asia Minor as their own; Ordericus Vitalis succeeded in integrating them into his history.[6] It is doubtful however whether one can speak of reciprocity in this case.

The word 'Norman' did not figure in the King of Sicily's titles, nor did contemporaries, either within or outside the kingdom, refer to it as 'Norman'.[7] It always was the 'Kingdom of Sicily' and indeed the Sicilian kings showed not the slightest desire to appear Norman. Their ambitions were almost entirely Byzantine and the same is true of their behaviour. Roger II had his Assizes or laws based on those of Justinian, he enjoyed state monopolies (the silk industry for example) and he issued documents in the Byzantine style sealed with a golden bull, an imperial prerogative indeed.[8] Byzantine artists worked in Sicily and when the king was portrayed he wore the clothes of a Byzantine emperor. After their death the Sicilian kings were buried like emperors, following a Constantinian tradition, in massive porphyry sarcophagi amid the Byzantine glories of Palermo and Monreale.[9]

Probably one has to agree with Davis's conclusion: 'The king of Sicily was one of the richest monarchs in Europe and a Hauteville too, but he was too busy with his own projects to bother about his Norman past'.[10] In such a situation one may guess that it is most fascinating to look for a Byzantine view of the 'Normans'.

Looking for information on Western Europe is somewhat disappointing for a reader of Byzantine historians. One thing that strikes is their evident ignorance of the history and geography of Western Europe. Part of this stems from a Byzantine preference for archaizing. The nations beyond the boundaries of Byzantium had to be disguised or dignified with Herodotean names. Donald Nicol has given some examples from thirteenth and fourteenth century sources. I quote: 'The Serbs become Triballians, the Bulgars Mysians, the Hungarians Paeonians and the Mongols Scythians (though here confusion arises because some historians apply the name of Scythians to the Bulgars as well). The confusion becomes worse confounded when the Italians are called Franks, the Franks Celts and the Catalans Italians. George Pachymeres (1242–c. 1310) calls Charles of Anjou an Italian and entitles him "king of Apulia" and "brother of the *rex Frantziskon*" which sounds like king of the Franciscans. Nikephoros Gregoras (1290/91–1359/60) can dismiss the Battle of Crécy with the illuminating sentence: "The Britons crossed over to the mainland of the Celts with their fleet and there was a great battle."'[11]

Confusions like these occur also in earlier times, when Turks are indicated as Persians, and σκύθης means Patsinak or Coman, tribes living north of the Danube. Even the well-known scholar Eustathius, Archbishop of

Thessalonica during the Norman Conquest of 1185, speaks in 1186 about ὁ Γερμανικὸς φύλαρχος, 'headman of the German tribe': he means the French king![12]; yet he knew better, since in the same text he refers to him as ὁ τῆς Φραγγίας ρήξ which is much closer to *rex Francorum* as the monarch entitled himself.[13] It is the more surprising because Eustathius, who was also a very fine philologist, had written a couple of years earlier an elaborate commentary on Dionysius Periegetes, the author of a description of the world in the second century A.D. In this description the Γερμανοί of course made an appearance.[14] Eustathius, however, hardly mentioned contemporary affairs, referring as he was to writers like Plutarch, but he showed nevertheless a deeper understanding of where those 'Germans' lived.[15] So we have to agree with Nicol's observation that 'quite different from the West where historians became better informed about the East as time went on, the Byzantines simply closed their eyes and ears. Ignorance gave way to calculated indifference'.[16]

Closely connected with this ignorance was the problem of royal and other titles outside the Byzantine world. Since Emperor Heraclius in the seventh century changed from Latin to Greek as the official language in the empire, the title of βασιλεύς could only mean one thing, 'emperor', with the exclusion of every other king. When Charles the Great had to be accepted as a βασιλεύς the Byzantine solution was to add to their own title βασιλεύς: τῶν Ρωμαίων, 'of the Romans', thus indicating that the ruler of New Rome was the only one, the elect of God, crowned by God and guarded by God. The Byzantine Empire was not like the kingdoms in Antiquity or those elsewhere in their own time. No, this empire was not a temporary phenomenon that would one day come to an end. The emperor, the βασιλεύς and αὐτοκράτωρ was the representative of Christ, who as παμβασιλεύς and παντοκράτωρ could only be one.[17]

This was all basic political theory to the Byzantines, generally taken for granted and therefore seldom spelled out in so many words. We can however reconstruct these ideas by looking in the opposite direction to this God-chosen people. The unhappy beings living outside the 'charmed circle of true believers' as Nicol calls them,[18] were mere barbarians, ἔθνη or 'nations', the New Testament expression for the Gentiles. In such a βάρβαρος we may discern three important features, more or less the same since Herodotus.

First, a barbarian does not speak the right language; he is just jabbering (or as you might say: he is speaking double dutch) and that is what the word derives from. Then, he has not the true religion. For people in the East, Arabs, Turks, one could feel compassion since they were victims of invincible ignorance, but the West was condemned as a group of wilful and unrepentant deviationists. Their barbarous situation was most of all apparent in a third aspect: a barbarian does not have the right state. What is more: he lacks the ability to arrange his affairs in a proper way. And here one sees an important reason why the West, once a part of the Constantinian Legacy, now was seen as disturbing the Divinely ordained scheme of things, and thus guilty of a form of heresy.[19] 'How did those Westerners dare to claim that the Empire of Byzantium was some other than that of Rome?' wrote John Cinnamus, a mid-twelfth-century historian, who tells us about the absurd pretensions of the popes and self-styled rulers of the West. I quote: 'The pope says: "I can designate emperors". Yes, as regards laying on of hands, as regards consecrating: these are spiritual matters. But no, as regards granting empires and innovating in such things. . . . Those whom, not long ago, while you were behaving properly toward the emperor, you did not receive when they requested it, since it was impossible, but enrolled among your grooms, now, I do not know how, you are accepting as emperors; you deem that he by whom and through whom and from whom you claim the papal throne, is not possibly identical with the barbarian, the tyrant, the slave.'[20]

This passage shows us the huge problem generally known as the *Zweikaiserproblem*. This is not the time or place to deal with it at length, but it is important to emphasize that the conflict between the Eastern and Western Emperors was for a very long time confined to words, most probably due to the geographical factor of the long distance between them. The appearance of the Normans at the common border in South Italy was doubtless complicating, the more so since the pope became involved in several pro- and anti-Byzantine treatises.[21]

Another aspect of this quotation is the use of the word tyrant, to indicate the usurpation of power in territory that ought to submit to the Byzantine emperor. This term of abuse was the common Byzantine 'title' for the Sicilian king. But also for less aggressive rulers the Byzantines preferred everything to the normal royal title we should expect. They are called ἔθναρχος (ruler of such an ἔθνος as we met) or φύλαρχος (headman of a φύλη, a tribe) and as time went on even ugly Latin expressions as ῥήξ or κόμης found acceptance.[22]

These examples explicitly emphasize another characteristic, apart from the ignorance, of the Byzantine mind, viz. the boundless pride in their city, their empire and their traditions. There was only one standard to measure the world, the Byzantine, and the rest of the world was τὸ πέριξ βαρβαρικόν 'the barbarians all around'. Not even Rome was an exception: how could one be Ῥωμαῖος, a 'true Roman', if one did not speak proper Greek? Therefore the Byzantines created a *Translatio imperii* from old Rome, πρεσβύτερα Ῥώμη, to New Rome, the queen of cities, lasting until the End of time.[23]

All these exalted ideas about the uniqueness of their empire were laid down in a somewhat over-blown style. The rhetorical expressions make strange reading. To see these texts in their true perspective we have to realize that there were two groups of literature. They were differentiated by language, designated by professor Mango as highbrow and lowbrow. The latter derived from *koine*, contemporary or biblical Greek, the former tried to be ancient Greek. We must keep in mind that most of the texts we are investigating now belong to this group and thus were written in a dead language, artificially kept alive and as such to be compared to the Latin and Greek compositions produced by countless generations of schoolchildren and university students. To an historian, the most important conclusion of this observation is that writing in a dead language about contemporary affairs inevitably results in the interposition of a certain distance. Texts are getting studded with qualifying clauses such as 'as it were' or 'as they call it', but most of the specific modern terms and concepts had to be converted into their nearest classical equivalents. Professor Mango therefore calls the Byzantine literature a 'distorting mirror'.[24]

This phenomenon may be discerned in highbrow literature as early as the fifth and sixth centuries, but exactly in our period there is an important classicist tendency, perhaps best known as the Comnenian Renaissance. It is often emphasized that Anna Comnena was writing a language she held for Attic Greek of the time of Thucydides, but which is at best Atticistic or Attiquarian as our Groningen colleague Dr Aerts calls this special type of Greek; it looks very much like a scratch collection of out-of-date words and forms.[25] The result of this literary practice is a dichotomy between literature and a changing reality. Byzantine highbrow writing tends to be diverting from the reality of its own time while remaining in an ideal past.[26]

That brings us, at last, back to our Normans. It goes without saying that they do not belong to the ideal arrangement of a Byzantine styled οἰκουμένη. But they did appear, not only in history, but also in historiography.

Let us first look at the list of the main historians and a couple of minor writers, where we find remarks on the Normans.[27]

John Scylitzes (eleventh to twelfth century) Σύνοψις ἱστοριῶν (811–1057)[28] with an anonymous continuation 1057–1079.[29] Almost literally incorporated in:

George Cedrenus (eleventh to twelfth century), same title (from the beginning of the world–1057)[30]

Michael Psellus (born 1018), *Chronographia* (976–1078)[31]

Michael Attaleiates (1028?–1085?), Ἱστορία (1034–1079/80)[32]

Nicephorus Bryennius (died 1137), Ὕλη ἱστορίας (1070–1079)[33]

Anna Comnena (1083–1148), Ἀλεξιάς (1069–1118)[34]

John Zonaras (twelfth century), Ἐπιτομὴ Ἱστοριῶν (from the beginning of the world–1118)[35]

Constantine Manasses (died 1187), Χρονικὴ σύνοψις (from Adam–1081)[36]

Michael Glycas Sicidites (mid-twelfth century), Βίβλος Χρονική (from the beginning of the world–1118)[37]

John Cinnamus (1143?–?), *Epitome* (1118–1176)[38]

Eustathius (metropolitan) of Thessalonica (died 1195/98), *De Thessalonica capta* (1185)[39]

Nicetas Choniates (c. 1155–1213), Χρονικὴ διήγησις (1118–1206)[40]

Some additional information can be taken from other texts, of which I give you only a few examples:

Cecaumenus (1071?), Λόγος νουθετητικὸς πρὸς βασιλέα (1075–1078) Στρατηγικόν, a kind of *mirror of princes*, respectively of aristocrats[41]

Some *poetical works* from the middle of the twelfth century, written by Prodromus (or Ptochoprodromos, 'the poor Prodromos') and John Tzetzes[42]

Some *rhetorical writing* like that of Michael and Nicetas Choniates, dating from the last decades of that century and the first of the next century[43]

A couple of *letters*, like those of Michael Italicus (early twelfth century), George and Dimitry Tornikes (middle and end of the twelfth century) or the brothers Choniates.[44]

Looking at this list it must be said that most of these writers were members of the highest ranks in society.[45] Psellus was the greatest scholar and clearest thinker of his day, but also for quite some time imperial secretary and thus able to use the official archives. On the other hand, as teacher of several princes and councellor of the emperor he helped to create the history he described. The imperial request to write the (second part of the) *Chronographia* explains quite a bit of its sometimes exceedingly tendentious character. Attaleiates held a high position at court too, as must Scylitzes about whom we do not know very much. About Cedrenus we know nothing, but his work has only very little original historical value, so this is for us not very important. Anna Comnena and her husband Nicephorus Bryennius were members of the imperial family. In Anna's writing we feel very clearly how much she dislikes her brother John's coming to the throne instead of herself.[46] Cinnamus and Nicetas Choniates were imperial secretaries, the latter, moreover, for about ten years μέγας λογοθέτης, a sort of Prime Minister. After 1204 his circumstances became less than glorious, which is the reason why he spent his last years rewriting his Χρονική in more or less positive versions, whereby he hoped to gain support.[47] Glykas was an imperial secretary too, but after a conflict with Emperor Manuel Comnenus about the latter's predilection for astrology, he ended in prison. A last secretary in this list is Tzetzes, who wrote on the widest variety of subjects in his *Historiae*. Returning to the eleventh century we meet Cecaumenus, a general belonging to the Byzantine aristocracy who wrote remarkable advice on a great variety of things, from how to read books ('always start from the front cover, don't pick out a few pages!') to how to appoint barbarians to important posts ('if they are not from a ruling family in the country where they come from everybody will laugh at you, both the barbarians and the 'Ρωμαῖοι'). Incidentally he gives as an example τὸν ἐξ Ἀγγέλης ἐθνικόν, 'a barbarian from England'.[48] Italicus, important philosopher and teacher of rhetoric, was later Metropolitan in Philippopolis. The Tornikes were rhetoricians too, without a very clear position in the civil service but very often writing for the emperor and his court. The last authors left are clerics: Zonaras was a monk, Manasses became Bishop of Naupaktos, Eustathius became Metropolitan of Thessalonike after a brilliant career as a philologist, and Michael Choniates, his pupil, became Bishop in Athens. The most problematical author is Prodromus. He was no doubt one of the most fertile authors of his age, but so many poems are attributed to him that a 'prodromaic question' has arisen around his identity.[49] For us it is important that he had to write in order to earn his money. That explains why he was writing in highbrow Greek, although sometimes incorporating fragments of the common lowbrow language just to make fun of it.

The majority of the texts written by the authors mentioned above belong to that complicated highbrow Greek literature we discussed earlier. There are different levels of purism of course, but all texts show elements of divorce from the contemporary scene.

After what I have said about the general view of barbarians in Byzantium it will not come as a surprise that if there is anything to be found in Byzantine sources about Normans, it usually concerns the careers of individuals, such as Robert Guiscard, Roussel de Bailleul or Bohemund. This is also the case in the Sicilian sources as Davis stated.[50] To the Byzantines barbarians are normally of no importance at all, unless they are involved in Byzantine history. As we have seen, Normans were known for their military activities, and consequently their leaders had to be dealt with. We must however keep in mind that if we find some considerable information in Anna Comnena's work, most of it was intended simply as an introduction to Robert Guiscard and his son Bohemund.[51] They were two of the main enemies of emperor Alexius, Anna's father and hero of her epic to whom she dedicated her work, for obvious reasons called Ἀλεξιάς, after the Iliad of Homer! What would be better than to gain the victory over almost invincible barbarians!

The early history of the Normans is therefore not very well known to the Byzantine writers. Anna knows quite accurately that Normandy was the birthplace of Robert Guiscard. She states this several times and she even uses the words Νορμάνος and Νορμανία.[52] That is rather unusual since the majority of writers speak about Φράγγοι 'Franks' or Κέλτοι 'Celts'. Psellus even uses Ἰταλοί 'Italians' for the auxiliary troops in 1056–1057, who were probably Norman.[53] The Sicilian commander of the contingent of Normans fighting in the north of Asia Minor is indicated as Φράγγος, 'Frank'.[54] The same word can be found in Cecaumenus' work, where Robert Guiscard is called Robert the Frank, spelled Ῥουπέρδος and Ῥουνπέρδος.[55] His army consists of Φράγγοι, 'Franks'.[56] Once the word Φραγγία occurs, and even in the clause ὁ βασιλεὺς Φραγγίας, who is perhaps the same as the one to whom Cecaumenus refers a couple of lines further on as ῥήξ Γερμανῶν.[57] Apart from the question whether these rulers were the same—probably the German emperor, but this riddle has not yet been solved[58]—we must consider the unusual title of Basileus for a barbarian. The rather informal style of Cecaumenus may have contributed to an easier use of this imperial title. We meet another βασιλεία, 'kingdom', this time that of Harald ('Aράλτης) and his brother Olav ('Ιούλαβος) who were heirs to the throne of the kingdom of Βαραγγία, which was identified by the editors as Norway.[59] Olav became king and Harald Haardrade went to Constantinople about 1040 from where he was sent to Sicily with the 500 noblemen (γενναίους) he had brought with him. There he performed great acts in the war carried on by the 'Roman' (Byzantine) army. From Sicily he went to several other campaigns in which he was useful.[60]

This brings us to a small excursus on the Varangians. The question of whence those 'axe-bearing barbarians' came is still not sufficiently answered, and even the origin of their name is not clear. An extensive survey of all the theories of a possible Scandinavian, Slavonic, Greek or other origin was given by Alexander Riasanovsky.[61] One of his suggestions was a corruption from *Frank* to *Varjag*, which might have come through the Balkans to Russia.[62] Our text may provide some additional support for this hypothesis. Cecaumenus tells us of a provincial governor in Sicily who had a garrison, among others consisting of 'Ρῶς καὶ Βαράγγους, 'Russians and Varangians'.[63] This fits perfectly well the story I just gave you about Northmen coming to Constantinople, for whom of course the Russian route is the shortest. The third and last passage in which he mentions the Varangians follows the above mentioned advice never to promote barbarians of low rank. We read that it is unwise to give the rank of *Patrikios*, a rather low one indeed, to a Φράγγος ἢ Βράγγος (pronounced as: 'Frángos i Vrángos'), 'a Frank or ...' what else? My point may be clear. The editors made out of Βράγγος, Βαράγγος: 'Varangian'.[64] Even without an *apparatus criticus* such an evolution may have been possible according to philological laws. Perhaps then this brief passage contains another argument for a western origin of the Varangians. Is this too much credit to the author? I do not believe so, since he was personally acquainted with Harald and probably knew what he was writing about.[65]

Let us return to the Normans. As a matter of fact only Anna shows some accuracy, though even she makes a few mistakes. After the Illyrian campaign in the 1080s followed by the first crusade, she tends to see a Norman in every Westerner. Normans behaving ill under Peter the Hermit were probably Germans and the Νορμάνων φοσσάτον, led by two chiefs from Flanders, consisted probably of Lombards and some German and French counts.[66]

More interesting are the qualities attributed to the Normans. They seem to have had some fame as horsemen.[67] Other positive characteristics are rather scarce, which may result from their being enemies of the Empire. Anna emphasizes the obscure origin of Robert Guiscard and his son Bohemund.[68]

Robert was a Norman by race, 'but nursed and nourished by manifold Evil'.[69] He was a pretender and therefore the word tyrant often occurs.[70] But he had his positive qualities too: he was very 'crafty in soul', noble in fight, most formidable in attacking the wealth and abundance of great men, unfailing in achievement, turning the objects of his aim into inevitable facts. Both he and his son Bohemund were good-looking: 'well proportioned from the top of his head to his feet' and his shout 'would put many myriads to flight'. Anna shows admiration for this Norman leader, who is twice fully described. 'He was of course no man's slave, subject to none of all of the world; for such are great natures, people say, even if they are of humbler origin'.[71] One quotation on Robert may serve to prove the fairy-tale impression Professor Davis indicated.[72] Anna writes: 'Robert then, being a man of such character, wholly incapable of being led, set out from Normandy with some knights; there were five of them and thirty footsoldiers in all. After leaving his native land, he spent his time amid the mountain peaks and caves and hills of Lombardy, at the head of a band of pirates, attacking wayfarers. Sometimes he acquired horses, sometimes other possessions and arms. The start of his career was marked by bloodshed and many murders.'[73] Then she writes of how he settles in Italy, of his growing imperial ambitions and his belief, real or pretended, in the cause of pseudo-Michael. The latter was a Byzantine who claimed the imperial throne and therefore was held in great honour at the Norman court, most probably just a puppet of Robert.[74] According to Anna there was indeed a reason why Robert could lay claims to the Byzantine throne. She admitted the folly of Michael VII in affiancing his son to Robert's daughter in that 'foreign and barbarious marriage contract' which gave the Normans an excuse for interfering in Byzantine affairs.[75] The main reason for Robert's eventual failure however was not his premature death, but his unrestrained insolence, ὕβρις, the reason why God became his great enemy.[76] That after three warnings not to fight 'against Christians' he nevertheless decided to do so, exposed him to the most terrible punishments by the 'almighty power of God'.[77] No personal courage (of which he admittedly had a great deal) could help him.[78]

How different is the picture in the other writers! Zonaras, for instance, says that Robert, ὁ Λογγιβαρδίας ἡγεμονεύων, 'the commander of Lombardy'—but also called 'Robert the Frank'—is just an ἀνὴρ πανούργος τε καὶ πολεμικώτατος, 'a mean man and very war-minded too'.[79] Zonaras seems to suggest that the Normans had only recently come to Italy, not saying that they are Lombards but are ruling there, and so did Bryennius who speaks about τὸ Φράγγων ἔθνος κατακυριεῦσαν τῆς Ἰταλίας καὶ Σικελίας 'the people of the Franks, who rule over Italy and Sicily', who were planning 'evil things for the Romans' in the 1070s.[80]

When did those Normans arrive in Italy? A first group came as mercenaries during the revolt of Mélès in the second decade of the eleventh century.[81]

Unfortunately we do not find much proof of this in Byzantine sources, although this revolution was aimed at the Byzantine government. It was suppressed in 1018.[82] A second group, about which we know more, arrived about 1040. The sources contradict each other on the question whether the Byzantines at first faced the Mussulmans only in Sicily or whether there was a 'Lombard' revolution too.[83] What concerns us here is the fact that the Byzantine general, George Maniaces, was sent to Sicily with 500 Franks in his army, $Φράγγους$ $πεντακοσίους$ $ἀπὸ$ $τῶν$ $πέραν$ $τῶν$ $Ἄλπειων$ $Γαλλιῶν$ $μεταπεμφθέντας$ 'sent for from *Gallia Transalpina*'.[84] All or most of these were probably Normans. When Maniaces is suspected of $ἀποστασία$, 'rebellion', he is summoned back to the capital, but he allows his troops to proclaim him emperor. He crosses over to Dyrrachium and marches on to Thessalonica. In 1043 however, in a battle as good as won, he was suddenly killed by an arrow.[85] In this period Franks were conquering Italy since the Byzantine Empire had proven to be too feeble to resist.

Some of these troops went to Asia Minor for reasons unknown to us. There they fought as mercenaries for the Byzantine Emperor against Turks and claimants to the imperial throne.[86] One of their leaders was a certain Frank named *Krispinos*, who served an official Byzantine army. He became a general but in 1069 he deserted for, as Bryennius says, 'he was long since an enemy of the Roman Emperor and felt hatred against him'.[87] This sentence was taken from Psellus, where Crispin was only $πολέμιος$ $Ῥωμαίων$, 'an enemy of the Romans'.[88] Bryennius however is writing several decades later and so he can add that after Crispin's death in 1073 another Frank, 'Ourselios', a companion of Crispin since Sicily, took over.[89] After these Normans had served in the army of Isaac Comnenus for a while another revolution started, which it took some time to suppress,[90] since this Ourselius was very skilled and succeeded in creating an empire of his own.[91] Anna speaks of 'the Celt Ourselius' as a 'hurricane', a 'thunderbolt' and 'irresistable in his attacks'.[92] Only by way of a trick could he be brought into prison where he died a pitiful death.[93]

From the moment the crusades are mentioned in Byzantine sources the authors are very vague in their use of names. This applies even to Anna, for although she is quite explicit on Sicily as 'an island lying near Italy', she uses 'Italian' and 'Lombard' for the whole peninsula. But further on crusaders are called indifferently Latins, Franks or Celts, thereby denoting anyone from the other side of the Adriatic.[94]

The most important qualities of the Normans so far are military both on land and at sea. As time goes on there are more texts speaking about an 'Italian' fleet of high quality. Anna's work, the last of our sources in this period, shows some reflection on the invincibility of the Normans. In her opinion Robert and his son Bohemund, of whom she says that he was 'inferior to the emperor only', were eventually defeated by the glorious Alexius

Comnenus.[95] Of great help to the *basileus* was the insolence of the barbarians, by which they evoked the divine wrath.

Another point I must emphasize is that the Normans in fact were regarded as barbarians also in the sense that they had pretenders instead of the only emperor.[96] On the other hand we see that there is no difference in religion so far: we do not find any reactions to the schism of 1054.[97] When the knights of the first crusade arrived, with many Normans among them, Alexius had two good reasons to send many Greeks with them. First he cared for them as Christians, secondly he hoped to extend the dominion of the Greeks by organizing the campaign in his way.[98] That it turned out quite differently had to be explained. Even in Anna's text we can read that the real problem started from Alexius' duplicity in not keeping the very oath he first extorted from the Latins.[99] That oath was something new to the Byzantines.

Exactly in this period of the Comneni the Byzantine Empire had to find a new structure in order to have faithful subjects. It was the time when there were several Latin councillors at Alexius' court, of whom several were Normans. Some even were from the very family of Guiscard, e.g. a certain Paulus Romanus.[100] As a try-out for a new system the agreements with the crusaders could serve. This is most clearly illustrated by the pact between Bohemund and Alexius near the walls of Dyrrachium in 1108. Anna tells us that her husband, the author Bryennius, played a very important rôle in convincing Bohemund to sign,[101] probably because he was one of the main advisers of emperor Alexius.[102] Bryennius really did know what those feudal forms were. He describes them in his story about the Franks, who after Roussel's capture first served Botaneiates but now deserted to the pretender, the older Bryennius: 'And all got off their horses and laid their hands in his, as is usual in their land, and they gave an oath'.[103] Anna was quite aware of the consequences of such a procedure as we can see from numerous remarks about the pact concluded at Dyrrachium.[104] This was laid down in the first formal charter concerning any oath of allegiance in Byzantium.[105] The feudal forms that gave a new impulse and a fresh look to the Byzantine system of *Pronoiai* may be regarded as a Norman legacy.

The second period of Norman menace was in the middle of the twelfth century, while the Comnenian Renaissance was in full glory. On every occasion poets are gathered to celebrate their emperor.

The Sicilians appear with their fleet in the years 1147–1149, once even before Constantinople, but every time they can be defeated.[106] Marguérite Mathieu investigated the poetical reactions to these events, sometimes very important indeed as historical evidence, but for our purpose of less interest.[107]

Only during the celebrations of 1149 and 1151 do we find explicit remarks. The content however is already known: 'Tyrant of Sicily, how dare you!' Since the Normans are operating this time mainly at sea, the qualifications show an emphasis on this naval aspect. The ῥήξ of Sicily is mostly called 'tyrant', like 'tyrant of the island', or 'tyrant of the Syracusans' but above all: 'dragon of the sea'.[108] Manuel Comnenus uses even in an official document of February 1148 the expression 'dragon of the West', and speaks of 'the common enemy of all Christians'.[109] The Normans are 'children of the water, by nature used to permanent travel on the sea, seamen, pirates, always busy with navigation and oars'.[110] Especially attractive to the credulous Byzantines and the superstitious Manuel must have been the magic witchcraft imputed to the Normans, who were thought to have power to rule the elements, storm and heavy weather were at their beck and call.[111]

In the following years no success could be mentioned—especially after peace was concluded in 1158—and Sicily was but a nightmare to which an allusion was made on rare occasions.[112]

It became reality again in the early 1180s, during the reign of Andronicus. No reasons for poetic eulogy could be found in the Sicilian conquest and massacre of Thessalonica, August 1185, but because this capture was the sign for a revolution against Andronicus who was replaced by Isaac Angelus, at least the end of this Byzantine 'tyrant' could be celebrated.[113]

The text of Eustathius on this capture, probably read as a sermon at the beginning of Lent 1186, was full of vivid paintings of the cruelty that was displayed by the Sicilian Normans.[114] This time it was not Western insolence that had caused the massacre. It was due to Byzantine faults. Eustathius points at the aggression of Manuel against Italy in the 1150s. Secondly he notes that the amphibious action of the Sicilians was urged by the appearance of Pseudo-Alexius, who claimed the throne in Constantinople and asked Γελίελμος for help. This William was different from Roger, who had his 'county' (κομητᾶτον) changed to a 'kingdom' (ῥηγᾶτον) and was an active and capable man. William was better at designing plans than fulfilling them.[115] But perhaps the main reason for the Sicilian attack on the Empire was, Eustathius says, the slaughter of 1182, when at the time of Andronicus' ascent to the throne many Latins who happened to be in Constantinople were murdered by the mob of the capital.[116] Furthermore Andronicus had appointed an absolutely incapable man as commander of Thessalonica, which was the reason why this city could be conquered.[117] Finally Eustathius inveighs his own sin and those of his kinsmen which were not the least reason for this disaster.[118]

The qualities ascribed to the Sicilians are for the greater part inspired by the behaviour of a plundering and pitilessly cruel soldiery. But we must note that it was an army of very mixed character, including several mercenaries other than Norman, that William collected. These enemies, Eustathius intimates, lacked any culture whatsoever and were unable to appreciate nice cutlery, clothing and silk, precious metals or stones, books and even good old wine, since that was not sweet enough for their taste.[119] Those 'Latins' are barbarians indeed, and Eustathius seems surprised in summing up difference after difference between the West and Byzantium: 'They really do not know a civilised and cultivated way of life'.[120] Apart from these barbarous features, there is still another remark to be quoted about West-Europeans: 'They think the world is not big enough for themselves and us'.[121] Very alarming indeed, but at the time when this sermon was read the Normans were already defeated.

It is time to conclude this paper. We saw that in the early years Cecaumenus and Anna Comnena were best informed but even their knowledge was not impressive. Personal acquaintance with respectively Harald Haardrade and an ambassador of a bishop of Bari about A.D. 1100 are probably the reasons for this knowledge.[122] The name *Νορμάνος* only occurred in the Alexiad. From the crusades onwards Westerners were often named indifferently Latins, Franks or Celts, Alemanoi or Germans. Sicilians kept their name most of the time, but even they lost their identity in the general amalgam of Western barbarism.

Normans were skilled horsemen, cunning politicians and—once settled in Sicily—fine sailors. On the other hand they suffered from all bad characteristics attributed to the Latins, with special emphasis on their insolence. Now and then they could be very cruel.

In military affairs they are almost invincible; they win until God sends his emperor to stop them. Alexius was glorious (the Byzantines did not give much attention to the sudden death of Robert Guiscard or the starvation in Bohemund's army). Manuel was glorious but his defeats are in historiography passed over in almost complete silence.

From 1183 until 1185 however God did not interfere and Thessalonica was conquered! The Byzantines had to explain this defeat. The Emperor Andronicus was a *τύραννος* himself because he ascended the throne by committing numerous crimes. The gaining of power of this anti-Latin emperor coincided with an enormous slaughter of Westerners. This brutish action against the West asked for revenge. And the Normans came to act like angels of vengeance.

This event is in my opinion very important. Later emperors were only weak rulers 'who sold services as fruits on a market' as Nicetas says.[123] Once again Byzantine shortcomings create a risky situation. There was a deeply felt fear of the West, not only of the Normans but also of the crusaders, led by Barbarossa, who came a few years later and who met with problems during their march through the empire. In 1196, when Henry VI, German emperor and king of Sicily, pleaded for money in Constantinople to organize another crusade, many people were scared. A special tax had to be levied known as *Ἀλαμανικόν*, 'the German one'.[124] A year later Henry died but again five years later a new crusade was organized which resulted in the conquest of Constantinople in 1204. In the eyes of Nicetas this was again a punishment from heaven which he hoped would not last very long.[125] If Sicilians were able to take revenge for injustice done in 1182, why could not the Latins conquer Constantinople after a period best described as 'Byzantium confronts the West'?[126]

The events of 1185 gave birth to the idea in modern historiography that 1204 was due to a growing anti-Byzantine feeling originating among the Normans. Proposed about 1900 by Norden, this notion was picked up by Sibyll Kindlimann in her 1969 thesis, in which she states that there was a growing demand in the West for a dependable, i.e. non-Greek, leadership in Constantinople.[127] A couple of years later a Groningen colleague of mine Dr Bunna Ebels proved there was no such growing demand in the Western sources. Above all after 1189 Norman Sicily was internally divided, and it did not play any rôle in the Fourth crusade at all.[128] This whole theory of blaming the Normans was based more on Byzantine fears than on Western sources.

The Normans were important to the Byzantines as we can read in a letter of 1193 sent by emperor Isaac Angelus to the pope. He complains about all recent troubles in the *oikoumene* and he makes an appeal for peaceful coexistence. The emperor laments: 'Nowadays it is a passion of all people bearing the name of Christians to detest and fight each other. This began with Ἀλεμανία and Σικελία but after reaching the Ocean and the Rhine it now turns over to the regions around the Danube.'[129]

I hope I have given an impression of the Byzantine knowledge of the Normans. How very little they knew! And yet the Normans were given an important rôle to play, but it was a Byzantine play, based less on reality than on a 'Norman myth'!

Henry I and the Anglo-Norman Magnates

C. W. HOLLISTER

To contemporaries, the most striking thing about Henry I's reign was its peace. In an age when violence was brutal and widespread, when the ideal of the *rex pacificus* was cherished but seldom realized, Henry kept England in a state of tranquillity throughout the last thirty-three years of his thirty-five-year reign (1100–1135). Normandy posed a greater problem because of the military threat of hostile and powerful neighbours. Yet even in Normandy the twenty-nine years of Henry's rule (1106–1135) were marred by serious violence only twice: in the crisis years of 1117–1119 when French, Flemish, and Angevin armies, breaking through the duchy's defences, joined forces with rebellious Normans; and again briefly in 1123–1124 when a small group of discontented Norman magnates enjoyed the military support of France and Anjou.[1] Baronial rebellion against Henry I was a hopeless prospect, not only in England but in Normandy as well, unless backed by outside intervention, and royal diplomacy limited such intervention to rare occasions. The Norman monk Orderic Vitalis describes Normandy at Henry's death as basking in abundance after a long peace under a good prince.[2]

Historians of the past two generations, while agreeing that the peace was long, have been less certain that the prince was good. Sir Frank Stenton, in the concluding chapter of his *First Century of English Feudalism*, used evidence from the Pipe Roll of 1130 and elsewhere to argue that Henry I controlled his magnates by extortion and repression. Stenton remarked on 'the fundamental insecurity of a government which, like that of Henry I, had rested on the enforced obedience of feudal magnates'.[3] This notion has evolved in the writings of formidably gifted historians such as Sir Richard Southern and Christopher Brooke into the sombre portrait of a cold, hard, inscrutable king—savage and ruthless, morbid and unforgiving, terrible and barbaric.[4] Still more recently Henry's regime was described as a 'reign of calculated terror'.[5]

As you will have suspected, I am unconvinced. Given the formidable resources of great magnates in any feudal regime, the notion of a medieval king keeping the peace for a generation by terrorizing his chief landholders seems to me implausible on *a priori* grounds alone. To see Henry's rule as a reign of terror is to miss its central point: that a substantial number of magnates supported Henry's peace and profited from his lordship, that Henry based his success on the shaping of a royalist baronage, bound to him not by fear so much as by gratitude for past and present favours and hope of future ones.

William the Conqueror had created a royalist baronage by sharing with his nobility the prodigious wealth of conquered dominions. As a result, one finds that his wealthiest magnates tended to be the most frequent attestors of his charters. This relationship between landed wealth and participation in the royal *curia* becomes clear when one follows Corbett's methodology of adding up the values of Domesday manors held by the Conqueror's major tenants-in-chief in 1086 and then compares the wealth of such tenants with the totals of their attestations of genuine royal charters between 1066 and 1087.[6] I have presented the results of this comparison elsewhere in tabular form.[7] To put it as simply as possible, the ten most frequent attestors of William I's charters include seven of his ten wealthiest lay landholders. Thus, Roger of Montgomery attested more charters of William I than any other layman; Odo of Bayeux, Geoffrey of Coutances and Robert of Mortain were second, third and fourth. In order of wealth, Odo of Bayeux was England's greatest lay landholder (and although a bishop in Normandy, he held as a layman in England); Robert of Mortain and Roger of Montgomery ranked second and third, Geoffrey of Coutances eighth or ninth. In short, William's closest companions in conquest tended to become magnate-*curiales* in the new regime—which is rather what one might have suspected even without the statistics. It will be obvious enough that this wealth-attestation analysis does not in itself encompass the complex details of royal-baronial interaction. Several of William's magnate-*curiales* were also his close kinsmen; neither kinship nor wealth nor frequency of attestations protected Odo of Bayeux from arrest and imprisonment. The Conqueror's creations could mount rebellions against him, and several of them did so in 1074–1075. Nevertheless, William's regime established itself firmly in a hostile land, exercising lordship such as England had never before experienced. And the strength of the new regime was clearly based, to a significant degree, on the intimate associations and community of interests between king and magnates.

William's was a one-time opportunity, never to be repeated. His successors, lacking the advantage of a fresh start, had to deal with powerful landholding families not of their own choosing. His immediate successors faced the further problem of divided baronial loyalties resulting from the separation of England from Normandy between 1087 and 1096 and again between 1100 and 1106. As a consequence of these problems, the relationship between king and magnates shifted drastically at the accession of William Rufus in 1087. A group of Anglo-Norman barons took up arms against Rufus in 1088 with the object of enthroning his brother, Duke Robert Curthose, thereby reuniting England and Normandy. Rufus's opponents included at least six of the realm's greatest nobles—Odo of Bayeux, Robert of Mortain, Roger of Montgomery, Gilbert of Clare, Geoffrey of Coutances, and Eustace of Boulogne—along with other barons of lesser wealth: Roger Bigod, William of Eu, Roger of Lacy and Hugh of Grandmesnil. Rufus was confronted, in short, with the hostility of the very men whom the Conqueror had enriched, or, in several instances, their sons. Only two among England's ten wealthiest magnates—William I of Warenne and Hugh earl of Chester— are known to have supported Rufus. He survived the uprising, thanks in part to Curthose's incapacity, and in 1095 he managed to put down a second rebellion in which he barely escaped being ambushed. The rebellion-conspiracy of 1095 once again involved a coalition of wealthy families—Montgomery, Clare, Lacy, Eu, Mowbray (the rebel Robert of Mowbray was Geoffrey of Coutances' nephew and heir)—whereas the sources name no major magnates who were committed to Rufus's cause.[8]

The split between king and magnates that these uprisings suggest is confirmed by an analysis of the witness lists of Rufus's charters. As we have seen, seven of the Conqueror's ten wealthiest landholders in 1087 were among the ten most frequent witnesses of his charters. To provide a similar ratio of wealth to attestations under Rufus is a bit tricky: as one progresses through Rufus's reign, drawing farther and farther from the Great Survey, one is obliged to supplement Domesday data with much more fragmentary evidence of landed wealth. One thing at least is clear: the ten most frequent attestors of Rufus's charters alive in 1100 include only one representative of the Conqueror's ten wealthiest families, Hugh earl of Chester—that bloated sinner and devoted royalist whom Orderic described so vividly. The heads of the remaining great Conquest families that survived to 1100 attested scarcely at all for Rufus. Some of the honours—those of Odo of Bayeux, Geoffrey of Coutances and (probably) Eustace of Boulogne—had suffered forfeiture. Others had passed during Rufus's reign from seasoned fathers to untried, sometimes adolescent sons. Several such sons were involved in the rebellion-conspiracy of 1095, and it is significant that the eight identifiable conspirators together attested Rufus's surviving charters only nine times.[9]

As far as I can determine from the Domesday and subsequent record evidence, Hugh of Chester, with Domesday estates worth about £800 a year, was Rufus's only frequent attestor whose wealth was comparable to that of the Conqueror's ten greatest magnates—the 'Class A' barons as Corbett called them. The nine remaining men among Rufus's ten major attestors tended to be landholders of middling wealth, often holding royal household offices—men such as Eudo *Dapifer*, Hamo *Dapifer*, Roger Bigod (also a *dapifer*), Urse of Abitôt (constable and sheriff), and Robert of Montfort (constable). Their holdings range between about £100 and £450 a year— comfortable, but not Class A.[10]

Rufus might well have adopted a policy of luring the wealthiest magnates to his court by patronage, but he seems to have made no serious effort in that direction. Alternatively, he might have chosen to bestow vast estates on his *curiales*, making magnates of them. He did of course enrich them, but only modestly—so far as the evidence discloses. He seized the estates of Odo of Bayeux, Robert of Mowbray and William of Eu, and kept them for himself. At the time of his death he seems to have been supremely confident, but perhaps unwisely so. His brother, Robert Curthose, was known to be returning from the Crusade with a rich wife and enough money to redeem Normandy. Rufus intended to fight for the duchy, but the response of the leading magnates to such a war would have been, to say the least, unpredictable. Sir Richard Southern, on the basis of different kinds of evidence than I have been using, makes the perceptive observation that when Rufus died 'the country was ready for a revolution, which might well have swept away much of the structure of royal government'.[11]

The split between magnates and *curiales* that marked Rufus's reign continued into the early years of Henry I's reign. In the months following his accession Henry did everything possible to win the support of his greatest landholders. The Coronation Charter was only one of many overtures toward the magnates. He appointed a Clare to the abbacy of Ely and a bastard son of Hugh earl of Chester to the abbacy of Bury St Edmunds; he offered his wife's blue-blooded but penniless sister in marriage to William count of Mortain, who rejected the proposal and demanded the earldom of Kent instead.[12] Despite these overtures, Henry's regime was nearly toppled in its initial year when Curthose, invading England in July 1101, attracted active or passive support from most of England's wealthiest magnates.[13] Henry was harvesting what Rufus had sown: the anti-royal coalition of 1101 involved, to a remarkable degree, the families that had been so conspicuously absent from Rufus's entourage and had conspired against him in 1088 and 1095: Montgomery, Mortain, Grandmesnil, Boulogne—the names will be familiar. As I have observed elsewhere, the nine identifiable supporters of Curthose in 1101 differed markedly in wealth and frequency of attestations from the nine identifiable supporters of Henry I.[14] Henry's supporters tended strongly to be the very men who had previously surrounded Rufus—landholders of middling wealth, stewards and sheriffs. Whereas Curthose's nine supporters had witnessed Rufus's charters a total of seven times, Henry's nine had witnessed 140 times.[15] The data on land values become increasingly tenuous as we drift fifteen years beyond Domesday, but according to what evidence is available to me—again, Domesday Book supplemented by subsequent records—Curthose's supporters commanded three times the landed wealth of Henry's supporters.[16] Norman England was clearly experiencing an ominous schism between magnates and *curiales*, and Henry, having survived the crisis of 1101, resumed his attempt to heal it. Magnates who supported his regime and attended his courts would enjoy his favour and profit from his patronage;

those who betrayed him risked forfeiture and exile. Trustworthy royalists could always be found to take their place.

Henry appears to have offered such a choice to all his magnate families with the single exception of the Montgomerys, who had conspired against the monarchy in 1088, again in 1095, and still again in 1101. By Rufus's death the bulk of the family's lands were in the hands of Roger of Montgomery's eldest son, Robert of Bellême, whom the chroniclers describe as brilliant, violent, cruel, and sadistic.[17] As earl of Shrewsbury and lord of Arundel he was England's wealthiest magnate in 1100; as heir to his father's Norman lands and his mother's inheritance of Bellême, he commanded tremendous wealth and power in the duchy and beyond its frontiers. To top it off, he married the heiress to the strategic county of Ponthieu, just to the northeast of Upper Normandy. Perhaps the chroniclers exaggerate Robert's villainy; perhaps not. In any event, Henry cannot have regarded him as a promising participant in the new regime. Relations between them would have been embittered by the fact that in about 1092, when Henry was a landless wanderer, the inhabitants of the Bellême citadel of Domfront had withdrawn their allegiance from Robert and taken Henry as their lord. Accordingly, once Henry had weathered the crisis of 1101 he began assembling charges against Robert— forty-five in all, according to Orderic. When Robert, very sensibly, declined to have his case heard at the royal court in 1102, he was disinherited and driven from the kingdom. 'All England rejoiced,' Orderic writes, 'as the cruel tyrant went into exile.'[18] A decade later, having supported Curthose's losing cause at Tinchebray and having subsequently conspired with the French king, Robert was arrested at Henry's court and imprisoned for life. His violent energy and his surpassing wealth, much of it in districts outside the royal control, were altogether incompatible with the kind of regime that Henry intended to build.

There were other forfeitures in the troubled period between Curthose's invasion of England in 1101 and Henry's victory at Tinchebray in 1106, and still others in the years just following, when certain Anglo-Norman barons conspired in behalf of Curthose's young son, William Clito. Some of Curthose's supporters of 1101 were allowed to keep their lands: Robert Malet, Robert of Lacy, Walter Giffard, and Eustace of Boulogne were all forgiven. Eustace married the queen's sister Mary of Scotland (whom William of Mortain had earlier rejected) and became Henry's good friend. Robert Malet was advanced to the master chamberlainship either just before or just after the 1101 crisis and held the office until his death, attesting frequently at Henry's court.[19] William of Mortain, England's wealthiest magnate after Robert of Bellême (his uncle), broke his fealty to Henry in 1104 and joined Curthose in Normandy, thereby forfeiting his English lands. He was taken captive two years later at Tinchebray and imprisoned for the remainder of Henry's reign.

These and other forfeitures gave Henry the opportunity of enriching his followers without excessively depleting the royal demesne. And in the years following Tinchebray, he succeeded by and large in reshaping the magnates into royalists and *curiales*. Despite the forfeitures, Henry lacked the freedom of action—the *tabula rasa*— that had enabled the Conqueror to enrich his *familiares* so magnanimously. The engine of conquest no longer rolled; lands, offices and privileges had to be distributed with caution and finesse. In this connexion, Henry's famous administrative reforms—the exchequer with its Pipe Rolls, the system of justicial eyres, the reorganized treasury and expanded chancery—are to be seen not only as revenue-raising devices but also as means of systematizing the distribution of royal patronage to great and small alike. It was important to modernize the instruments of revenue collection in order to supplement the income from a gradually diminishing royal demesne with new sources of income, or old sources more rigorously audited. But it was likewise important to have exact records of exemptions from danegeld, *auxilium burgi* and *murdrum*; of the marriages of heiresses to royal favourites; of debts that might be collected swiftly or permitted to run on year after year, or pardoned altogether because of the king's love of the earl of Leicester or the lord of Pontefract. The Pipe Rolls are records not only of debts and payments to the crown but also of debts pardoned, taxes forgiven, income relinquished for the sake of patronage. The Roll of 1130 records payments into the treasury of about £24,200, but it likewise records exemptions and pardons totalling £5500.[20]

The great difficulty in comparing Henry I's baronial policies with Rufus's is that the nature of the evidence changes. We have fewer than 200 of Rufus's charters but nearly 1500 of Henry's, which permits a far more comprehensive and sophisticated analysis of Henry's attestors than of Rufus's. Conversely, Domesday Book becomes an increasingly poor index of baronial estate values as Henry's reign progresses. Some impression of baronial wealth can be derived from the Old Enfeoffment totals in Henry II's *Cartae Baronum*: any magnate who had enfeoffed 100 or 150 knights on his estates by 1135 must have been, to say the least, comfortably well off. Again, the danegeld exemptions on baronial demesnes recorded in the Pipe Roll of 1130 reflect baronial wealth in some instances, but unfortunately not in most. The difficulty is that danegeld exemptions measure not only demesne values but royal favour as well; magnates who were seldom at court received minuscule exemptions, if any.[21] Despite these difficulties, I have constructed a list of Henry's magnates divided according to their landed wealth. The division is based on Old Enfeoffment totals, supplemented by Domesday data when the honours in question seem to have remained very stable, and by 1130 danegeld exemptions when they are high enough to suggest that the entire demesne is exempt. As far as possible, I have tried to follow Corbett's classification system though, to repeat, my data are distinctly less reliable than his. I begin with Class AA: three 'supermagnates'—Robert of Gloucester and Stephen of

Blois with about 300 fees each, and Roger of Salisbury whose danegeld exemption total suggests comparable wealth.[22] Next, Class A: eight lay magnates with 100 to 200 fees. Then, Class B: a dozen or so laymen with about 60 to 90 fees. And finally, Class C: about thirty laymen with 30 to 60 fees. The methodology, though admittedly precarious, does provide a valuable general picture—blurred, yet not seriously misleading. And one can hardly arrive at any meaningful conclusions about Henry's policies toward his wealthiest barons without having some reasonably clear notion as to who they were.

Historians have sometimes restricted the term 'magnate' to the heirs of the 'old Conquest baronage'. I prefer the more straightforward definition: a magnate is, quite simply, a very wealthy landholder. The traditional distinction between old and new families raises the question: what do we mean by 'old'? Were there, indeed, any 'old' magnate families in England at Henry's accession? Henry's so-called old Conquest magnates in 1100 were William I's 'new men', or their sons—the beneficiaries of a prodigious land redistribution that had occurred in stages over the previous thirty-odd years. Moreover, as David Douglas has taught us, the Conqueror's companions themselves represented a Norman aristocracy 'of comparatively recent growth'.[23] Most of the Conquest families had been dominant in Normandy for only a generation or two. William's half brothers, Robert of Mortain and Odo of Bayeux, recipients of tremendously lucrative earldoms in England, were sons of a relatively obscure Norman *vicomte*, Herluin de Conteville, and his wife Herleva, whose liaison with Duke Robert I had had such momentous consequences but who was herself a mere tanner's daughter. Odo became bishop of Bayeux only in about 1050: Robert became count of Mortain in 1055. Accordingly, the forfeitures suffered by Odo in 1088 and by Robert of Mortain's son William in 1104 can hardly be viewed as a ruthless uprooting of ancient families.

Henry's wealthiest magnates of c. 1125–1135 came from a variety of backgrounds. Some were heirs of the wealthiest (Class A) conquest families: Clare, Chester, Richmond, Warenne. Others represented lesser but ascending aristocratic families: Beaumont, Bigod. Still others were younger sons or bastards of royal or comital fathers: Robert earl of Gloucester, Stephen of Blois, Brian fitz Count. Only one among the eleven Class AA and Class A magnates, Roger of Salisbury, had truly risen from the dust.[24] (And I venture to suggest that a political regime so conservative as to prohibit the rise of new men would be neither very successful nor very attractive.)

Four of Henry's eleven wealthiest magnates—Roger of Salisbury, Robert of Gloucester, Brian fitz Count and Hugh Bigod—figure among the ten most frequent baronial attestors of his charters, and three others were bound to the king by ties of kinship, gratitude or both: Stephen of Blois owed everything to Henry; Ranulf le Meschin had been advanced by royal favour to the earldom of Chester; and Robert earl of Leicester owed his substantial Norman honour of

Breteuil to Henry, and his English earldom to Henry's generosity toward his father, Robert of Meulan. Seven of the eleven represented families of either the greater or lesser baronage under William the Conqueror.[25] Eight were receiving substantial danegeld exemptions ranging from £20 to over £150 in 1129–1130.[26] One of the eleven, Stephen of Richmond, was absent for most of the reign attending to his considerable estates in Brittany. He caused no trouble, did no personal service to the king, and received no exemption. Nine of the remaining ten were men, or the sons of men, who had profited substantially from Henry's favour. From the truce of 1101 until Henry's death in 1135, none of the eleven, or their fathers, had opposed the king either in England or in Normandy.

My division of the magnates into classes is obviously fuzzy at the boundaries separating Class A from Class B and Class B from Class C. But the trend toward royalist magnates pierces these boundaries. At the top of Class B one encounters two *curiales* and royal servants, Geoffrey of Clinton and Nigel of Aubigny, along with David king of Scots who owed everything to Henry. Farther down among the Bs are William of Aubigny *pincerna*, a frequently-attesting member of the royal household, Walter fitz Richard who received his barony of Netherwent from the king sometime before 1119, Robert fitz Richard to whom Henry gave the Baynard honour of Little Dunmow, and William Maltravers whom Henry had planted in the forfeited Lacy honour of Pontefract.[27] These last two elevations exemplify a policy, to which Professor Davis has called our attention, of creating royalist magnates by placing them on the forfeited lands of the king's enemies. Robert of Lacy and William Baynard had both been disseised for treason in about 1110–1113, presumably for conspiring to support Curthose's son, William Clito. Should Clito ever prevail over Henry, the Lacy and Baynard honours would doubtless be restored to the families that had held them previously. The new holders thus had a compelling reason to back their king.

Notice, too, that Walter fitz Richard of Netherwent and Robert fitz Richard of Little Dunmow were younger brothers of Gilbert of Clare and Roger lord of Bienfaite and Orbec in Normandy. Gilbert of Clare was a Class A magnate whom Henry had favoured in 1110 with the lordship of Ceredigion in Wales. All Gilbert's lands passed, on his death in 1117, to Richard, his eldest son. Henry's generosity to Gilbert and the two Clare cadets had the effect of putting the entire cross-channel Clare family in his debt. And if any of the Clares had been tempted to betray Henry for Clito, the temptation would have been dampened by the realization that a Clito victory would probably cost their kinsman Robert his lucrative barony of Little Dunmow. At the climactic battle of Brémule in 1119, Roger fitz Richard, the Norman Clare, was in the first rank of Henry's army.[28] As the French were fleeing, William Crispin, a baron of the Vexin, struck at Henry's head with his sword; it was Roger fitz Richard who knocked William Crispin to earth.[29]

The conversion of the Clares was an impressive achievement. The family had been involved in the rebellion against Rufus in 1088; they had conspired against him in 1095; they had bullied Henry in the early months of his reign;[30] when Curthose invaded in 1101 Gilbert of Clare apparently sat on the fence while his uncle, Walter Giffard, joined the duke's army.[31] But Henry's gift of Ceredigion to Gilbert and his handsome provisions for Gilbert's younger brothers evidently had their effect. The Clares and Giffards remained royalists for the rest of the reign.

Henry's baronial policy shows to even greater effect in his handling of William II of Warenne, earl of Surrey, whose father's Domesday estates were exceeded in wealth only by those of Odo of Bayeux, Roger of Montgomery and Robert of Mortain.[32] William I of Warenne had fought for the Conqueror at Hastings, helped crush the earls' rebellion of 1075, and died in June 1088 of a wound received while fighting for Rufus shortly before at the siege of Pevensey. In that year Rufus had made him earl of Surrey, either to ensure his loyalty or reward it. William II of Warenne succeeded to his father's new title and English lands and also seems to have inherited the Norman patrimony centring on the castles of Mortemer and Bellencombre in upper Normandy. Like other magnates of his generation, he was not the royalist his father had been. He played his part in the sporadic baronial warfare of Curthose's earlier years in Normandy. Sometime in the 1090s he sought the hand of the Scottish princess Edith-Matilda and seems to have been deeply irritated at her subsequent marriage to Henry I. Master Wace, an untrustworthy but fascinating source, describes him as ridiculing Henry's obsessively systematic approach to hunting. Henry tried to win William over by offering him a royal bastard daughter in marriage, but Anselm blocked the project on grounds of consanguinity. William joined Curthose's invading army in 1101, and Henry responded by seizing his lands and banishing him to Normandy. Two years later, Henry reinstated William in his earldom at the request of Curthose, who, in exchange, relinquished the annuity of 3000 marks that Henry had agreed to pay at the truce of 1101.

For a time William of Warenne was seemingly unwelcome at Henry's court: he attested no royal charters known to have been issued between 1103 and 1107. But he fought in Henry's victorious army at Tinchebray, perhaps inspired by the fact that his younger brother, who had been fighting in Curthose's behalf, had fallen into Henry's hands shortly before the battle. Whatever the case, William began appearing at Henry's court more frequently in the years that followed. And in 1110 or shortly thereafter, Henry secured William's loyalty for all time by giving him the castle and lordship of Saint-Saens in Upper Normandy. Henry had seized the honour when its previous lord, Elias of Saint-Saens, guardian of the young William Clito, spirited him out of Normandy just ahead of the royal officials whom Henry had sent to arrest him. It happens that the castle of Saint-Saens lies about three miles up the River Varenne from the Warenne castle of Bellencombre. In Orderic's words, Henry gave William Saint-Saens 'to secure his loyal support and resolute defense against enemy attacks'.[33] It was an astute move, for the lordship was a valuable and strategic addition to the Warenne holdings in Upper Normandy, and William would have realized that, should Clito ever return in triumph, Saint-Saens would be restored to Elias—Clito's guardian, brother-in-law, and companion in exile.

Accordingly, William of Warenne now became a *curialis* and ardent royalist. Having attested only once or twice for Rufus, he witnessed a total of sixty-nine of Henry I's surviving charters. In 1111 he was sitting as a judge in Henry's court in Normandy. And in 1119, at the battle of Brémule, William fought alonside Roger fitz Richard in the forward rank of Henry's victorious army. William is quoted as telling the king on the eve of the battle,

> There is no one who can persuade me to treason. . . . I and my kinsmen here and now place ourselves in mortal opposition to the king of France and are totally faithful to you. . . . I will support this undertaking, with my men, in the first rank of your army and will myself sustain the full weight of battle.[34]

William's danegeld exemptions in 1130 came to the tidy sum of £104—the third highest figure among the English baronage—testifying not only to the wealth of his lands but to the warm affection of his monarch as well. When Henry lay dying at Lyons-la-Forêt in 1135 Earl William was at his bedside, and afterwards was one of the five *comites* who escorted the royal corpse to Rouen for embalming.

Henry did not squander lands and privileges on his magnates, for his resources, unlike William I's, were limited and he intended neither to impoverish himself nor to raise magnates to such heights as to rival their monarch. When his old friend Hugh earl of Chester died in 1101, Henry reared Richard, Hugh's seven-year-old son and heir, at the royal court and, in time, arranged a distinguished marriage for him. Richard's bride was Matilda of Blois, sister of Stephen and Count Theobald and the king's own niece. Richard of Chester, like Roger fitz Richard and William of Warenne, was absolutely loyal to Henry in the crisis of 1118–1119.[35] Henry had meanwhile raised Othuer, Earl Hugh's bastard and Richard's half-brother, to a position of considerable wealth, entrusting him with the education of the royal offspring and with the custody of the Tower of London.[36] As it happened, Richard of Chester, Matilda of Blois, and Othuer all perished in the White Ship disaster of 1120. Since Richard and Matilda had no offspring, the flexible inheritance customs of the time would have permitted Chester to revert to the king.[37] Nevertheless, Henry granted the earldom to Ranulf le Meschin, Richard's first cousin, a devoted royalist of long standing who had fought heroically for Henry at Tinchebray and had given him staunch support in the crisis of 1118–1119.[38] Ranulf was already a wealthy Anglo-Norman baron—

vicomte of the Bessin, lord of extensive lands in Cumberland, and, through his thrice-married wife Lucy, a major landholder in Lincolnshire. In exchange for his advancement to the earldom of Chester—England's seventh or eighth wealthiest Domesday honour—and to Earl Richard's Norman vicomté of Avranches, Ranulf gave the king most of Lucy's estates, apparently with her assent, and his own lands in Cumberland.[39] The exchange aroused conflicts in later years between the monarchy and Lucy's heirs, but Ranulf le Meschin seems to have accepted the arrangement with good cheer: he had gained a title and a fortune, and Henry had prevented the formation of a baronial agglomeration of dangerous proportions.[40] Although not a major *curialis*, Ranulf attested Henry's charters with some frequency, particularly after his advancement to the earldom.[41] His loyalty was such that Henry entrusted him with the defence of Normandy when rebellion and an Angevin invasion threatened the duchy in 1123.[42] At Ranulf's death in 1129, the earldom passed quietly to his son, Ranulf II, who is reported in the Pipe Roll of 1130 as owing 1000 marks of his father's debt for the land of Earl Hugh.[43]

This Pipe Roll entry is of exceptional interest in that it suggests a form of royal patronage—the deliberate non-collection of a debt—that occurs repeatedly in the pipe rolls of Henry II. The run of annual Pipe Rolls from 1156 onward discloses a pattern on which royal favourites often pay little or nothing on a debt over a long period of years and, in the end, are sometimes pardoned altogether.[44] This kind of policy is virtually impossible to perceive in Henry I's reign, where only the single Pipe Roll survives. Stenton and others have built their theory of Henry I's repression on evidence from the roll of 1130 of baronial debts rather than baronial payments. To quote Stenton, 'the £102 16s. 8d. laid on Simon de Beauchamp because he had been the pledge of a man whom he did not produce in court seems grotesquely severe'.[45] But Simon in fact paid less than a third of the fine (£33 6s. 8d.) and, for all we know, may never have paid the rest. The Chester relief seems to disclose precisely such a policy of non-collection. The round figure of 1000 marks suggests that it may have been the full, original assessment. Earl Ranulf II paid nothing on it in 1130. It is described as his father's debt, which probably indicates that it represented the full relief assessed on the earldom when Ranulf le Meschin received it back in 1121. Further, the designation of the honour as the land of Earl Hugh could be taken to imply that Earl Richard, who acceded to the earldom as a child on Hugh's death in 1101 and grew up in the royal court, had paid no relief at his own death in 1120—probably because the king had the custody of the honour during Richard's long minority. Whatever the case, Earl Ranulf le Meschin was clearly permitted to leave unpaid throughout his eight-year tenure either the whole relief on his earldom or, at the very least, a considerable portion of it. Such was Henry's policy toward a faithful and singularly wealthy earl. It demonstrates how king and magnates could prosper together in the new era of exchequer accounting just as in the land-grabbing, swashbuckling years of William the Conqueror.

Thus far I have been concentrating on the great Domesday honours that remained intact or expanded only moderately under Henry I. Other families, moderately wealthy under the Conqueror and Rufus, were raised to the heights of Class A only under Henry I. Orderic tells us that immediately upon his accession Henry, apparently in contrast to Rufus, eschewed the advice of rash young men and followed the counsel of wise and older men, among whom Robert of Meulan, Hugh of Chester, Richard of Redvers and Roger Bigod are singled out by name.[46] The notion of the king surrounded by wise and seasoned advisers is of course a medieval political cliché, and, despite Orderic's implication, three of the four men he names had been *curiales* of William Rufus. Only Richard of Redvers was new to the *curia*. A baron of western Normandy, he had been a loyal friend during Henry's troubled youth and now became a very frequent attestor of royal charters. Henry granted him a Class B barony, chiefly in Devon and the Isle of Wight, carved out of *terra regis* and the vast honour forfeited by Roger earl of Hereford in 1075. Although Roger Bigod and Robert of Meulan had been major attestors for Rufus, it was Henry who catapulted them into the top echelon of the English aristocracy. Roger Bigod's Domesday lands, worth £450 a year, put him in the lower circles of Corbett's Class B barons. But the family prospered, chiefly through Henry I's gifts to Roger, and to such a degree that the Bigod *carta* of 1166 reports the very impressive total of 125 knights having been enfeoffed by 1135. Roger and, later, his son Hugh served as royal stewards and figured among the most frequent lay attestors of Henry's charters.[47]

Robert, count of Meulan and lord of Beaumont, held a Domesday estate of about £250, placing him toward the bottom of Corbett's Class C. Under Henry he was permitted to acquire, through sharp tactics, the considerable Grandmesnil estates centring on Leicester, plus chunks of the forfeited earldom of William of Mortain in the Rape of Pevensey and elsewhere, along with lands from the royal demesne.[48] He became the first earl of Leicester, a notable achievement in a regime that did not create new earldoms with careless abandon, and his successor in early Angevin times answered for 157 knights' fees,[49] a figure that suggests prodigious wealth. Robert earned his fortune by serving as Henry's chief adviser, his most frequent lay attestor, his *alter ego*.[50] Robert's twin sons, Waleran and Robert, were raised in the royal court. The young Robert became earl of Leicester on his father's death in 1118 and, as we have seen, was given the wealthy Norman lordship of Breteuil shortly thereafter. He remained strictly loyal to Henry I, supported Stephen almost to the end, and served Henry II as chief justiciar. Waleran became lord of Beaumont and count of Meulan. Surprisingly, he joined the Norman rebellion of 1123–1124. It was an almost calamitous error, for he was captured at Rougemontier and remained Henry's prisoner for five years. But Henry released him in 1129, following Clito's death, and restored his lands and the royal friendship—though the king's garrisons remained in Waleran's Norman castles.[51] The Pipe Roll of 1130 discloses the fiscal dimensions of both the royal anger and the royal love. Waleran is charged 100 marks for the recovery of his estates in Dorset (but pays none of it), while at the same time the flow of royal patronage is resumed: he receives danegeld exemptions on forty-six demesne hides in 1129, fifty-two in 1130, and is among those royal favourites exempted from the *murdrum* fine.[52] Waleran learned Henry's lesson well: he attested the king's charters regularly after his release and never rebelled again.[53] The remainder of his career, under both Henry and Stephen, was a model of baronial circumspection.

An important minority of Henry's Class A and AA magnates inherited nothing in England or Normandy and owed their entire fortunes to Henry. Brian fitz Count, with danegeld exemptions on 720 demesne hides, rose through royal gifts and a marriage to the heiress of Wallingford to become one of Henry's wealthiest magnates and most active *curiales*.[54] Robert earl of Gloucester and Stephen of Blois rose still higher, again through royal gifts and strategic marriages.[55] Stephen of Blois' English fortune derived primarily from the forfeited honours of Henry's enemies, William Malet and Roger of Poitou (a disinherited Montgomery), and from his marriage to the Boulogne heiress, the offspring of Eustace's marriage to Henry's sister-in-law, Mary of Scotland.[56]

Henry's three wealthiest landholders—Robert of Gloucester, Stephen, and Roger bishop of Salisbury—were in a class apart. Nobody else approached them in landed wealth. And all three were Henry's creations and unswerving *fideles*. Stephen's ascent has been described as Henry's single act of folly— forced on him by his need of an alliance with Theobald of Blois, Stephen's brother.[57] My own reading of the evidence persuades me that Theobald needed Henry more than Henry needed Theobald, and that the elevation of Stephen and Robert of Gloucester is to be seen as a product of deliberate royal policy, uninfluenced by diplomatic considerations. A comparison of Corbett's classification under William I with my own parallel classification under Henry I discloses a remarkable similarity in the overall distribution of baronial wealth between 1086 and 1125–1135. William I's 'super-honours'—those of Odo, Robert of Mortain, and Roger of Montgomery—had all perished by 1104, but by the mid-1120s others had been built in their places. Henry I's 'super-honours' seem to have been of approximately the magnitude of William's. And, significantly, Henry's two greatest hereditary honours were both granted to close kinsmen—a nephew and a natural son—just as two of William's three had been created for his half-brothers.[58] Both kings were, in effect, creating apanages—placing trusted kinsmen in positions atop the baronial hierarchy. The policy had been followed by the Conqueror's ducal ancestors, who entrusted their kinsmen with the great frontier counties of Eu, Évreux and Mortain. It was of course a Capetian policy as well; in one form or another it influenced most of the rulers of medieval Christendom. It often led to difficulties: Odo and Robert of Mortain rebelled against Rufus; Stephen seized the throne after Henry's death and against his wishes. But so long as Henry lived, Stephen and Robert of Gloucester remained the most ardent of royalists.

During the last decade of the reign, Henry's restructured baronage was firmly in place. The forfeiture of honours that marked Henry's early years had diminished after Tinchebray and ceased altogether after about 1113.[59] By 1125 the honours of Robert of Gloucester, Stephen, and Brian fitz Count had been formed. The magnate class was by now solidly royalist and even, to a degree, curialist. The extent of the transformation will be evident when one contrasts the struggle between magnates and *curiales* in 1101 with the backstairs manoeuvering twenty-five years later between the supporters and opponents of the Empress Maud. Two factions appear to have been at odds in autumn 1126 over the question of the Anglo-Norman succession. Maud's candidacy was backed, so the evidence suggests, by Robert of Gloucester, David king of Scots and Brian fitz Count, and opposed by Roger of Salisbury, his kinsmen Alexander bishop of Lincoln and Nigel the Treasurer, and possibly the *curialis* Payn fitz John. The issue was resolved, for the time, entirely within the confines of the court, and with such adroitness that Roger of Salisbury himself was put in charge of the oath-taking ceremony.[60] Maud must have enjoyed that.

The political factions dimly visible in 1126 emerge in the glare of Stephen's early years as the nuclei of the two contending parties of the Anarchy. Roger of Salisbury's group, still opposing Maud, leapt to Stephen's support the moment he crossed the Channel, while Maud's supporters of 1126–1127— Robert of Gloucester, David king of Scots and Brian fitz Count—became the champions of the Angevin cause. The most interesting thing about these two parties is that, unlike the rival groups of 1101, they were composed of similar kinds of men. All had been enriched by Henry I; all had frequented his court and attested his charters; all were royalists. They made war in Stephen's reign not because they sought freedom from a predatory Anglo-Norman regime (for they had been a part of it), but because they sought effective royal lordship and could find it nowhere.

Why, then, was there a civil war at all? Historians have traditionally viewed Henry's succession plan as unworkable and have attributed its failure to the bias of the Anglo-Norman baronage against Angevins and women (usually in that order). But Stephen's dash for the crown was made possible only by Maud's ill-considered diplomatic break with Henry in mid-1135 and her consequent absence from his court at the time of his death a few months later.[61] Maud and Geoffrey had demanded custody of some of Henry's castles and the restoration of the castles of William Talvas, son of Robert of Bellême. The result was a minor war along the Norman frontier, in which Henry's most faithful magnates—the very group that might normally have been expected to back the Angevin succession—were in arms against Anjou. It was Maud's impetuousness, and a trivial border conflict, that cleared Stephen's path to Westminster. The Civil War was not an exploding furnace of baronial discontent but the product of a political stalemate in which Henry's designated successor, to whom the baronage was oath-bound, found herself pitted against a crowned, anointed king. 'Stephen's reign is so confused and so messy,' writes Edmund King, 'not because the aristocracy was reacting against strong government but because they had accepted it. . . . Having learned to live with a strong king, to accept his peace and adapt their strategy to his power, they found it difficult to manage without one.'[62]

Much more could be said about the men on whom Henry depended for his power and his peace—the bishops and abbots, the *curiales* and royal officials of lesser wealth whom Sir Richard Southern has analysed so brilliantly. Even the magnates have been viewed here in an insular perspective, with no serious attention given to their landed wealth in Normandy (where the evidence is even thinner than in England). Nevertheless, it should be clear that the stability of Henry's regime was based on the support of great landholders. From beginning to end Henry worked to create a royalist baronage. He realized that most barons, even Norman barons, were by nature neither turbulent nor particularistic, but anxious simply to safeguard their family wealth or, better yet, increase it. Henry's magnates discovered that rebellion involved high risks but that loyalty to the king and association with his court brought security and enrichment.

That is the key to Henry's peace. I wish I could claim to have discovered it myself, but it was well known to Henry's own contemporaries. Orderic Vitalis, who understood the Anglo-Norman aristocracy as well as any writer of his time, sums up Henry's baronial policy, and my paper, in these words: 'He treated the magnates with honour and generosity, adding to their wealth and estates; and by placating them in this way, he won their loyalty.'[63]

Anglo-Norman as a Spoken Language

M. D. LEGGE

Shortly before her death, Professor Pope said to the reader: 'I've come to the conclusion that Anglo-Norman is just spoken French.' Unfortunately, she never committed this remark to writing, but it is something which strikes oddly and has never been pursued. It is the object of this paper to develop this train of thought, and to show that it sheds light on both Anglo-Norman and French.

There is a heresy that Anglo-Norman is not a vernacular, and it started on the other side of the Atlantic. In 1910 a young lawyer named George Woodbine published as his thesis an edition of *Four Thirteenth-Century Law Tracts*.[1] These were all in French. This edition was a first-class piece of work. It was not until 1943 that he followed this up with an article in *Speculum* entitled *The Language of the English Law*.[2] It has been cited in a wider context, but even if read in application to the law only, it is based upon a false premise. He seems to think that because it is in the thirteenth century that we have written evidence that French was used in the courts, therefore lawyers did not use French before that date. Now Professor William Rothwell has taken up the cudgels on this side of the water,[3] and speaks of French in the thirteenth century as a second *learned* language like Latin, and not as a vernacular! Oddly enough, a far more balanced view comes from an English specialist, Derek Pearsall, in *Old English and Middle English Poetry*, 1972. Here he counts Anglo-Norman as a vernacular alongside English, and points out that advance in both speech and writing proceeded side-by-side in the two languages.

Only in the thirteenth century did the French themselves become aware of dialect. The first writer in England to boast of the purity of his French was Guernes de Pont Sainte-Maxence,[4] soon after 1170, but a sojourn in England had left its traces. In the 1160s the Nun of Barking had apologized for her French in an introduction to her *Life of Edward the Confessor*.[5] She says that she mixes her cases, but she was inspired by Gregory of Tours' apology for his Latin, in which he mixed his cases, bearing in mind that this was in his introduction to a book on Confessors. For in the list of remarks about French dialects, we are indebted to Brunot's *Histoire de la langue Française*, newly edited in 1966. In 1180 Aymon de Varenne's lyonnais was not acceptable.

Very well known is Canon de Bethune's complaint that the Court laughed at him, in the hearing of the Champenois, even of Alice the Countess, adding insult to injury. That was before 1224, when he died. Jean de Meung protests about the domination of Francien in his *Boece* towards the end of the thirteenth century. Breton French was fair game. French jeers at Anglo-Norman take the form of parody. Nobody ever talked like the Earl of Gloucester in Philippe de Beaumanoir's late thirteenth-century romance *Jehan et Blonde*.[6] Sometimes there is a basis of truth. The riotously funny *Fabliauce des Deux Angleys et l'Anel*[7] has the Englishman's chronic inability to pronounce the *n mouillé* as its starting point. The result is a confusion between the French for lamb and for donkey.

Edward the Confessor, that half-Norman hero of the Anglo-Saxons, imported Norman clerks into England. They left no traces on language,[8] but they provided a foundation of civil servants who were acquainted with English ways and English law on which post-Conquest clerks would build. These clerks at Winchester who worked on the Domesday Book returns were probably Edward the Confessor's men, who could sometimes even correct the spellings of English place-names. It was the army of the Conquest which talked Norman and brought about the phenomenon of Anglo-Norman which coexisted for centuries with English, and finally transformed it into the amalgam we talk today. The army was accompanied by various servants and cooks as well as clergy depicted on the Bayeux Tapestry, and these had a profound but scarcely recognized influence on our vocabulary.

Ladies followed with Queen Matilda the next year, and this meant Anglo-Norman homes. The children who arrived were French-speaking, but it is often remarked that post-Conquest babies learned to speak from their nurses. No doubt they did, but great ladies would see to it that their offspring did not lose caste by not knowing French. Professor Rothwell has compared such children to those of immigrants, who rapidly substitute English for their own languages.[9] But immigrant children go to school and go into shops and public transport. Baronial children did not. Moreover, at seven boys and girls were sent to other households to be fostered, and to act as pages and maids-in-waiting to their hosts, mixing with the knights and ladies and learning to read and write from the chaplain. A better comparison than with immigrants would be with our great-grandparents in the Highlands, who were beaten if they were heard talking in their native Gaelic, which they picked up from the servants. Before the loss of Normandy contact was kept up with families across the channel. William Marshall was sent to a cousin, Guillaume de Tancarville, Chamberlain of Normandy.[10] Gervase of Tilbury, his contemporary, says that people sent their children to France to learn French;[11] they also, like the Marshall, acquired polish. Speakers of Anglo-Norman were always distinguished between those who had had contact with France and those who had not. Giraldus Cambrensis, whose own French pronunciation was not above reproach, tells of a John Blount whom he commended for his pronunciation, supposing him to have been to France. He had not, but his uncles had, and he had talked with them.[12] Even in the last days of Law French, Roger North says that his brother, Chief Justice in 1675–1682, coped with it better than his fellow-judges because he was familiar with the French of France.[13] Froissart, who is too pro-French on occasions to be quite trustworthy, says that in 1360 the English negotiators of the Treaty of Brétigny complained that the French of the French clerks was different from the French that they had learnt in childhood.[14] As they included the Duke of Lancaster, author of *Les Seintez Mediceines*,[15] and who had served for long periods on the Continent, and the Duke of Gloucester, this looks like delaying tactics. Froissart, however, remarks that David II's French was superior to that used at Edward III's court, because of the seven years he had spent at the French court.

But what of the English themselves in 1067? Not everybody perished at Hastings. The nobles' estates were given to William's followers, and the St Wulfstans, the Waltheofs, the Edwins and Morcars soon disappeared. Many of the Normans settled on the lands of their overlords, like the Thaons in Kent. They formed what the historians call networks. If families were not intermarried already, they intermarried after their arrival. It is difficult, for instance, to disentangle the Lovels. Was there originally one family or two? but all this was not enough, and in a recent article in *Speculum*[16] Cecily Clark has shown how much racial intermarriage there was. The results must have been bilingualism. To be bilingual does not imply complete equality of languages, and the languages may have been used for different purposes. As French had become very quickly the language of the Church, the law and diplomacy, the Norman husband would have to keep up his language, while his wife could retain hers for domestic use, while if the husband was English he would have to learn French. Cecily Clark has also studied English Christian names given to women. This, as she acknowledges, is slippery ground. It was the custom to christen children after a grandparent. Men's names were more often Normanized or Latinized by clerks, women's more rarely so. Occasionally it can be proved to have occurred. The Viking-descended Prioress of Iona, who ordered the Psalter executed in Oxford, was called Bethog, a sister of Reginald Lord of the Isles. His real name was Ranald, and she acquired the name of Beatrice. Such doublets still exist—Aeneas exists side-by-side with Angus, Hector with Aechan.

The late twelfth-century romance *Boeve de Haumtone*[18] has a rare reference to a Norman household with English servants.

> A taunt estes vous la dame venaunt de son polais,
> Ele fu bien vestue de une paile Gregeis,
> Les boucles de ses soulers sunt d'orfreiss.

Mult fu bele femme, mes quer out pugneis.
Sabot la dame apele, si li dist en Engleis.
'Ou est Boefs mun fis, le fin maveis?'

Here is a very grand lady, most expensively dressed, who knows enough English to address an inferior. Again, and again, one is reminded of India today, where English is the lingua franca and the memsahib of yesterday learned to converse with the servants.

The evidence of lingualism is hard to come by. People do not write down what everybody knows. Professor R. M. Wilson collected in his article 'English and French in England 1100–1300'[19] examples of English quoted in chronicles. Here it must be remembered that these are not eye-witness accounts, and that it was a well-known trick to insert something in a vernacular into a document or chronicle in Latin in order to give an air of authenticity to the affair. What can be deduced is that it was accepted that the upper classes did know English. The most oft-quoted example comes from the *Vita Sancte Thome*,[20] the point of which has been missed. The advances of an Englishman had been rejected by Helewisia, the wife of Hugh de Moreville, one of Becket's murderers. Both were of Norman descent. Helewisia pretended to help Liulf to murder her husband, but when he appeared with a sword behind his back, she called out: 'Huge de Moreville, ware, ware, ware, Lithulf heth his sword adrage.' This is supposed to indicate that the Morevilles habitually spoke English together. Perhaps they did, but Helewisia was anxious to make clear to young Liulf that she had betrayed him. He was scalded at once. He would have done better to learn French.

The chronicle evidence is not all one-way. Fordun's chronicle reports a conversation between Edward I and Bruce the Competitor after the Battle of Dunbar in 1296, when the king repudiated a promise to support Bruce's claim to the Scottish throne.

'Ne avoms ren autres choses a fer, que a vous reams a ganere?' Quod est dicere: 'Nunquid non aliud habernus facere, quam tibi regna lucrari?'

Then again, he shouted at Anthony Bek, Bishop of Durham:

'quasi caput concutiens: Par le sank Dieu, vous avez bun chanté Quod est dicere: Per sanguinem Christi, tu bene cantasti.'[21]

This shows that Edward was expected to speak in Anglo-Norman, even when he had completely lost his temper, a not unusual occurrence.

There are two references on either side which have the ring of authenticity. Walter Daniel reports the last words of Alfred of Rievaulx:

'Festinate, for crist luve'

Ailred, that son of a Northumbrian married priest, was in old age mixing his languages, but his original English came from the heart.[22] This story rings true. There are French quotations in a letter addressed to the Bishop of St Davids by Giraldus Cambrensis, complaining of scurrilous attacks against him.[23] His adversaries had quoted two scurrilous proverbs. Roger de Becke had said:

'Bien set chat ki barbe il leche'.

and Jocelin, the Dean:

'Tant giwe li purcel Cume volt li chael'.

All three Edwards are believed to have understood English, but not to have been able to speak it. Froissart was naively astonished to find Richard II's Court talking English when he had witnessed Richard's christening at Bordeaux, and expected that the French tradition would have continued. However, the king was able to express pleasure at Froissart's reading from the book of poems which he had been graciously pleased to accept.[24] Henry IV is credited with being the first king since the Conquest whose mother-tongue was English, yet he made a cruel joke when he said that James I, unlawfully kidnapped on the high seas on his way to be educated in France, would have learnt the language just as well at his own court.[25] We possess a postscript added in his own hand to a signet letter in 1403,

'Nessescitas non habet legem Et pour tant volons que noz lettres de protection soient fais selonc la contenue de cestes noz lettres, consideranz q'a cause de guere move contre nous dedeins nostre reaume nous pourrons fere toutes noz Courtez cesset, en sauvacion de noz et nostre reaume.'[26]

So, as Professor Wilson acknowledges, the evidence is confusing. What is clear is that Anglo-Norman remained, as we should say today, *U*. It was in the mid-thirteenth century that a noble lady Dionysia de Munchessy asked the crusader-poet Walter de Bibbesworth for a book to instruct children in French.[27] This is based on homonymics. That it is intended for the gentry is proved by the subject-matter. It progresses from parts of the body to common animals and then household affairs necessary for a householder to know in order to supervise servants, then to agriculture and hunting, and finally to the menu for a great banquet. It was evidently very popular, since fourteen manuscripts, some fragmentary, survive. None is earlier than the fourteenth century. The Prologue, which occurs in four manuscripts, ends with the words: 'Dount tut dis troverez-vous primes le frounceis e puis le engleise amount.' We do not know when and by whom this prologue was written. In all the copies of the text which survive, English words are often written above the

French, but these so-called glosses increase in the later copies, and, indeed, the treatise teaches English as well as French, for many of the words would not be known by a child. Bibbesworth is indeed a portent, but not for the reason put forward by the anti-Anglo-Normanists alone. This tiny work is a testimony to the growth of literacy. There had always been bluestockings like the convent-bred Queen Maud, but an ordinary baron's wife demanding a child's primer as a substitute for oral tradition was something new. In the fifteenth century a verse treatise with interposed English lines is preserved in a solitary manuscript. It is called '*Femina*'[28]

quia sicut femina docet infantem loqui linguam
maternam sic docet iste liber juvenes rethorice loqui gallicam'.

This is not, like Bibbesworth, meant for children and belongs to a later age.

So much for the upper classes. But what of the lower, whose knowledge of French has been denied? Norman servants imposed their vocabulary on their underlings—the chefs changed the names of *beasts* in the lord's kitchens, not on his table, as Miss Pope has pointed out,[29] and words like beef, mutton, veal are in dialect, while gammon keeps the picard g. The picard carpenter used chisels and planes. Professor Woodbine laments that we do not know how the Conqueror pronounced his French. But we do, not only by the English words listed above, but because it is the language of the *Chanson de Roland*.[30]

'Cinquante carre qu'en feront carrier—Fifty carts for carrying'

Abbot Samson, an Englishman, is often used to supply evidence that countrymen knew no French, because he confirmed a manor to an Englishman, a serf, mark you, because he was a good farmer and knew no French. But, as Professor Wilson[31] has pointed out, this means that some serfs *did* speak French. Already we see them as described by Higden—I quote from Trevisa's translation:

'uplondisshe men wil liken hymself to gentilmen, and fondeth with greet besynesse for to speke French; for to be i-tolde of'.[32]

English was never proscribed, but French was naturally the language of clerks, and became therefore the language of law and administration and of the Church. Law and administration were built on the foundation of the Winchester clerks imported by Edward the Confessor. The second in date of Anglo-Norman texts is the *Cumpoz* by Philippe de Thaon, for his uncle Humfroi in the household of the royal steward. It is a highly technical performance, in verse because it was easily memorized.[33] The indication is that clerks were talking Anglo-Norman even if most of their work was recorded in Latin. The law presents a paradox. English law was taken over, and much of its vocabulary was adopted. In the thirteenth century glossaries of law-terms appeared. These give definitions, but not translations of terms like 'infang thief' and 'outfang thief'. One of the difficulties was that only Canon and Civil Law were taught in the Universities, and these were often in conflict with the native variety. To remedy this state of affairs, the Inns of Court were set up in the reign of Edward I. This was coincident with other educational developments. The grammar masters of Oxford taught boys in the mornings in the ordinary lecture hours, and gave business courses in the afternoons, including French and the English manner of pleading, besides the drafting of charters, examples of statutes and forms of letters in French. Thomas Samson used the best-known of these treatises on spelling, the *Orthographia Gallica*.[34] His course was studied by I. D. O. Arnold in *Medium Aevum* in 1937.[35] His son-in-law, William of Kingsmill, who seems to have succeeded him, used the *Tractatus Orthographiae*, written by T.H., a former student at Paris. This I described in the Pope festschrift in 1939.[36] Miss Pope, who edited the *Tractatus* in the *Modern Language Review* of 1910,[37] thought on linguistic grounds that it must be earlier than the *Orthographia* but as Kingsmill seems to have preferred it, it may be later. It is the source of Coyfurelly's treatise—the *Orthographia* was taught in French, and glosses have been added in the manuscripts. These are usually attributed to the Masters, and their inefficiency mocked. But, as Professor Arnold pointed out, these manuscripts are students' notebooks, and it is incredible that University teachers should blame students' mistakes on their masters. Have they never read an examination script? It is well known that after the first plague of 1348, two Cornish schoolmasters substituted English for French in the teaching of Latin. With Thomas Samson and William of Kingsmill we are dealing with the second half of the fourteenth and the beginning of the fifteenth centuries. Evidently, as members of the sub-faculty of grammar, paying to the University thirteen shillings per annum, and bound to observe the statutes, they were complying with the statute, unfortunately undated, enjoining the teaching of French, 'lest the Gallic tongue be utterly forgotten'.[38] Trevisa says: 'Also gentil-man children beeth i-taught to speke French from the tyme that they beeth i-rokked in her cradel.' Thus far Higdon, writing in 1342 or '44. Trevisa adds sadly; that after the 'first dethe', the two Cornish Masters of Grammar, Cornwalle and Pencrich, had changed to teaching in English, 'the disadvantage is that now children of gramer scole conneth no more Frensche than can hir lift heele. Also gentil men haveth now moche i-left for to teche here children Frenssche.' That was in 1385.[39] These men were scriveners dwelling in houses clustered round the church of St Mary the Virgin, on sites now occupied by parts of Brasenose and All Souls. It is not true that the Colleges in general insisted on the speaking of French as well as Latin. Only three colleges mention French in their statutes. They are Exeter, 1322 and 1325, Oriel 1326, and Queen's 1340. The founders of these Colleges were men in the Royal service, and their object was to ensure that there were sufficient graduates to serve the church and the state. The 'civil service' as one might term it, long worked in Anglo-Norman. Chaucer's English was heavily Gallicized—documents survive drafted by his fellow-poet Hoccleue.

It is not true that the spelling treatises had no effect. Either some are lost, or those that we have are older than we think. Henry III's clerks were spelling *st* after a vowel *ht*. Edward I's clerks knew better, and the express point that the sound *-ght* must be written *-st* is made. This coincides with the passing of statutes in Anglo-Norman, the foundation of the Inns of Court and the beginning of the Year-books.

As Trevisa puts it—'Hit seemeth a greet wonder how Englisshe, that is the birth-tongue of Englisshemen and her owne language and tongue, is so dyversse of soune in this oon iland, and the language of Normandie is comlyng of another londe, and hathe one manere soun among ale men that speketh hit aright in Engelond—Nevertheless, there is as many dyvers manere Frenssche in the reem of Fraunce as is dyvers manere Englisshe in the reem of Engelond. For a man of Kent, Southern, western and northern men speken Frenssche al lyke in soune and speche, but they can not speke theyr Englyssche so.'[40]

This passage tells us two things: why Anglo-Norman became a *lingua franca*, and so retarded the emergence of a standard English, and why the teaching of French was forced to change. It was useless for a commercial traveller to try to sell wool in North-Eastern France in high Francien. A fifteenth-century glossary gives Picard variants of Francien words where they differed. *Manieres de Langage*,[41] giving delightful glimpses of social life, give instructions about different ways of addressing people of different classes, so as to help the traveller not to make a fool of himself. Inn Dialogues, curiously, deal with life in England. In one of these, William of Kingsmill advertises his school through a little poem recited by a small boy, son of the landlady:

'l'ay a noun Johan, bon enfant,
Beal et sage et bien parlant
Engleys, frmaunceys et bon Normand.'

Anglo-Norman made its way in the Church. After the Conquest, monks like Eadmer at Canterbury, author of the Life of St Anselm, settled down with Norman incomers. Some clergy could preach in English, but others could or would not. Here dialect played a part. Abbot Samson exhorted his monks to preach in English, or French if they could not manage it, rather than Latin. He himself preached in his native Norfolk, but his Suffolk hearers could not follow him. Their French, however, was an acquired tongue and differed from Continental French. When it was proposed to elect as prior a native Norman who was more fluent than his fellows, he objected that he was a bad preacher. He was told to take his sermons out of books, like other people.[43] Here there is comparison between Anglo-Norman a mere hundred years old, and the parent variety. French took over to such an extent that a young man who appealed to St Hugh of Lincoln to free him from temptation, told his tale through an interpreter, since he knew little French and the bishop little English. This is told in the *Magna Vita*, by Adam, who was an Englishman belonging to an Oxford town family. Less surprising is the story of the countryman possessed of a devil, for whom St Hugh required an interpreter. Apart from the fact that countrymen knew no French and that a young man might know little, there is a further deduction to be made. St Hugh, a Burgundian, Bishop of Lincoln 1186–1200, communicated with his English fellow-Carthusians in French. There is also proof here that his contemporary William Longchamp's unpopularity, which caused him to be stoned, was only slightly due to his lack of knowledge of English.

Choir-monks took their professions in Latin or French, rarely in English. Lay brothers took theirs in English and it was forbidden to teach them to read.

The explosion of works such as *La Lumere as lais* and the *Manuel des Peches* after the 4th Lateran Council of 1215, really designed to help the clergy instruct congregations in the essence of the Christian faith, are in French. In about 1300 Nicole Bozon wrote his aids to preachers—his *Contes*—in French.[45]

It is therefore not true that Anglo-Norman died during the thirteenth century. Not only is Sir Thomas Gray of Heton's *Scalacronica*, finished in 1369, written in fluent Anglo-Norman, but he records that his father, like Henri IV, swore 'jarnidieu' and knew that there was a connexion between the words 'cheval' and 'chevalier', which exists only in French.[46] The language survived perhaps longest in the ports, witness the words in The Oak Book of Southampton[47] and The Register of Daniel Rough,[48] both fourteenth century. Not only were the clerks trained to write Anglo-Norman, but their spellings prove that the language was actually pronounced.

Nobody, even with an Anglo-Saxon name, can claim to have no Norman blood, and when in 1944 we landed in Normandy, countless Beaumonts, Bruces, Colvilles, Granvilles, Gurneys, Harcourts, Hays, Montgomeries, Percies, Sinclairs, Somervilles and Warrens found themselves at home, and hinted to their families where they were in defiance of the censors. What the Dialogue of the Exchequer says is still true.

Our present-day language is a mixture of Anglo-Norman, Anglo-Saxon and Danish. Woodbine lamented that we do not know what Anglo-Norman sounded like. But we do. It is the language of the *Chanson de Roland*, and many of the words in that survive in English with their original pronunciation, as 'charge', 'castel', 'Apostle', 'verai'. The spelling was semi-phonetic and since the publication of Hans Goebl's *Die Normandische Urkundensprache* in 1970[49] we know that the much-derided Anglo-Norman spelling was just plain Norman.

What, finally, of the law? When Woodbine says that the judges quipped in

Latin or in English but not in French, he forgot Maitland.[50] We have what he called a photograph of pleadings in the reign of Edward II, 1307–1327. The chief justice, Sir William Bereford, was fond of proverbs—'Il vodreient volunters avoir la gelyne et la maille'—in Yorkshire they still talk of the chicken and the halfpenny—and of stories, mostly about hanging and gallows. There is one, however, which Maitland could not bring himself to translate, and is pure fabliau: 'Cum la pucelle dist au vallet ge li demanda si elle fust pucelle "assaiet, assaiet", auxi assaiet vous, et si la seute ne sera aporcioné, mei blamet.' Thanks to the reporters, who could not afford to leave anything to chance, we can catch the very tone of voice in which these things were said. 'Est ceo un a relesser terre demeine et dreit de comune'. (Quasi diceret non.)

'*Mutford*   Les uns de vous unt moult parlé encountre qe soleit estre lay.
 Bereford   Certes, c'est verite; mes jeo ne die point q'il sount. Et ascuns entendirunt q'il dist ceo de Stonore'.[51]

I submit that this is still a vernacular. The famous statute, allowing pleading in English, itself in French, remained a dead-letter down to Cromwell's time, though, alas, the judges had long ceased to participate.

Magnates, Curiales and the Wheel of Fortune: 1066–1154[1]

EMMA MASON

The definition of my title, like all Gaul, is divided into three parts. The magnates may be defined as 'the great men' of the realm in terms of feudal power at their disposal, and hence of their political consequence. Great men rose and fell, and some rose higher than others, but at any given time there was little doubt as to who *were* the magnates.

The *curialis* hoped to make his fortune in the royal court, but in doing so, he sought enrichment and the establishment of a landed family, when his interests would merge with those of the older baronage. Many families which were undoubtedly çurial in the reigns of the Norman kings were clearly baronial by the end of the twelfth century, and often well before that. Moreover, it often happened that an undoubted *curialis* also had specific powers, perhaps as sheriff or castellan, which gave him territorial pre-eminence within a limited radius, so that here, at any rate, he was regarded as a magnate.[2] No family could be classified indefinitely as curial. Either its members prospered, and became baronial, or failed to make their mark at court, and faded from the administrative hierarchy, leaving little further trace. The term *curialis* covers a wide range of the tenurial spectrum, ranging from great barons who were closely associated with royal policies, down to minor administrators who might never rate more than a chance entry in the Pipe Rolls. We shall take the *via media*, and emphasize those considerations which applied to families of modest origins whose fortunes steadily improved in the period under discussion.

The rotating Wheel of Fortune appeared towards the end of the eleventh century, as a literary and artistic image, probably in response to a general awareness of increasing social mobility.[3] Its imagery had a dominating influence on men's minds in the period covered by this paper. Orderic Vitalis depicts Amaury de Montfort encouraging Louis VI after the battle of Brémule with the words: 'Fortune is like a turning wheel. One moment she suddenly lifts a man up, the next throws him down, and conversely she raises the man who is prostrate and trodden in the dust more generously than he could have hoped.'[4] It was generally held that an individual was driven by blind Fortune.

What became of him was largely a matter of luck, and it was entirely due to the grace of God that he was occasionally favoured. Individual success was due to an ability to see and seize opportunities, like the man who jumped on Fortune's Wheel as it ascended.[5]

The magnates of the Conquest era were themselves comparatively 'new men', ambitious and greedy, like other emergent social groups.[6] Their behavioural patterns were undergoing reappraisal, in order to meet the challenges, first of intensified ducal rule, and then those offered by the conquest of England. It was traditionally observed that fortunes were to be made in warfare, whether in the shape of rewards handed out by a grateful ruler to a dutiful vassal, or in the more insecure forms of land-grabbing and looting. Warfare was glorified in the popular literature of the Anglo-Norman period, such as the Song of Roland, the Gesta Francorum or the Song of Hastings. There was, however, a marked contrast between the self-sacrificing behaviour of an idealized hero such as Roland and the strictly practical objectives of magnates who actually engaged in warfare. In recognition of this dichotomy, Roland, the traditional hero-figure, was joined, early in the eleventh century, by the complementary character of Oliver, who personified the virtues of prudence required to modify unthinking valour. By the time William Rufus came to the throne, narrative texts were beginning to cite prudence, rather than courage, as the most estimable virtue in a worthy knight. Essentially, prudence was understood to comprise useful intelligence,[7] and a comparison of the careers of William II and Henry I with that of their brother Robert Curthose suggests that they, but not he, had absorbed the lesson offered by Oliver's arrival on the literary scene. Virtues displayed by the king must of course be emulated by the more ambitious of his subjects, and 'useful intelligence' was a denominator common to those magnates and *curiales* who successfully charted the wreck-strewn shoals of Anglo-Norman politics. In Stephen's reign, when the king himself reverted to Roland's behavioural patterns, and the framework of society collapsed in consequence, would-be survivors were even more in need of Oliver as their guide.

Parallel with the adoption of prudence went the assumption of Frenchness. By the time of the conquest of England, the Northmen of Normandy had been transformed into the 'French of France',[8] and a Norman was defined as a Frenchman who happened to come from Normandy. There were sound demographic and cultural reasons for this transformation,[9] yet in addition to these there was no doubt a tacit recognition that the old modes of conduct could not be upheld in face of the strengthening of government under Duke William. To a certain extent, awareness of the Scandinavian past reappeared as a literary theme later in the Anglo-Norman period,[10] but behaviour appropriate to saga heroes was not then politically acceptable. Lapses did of course occur whenever the heavy hand of government was relaxed, but this reaction can be paralleled in most unstable societies, of whatever ethnic

composition. Real-life manifestations of Norse characteristics were being steadily depreciated. An episode in the Gesta Francorum records the valuable service at the siege of Antioch of a berserker in the service of Godfrey of Monte Scaglioso,[11] but in general heroics were no longer given a Nordic gloss. By the time the Song of Hastings appeared, about 1125 to 1140,[12] the Viking burial which it depicted Duke William according to Harold had an air of dismissing from view a brave yet anachronistic rival.[13]

Peaceable means must now be used by the magnate who wished to keep his balance on the revolving Wheel of Fortune. The search for enrichment through the marriage market was exploited to considerable effect both within and beyond the frontiers of Normandy by the families which will be discussed below, the Beaumonts and the Tosnys.[14] Together with their contemporaries, they gave increasing attention to marriage policies and to the snapping-up of political windfalls to counteract the growing strength of the king-duke. The rights of overlordship which William I asserted as king in England quickly had repercussions on the tenurial position of the great lords in Normandy. Whereas in 1050 the Beaumonts, Tosnys and their equals would have resisted in practice the ducal assertion that they held their lands by conditional tenure, some twenty years later, as tenants in chief in England, they acknowledged their obligation to render large quotas of knight service. By analogy, this recognition rapidly affected their position in Normandy too.[15] The conquest of England brought such baronial houses a vast increase in their resources, but the joint effects of the enlarged powers of the ruler and the prevailing custom of dividing the hereditary and acquired lands between elder and younger sons meant that the gains of the conquest were often soon diminished.[16] That this did not always prove to be a bad thing in the long run will be argued from the respective fortunes of the families discussed in this paper.

Enrichment was traditionally sought at the expense of wealthy religious houses at times when central authority was relaxed. This was a major theme of both English and Norman chroniclers, one of whose stock characters, under a variety of names, was the revolting baron who molested the patrimonies of their patron saints, but whose career was brought to an abrupt end, with just enough time to disgorge his ill-gotten gains before his last gasp. The two obvious questions which emerge from this are, firstly, how precise a version of events are we given in such stories, and secondly, where they are substantially accurate, how often did permanent enrichment result from these activities?

Many of the Norman baronial families had enriched themselves at the expense of the older religious houses in the early decades of the eleventh century,[17] and we know from later events that there were those who attempted to repeat the process at intervals, usually when the machinery of government was weakened. The business of monastic chroniclers was to note what was remarkable, not what was typical, but the cumulative effect on the modern reader of entries recording such depredations is to imply that religious houses suffered from them more often than was actually the case. In the period under discussion, the major patrons of religious houses, apart from the king-dukes themselves, were these same nobles. For this very reason, some of the strongest criticism of the magnates was a back-handed compliment. When a noble acted wickedly, no rebuke was too strong for him because, under other circumstances, more was expected of him.[18] Even in peaceable times, the relationship between patron and protegés was one fraught with unspoken tensions, engendered by ambivalent expectations on both sides as to the implications and durability of the commitments existing between them. In these circumstances, any account of baronial activity was bound to be tendentious.[19] Moreover, chronicles of the period were written by men who, although often born into landed families, comprised those who had been denied a share of the good things inherited by big brother,[20] together with others temperamentally unsuited to normal, that is, aggressive, behaviour, as Roland is made to put it so forcibly.[21] Chroniclers therefore brought to the writing of history an entirely different perspective from that held by those who made it, but were quite ready to condone the outcome of baronial rapacity when this resulted in their houses receiving a share of the spoils.[22]

As to how far encroachments on monastic property contributed to a baron's rise on the Wheel of Fortune, it might almost be said that the louder and longer the chroniclers complained, the less effective was the transfer of economic resources from monastery to barony. The classic place and time for permanent enrichment was Normandy in the early decades of the eleventh century. Subsequently, however, the centralizing activities of the king-dukes ensured that baronial gains at the expense of monasteries were normally of short duration. The lesson took a long time to sink in, and in consequence, a major activity of the Chancery was the issuing of writs ordering the restoration of monastic properties and privileges. In the earlier examples, some doubt as to their effect is suggested by the phrase roughly translated as 'and if X does not compel you to do this, then Y will'. However, with the steady expansion of the judicial machine, an increasing number of such restorations were effected. This is not to say that baronial houses abandoned all hope of enrichment at the expense of the local monasteries, as numerous episodes in Stephen's reign make clear, although in many of these cases the lands were restored early in the next reign. Throughout the Anglo-Norman period, men who proved exceptions to the rule were those who effectively acted as judge and jury in respect of their own misdeeds. The wicked sheriff was beginning to emerge as a stock literary character, and as we shall see, there were conditions under which he was admirably placed to evade the normal consequences of conduct increasingly deemed anti-social.

Considerations affecting the fortunes of magnates may be further demonstrated and qualified by a survey of the respective fates of the Tosny family and the Warwickshire branch of the Beaumonts. The genealogy of both

has been fully documented elsewhere,[23] and the present account therefore concentrates on the responses of their members at crucial stages in their histories. Tosnys and Beaumonts alike had taken advantage of the disorders during Duke William's minority to augment their resources.[24] In the years preceding the conquest of England, they were two of the leading baronial dynasties, and their respective heads were among those involved in the deliberations on the invasion. Representatives of both families fought at Hastings,[25] and both houses were among the few who did really well out of the subsequent redistribution of land in England.[26] There were, however, significant differences both in the distribution of their estates and, perhaps in consequence, in their political responses to the growing claims of the royal government. These factors in turn had an impact on the respective positions of the families, both as regards formal status and political influence.

The Tosny family was founded by a Frenchman named Ralph, brother of Hugh, archbishop of Rouen (942–989). Tosny (Eure, cant. Gaillon), across the Seine from Les Andelys, pertained to the archiepiscopal demesne, but was given by Hugh to his brother. In the twelfth century, in an attempt to bring the family's ancestry into line with current fashions, descent was claimed from an uncle of Rollo,[27] but the Tosnys, despite their saga-like exploits, had little genuine Scandinavian blood in their veins. The family's fighting image was created by the deeds of Ralph (or a son of the same name) at the defence of Tillières and the siege of Salerno,[28] and upheld by the adventures of his son Roger (I) in Spain, where he went in the 1030s when Normandy became too hot to hold him. On his return journey, he reputedly acquired from the monastery of St Foy at Conques, in Rouerge, the relics of its saint, which he bestowed on the monastery he founded at Chatillon about 1035.[29] In consequence, the monastery acquired the alternative name of Conches,[30] which was soon bestowed on his son too. Roger himself was additionally nicknamed 'the Spaniard', and acquired a semi-legendary reputation.[31] In or around 1039 he was killed in a private feud with Roger de Beaumont. Orderic Vitalis reported that two of Roger's sons, Elbert and Elinant, were killed with him.[32] These men have not been traced from other sources, and their distinctly un-Norman names bear an artificial alliteration frequently found in the chansons de geste.[33] We have only to compare this doomed pair with others in the Song of Roland, such as Gerin and Gerier, or Basan and Basile,[34] to see that within a century of his death, Roger and his kindred were well on the way to becoming epic heroes. It is debatable, however, to what extent this representation was the work of Orderic, influenced by current literary fashions, and how far it is the outcome of deliberate propaganda on the part of the Tosny family.

By the twelfth century, the strong government of the Anglo-Norman kings was bearing heavily on families such as the Tosnys, and the creation of a literary propaganda campaign was one way in which they might hope to stabilize their position in relation to their neighbours and their tenants. *Pretz*, reputation and prestige, was the proper objective of a seigneur, according to Bertran de Born, writing perhaps two generations after Orderic.[35] In Bertran's world, the turbulent Limousin of the later twelfth century, warfare was the one way in which lands were won and augmented. The more territory a lord controlled, the greater his *pretz*, but this must be retained by continuous fighting. A successful seigneur must continue to win lands, subdue vassals, assert his suzerainty and avoid compromising his strength.[36] The turbulent condition of Normandy both in the later 1030s and again in the early part of Stephen's reign resembled that of the Limousin in Bertran's day, and his analysis of appropriate seignorial behaviour would have been equally applicable in these periods.

The aura which surrounded the grandest seignorial dynasties was perceived most clearly by their own members, and was the light in which they viewed their own position in relation to their equals and superiors. The founder of a house might encourage a belief in his *pretz* from pure opportunism, but the exalted position which he attained by the end of his career was the launching point of his heir, who transmitted to his own descendants an unshakable belief in the collective *pretz* of the dynasty, which in turn justified anything they might do to enhance it still further. Men took a proper pride in the deeds of their ancestors, and drew the appropriate lessons from them. The *pretz* of a baronial house was enhanced if the exploits of the dynasty, whether historical or legendary, were celebrated in poetry or prose. Such works romanticized those activities of the family which had ensured its pre-eminence in its own locality, while projection of its heroic image was intended to promote acquiescence in the material gains on which the family's *pretz* was based. The thirteenth-century romance of Fouke le Fitz Waryn is a well-known example of this type of literature, which was most popular, for obvious reasons, in unstable marcher societies. The legendary aura surrounding Roger de Tosny (I) seems to represent an early prototype of this genre, and its projection may well have been deliberate policy, either on the part of his immediate descendants, or perhaps more likely, by those in the earlier twelfth century. Roger's Spanish adventures enabled him to be depicted as an early example of the Christian warrior engaged in the Holy War against the infidel,[37] although that is not the chief component of the Tosny family's reputation as it has survived in the pages of Orderic Vitalis.

Towards the end of the eleventh century, a new spate of pillaging and killing was triggered off by insults bandied between Isabel de Tosny, wife of Roger's son Ralf (II), and Helwise, countess of Evreux.[38] The rôle played by these ladies has remarkable affinities to that of Bergthora and Hallgerd in promoting the vendetta in *Njal's Saga*.[39] Orderic Vitalis likened the forceful and adventurous Isabel to the legendary Amazon queens, but it is more appropriate to see her as a saga heroine. Her character as described by

Orderic, who rather admired her,[40] has strong literary overtones, and while the writing of all but the most embryo of the sagas lay well in the future,[41] one wonders whether he embellished the character of Isabel, and, to some extent, those of her menfolk, with traits drawn from some residual Scandinavian oral tradition, linked with the current literary fashion for things Nordic.

Orderic is our chief source for the early history of the Tosny family, and there is in his work a dichotomy between the Job-like literary effects he was attempting to achieve when recounting their recent misdeeds, and the fact that a good deal of the information he acquired about them seems to be coloured by propaganda. It is arguable whether Orderic himself had a conscious part in creating the heroic aspect of the family's image. It is true that St Evroul received considerable benefactions from the Tosnys, but a large proportion of these were in recompense for Ralph (II)'s burning their town.[42] Chroniclers were certainly expected to praise the patrons of their houses, but when these men took away with one hand while they gave with the other, it is not surprising that an ambivalent attitude towards them can be discerned.

The Tosny patronage of religious houses in Normandy did not deplete their growing resources to any great extent. Following the conquest of England, some of their protegés received endowments here,[43] but tithe income given to Conches was subsequently diverted to a series of English houses in turn, and commitments to Tosny foundations in this country were kept under stringent control.[44] Like most lay patrons, the Tosny family expected their donations to 'their' religious houses to be a sound investment in terms of status, and their parsimonious and ambivalent attitude towards their foundations was one which they shared with most of their baronial contemporaries.[45]

At the accession of Duke William, the Tosny family was already among the grandest of the Norman baronial dynasties, and Roger (I) de Tosny allegedly declared that no bastard was going to rule in Normandy.[46] The succession was not, however, at his disposal, and with the increase in stability under this duke's rule, the Tosnys were expected to conform to more tranquil ways, although self-restraint did not come easily to them. Their reversion to their old habits led to the short exile of Ralph (II) in the early 1060s, but political difficulties within the duchy led to his being summoned back within eighteen months or so.[47] By this time, the family, with their widespread lands and influential connections, were too great to ignore. Orderic Vitalis emphasizes their place in the group of dynasties whose political opinions counted.[48] The Tosnys were standard-bearers of Normandy, and in that capacity Ralph (II) is one of the small number of men who can definitely be said to have fought at Hastings.[49] That the office was a hazardous one is graphically illustrated by the account given in *Njal's Saga* of the rapid demise of several standard-bearers at the Battle of Clontarf in 1014.[50] The courage of the Tosnys in the performance of their hereditary duties was not impugned, but equally it must be observed that Fortune smiled on them to the extent that no member of the family is reported as having suffered death or serious injury in the course of his duties.

Their feudal stature earned the Tosnys a generous share of the spoils. Their Domesday fief stretched from East Anglia, across the Midlands and into the Welsh Marches.[51] In particular, their manors were heavily distributed in the West Midlands, yet it cannot be said that they enjoyed a pre-eminent position either there, where they were in effect non-resident, or in the Marches, owing to the proximity in each case of neighbours as powerful as themselves. The *caput* of their English honour was Flamstead in Hertfordshire, isolated from most of their other properties, but perhaps chosen as a conveniently central point between the major groupings of their manors.[52] The failed rebellion of 1075 enhanced their position still further. The dispossession of Roger earl of Hereford gave the Tosnys an increased status in the Welsh Marches, where they were able to take over Clifford Castle,[53] and the execution of Earl Waltheof left his young daughters as prizes on the marriage market. The younger girl, Alice, was given in marriage to Ralph de Tosny (III),[54] and this match brought welcome additions to the Tosny lands in East Anglia, although surviving documentation of their estates here suggests that Waltheof's elder daughter, the wife successively of Simon de St Liz (I) and of Earl David, carried not only her father's titles but also a disproportionately large share of his inheritance to her successive husbands.

The lack of an undisputed power base in England probably contributed to the fact that the Tosnys concentrated their main attention on Normandy in the later eleventh century and the twelfth, when their attestations to royal charters suggest that they spent most of their time in the duchy. Their Norman fief comprised well over fifty fees in the reign of Henry II, whereas the size of that in England and the Welsh March, although clearly a large one, is more difficult to evaluate.[55] Since Roger de Tosny (III) chose to render allegiance to King John rather than to Philip Augustus in 1204, his English interests were probably the more valuable. Against this, however, must be set Roger's long-standing political ties with John from the latter's period as count of Mortain,[56] and the fact that Roger's wife Constance de Beaumont, a descendant of Henry I, was acknowledged by King John as his kinswoman, a relationship which usefully assisted Tosny interests.[57]

In addition to the great gains made as a result of the conquest of England and the collapse of the 1075 rebellion, the Tosny fortunes took a further providential turn, although of a somewhat backhanded kind. According to Orderic Vitalis, Roger, the eldest son of Ralph (II), was a young man of benign and religious disposition, and was being groomed for the great political rôle which it was expected that he would eventually play. Roger died young, however,[58] and the heir was his younger brother Ralph (III).[59] Roger's admirable qualities were not those which had brought the family to its existing position, and Ralph was probably better equipped by temperament to inherit

the family mantle. It was Ralph (III) who married Earl Waltheof's daughter, and their own heir, Roger (II), married Ida, a daughter of Count Baldwin of Hainault. Although this match carried with it a potential political risk, Henry I bestowed a large estate in East Bergholt (Suffolk) on the young couple.[60] Henry's strong rule was not congenial to the Tosnys, who took advantage of Stephen's accession to revert to their old feuding habits. Roger (II)'s political views may be fairly expressed as anti-Beaumont rather than pro-Angevin, and his actions were perhaps motivated both by old territorial rivalries and by jealousy of a dynasty which had done well out of working, for the most part, with new political trends, instead of resisting them. The looting and butchering in which Roger (II) indulged at this time were thought excessive even by contemporary standards, and no-one was sorry when his greed caused him to fall into an ambush. Normandy was more peaceful with him behind bars, yet Orderic seemed stunned that so great a noble had reached this sorry pass.[61] A winter enduring harsh imprisonment did nothing to sweeten his temper, and he was a distinctly unreformed character on his release. A sudden reconciliation with the Beaumonts[62] led to the making of a match between his son Ralph (IV) and Margaret de Beaumont, daughter of Robert, earl of Leicester. Ironically Beaumont kinship now stood the Tosnys in good stead, for Ralph died young, and his own son Roger (III) found it expedient to claim the backing of his maternal kindred by styling himself 'son of Margaret' during and even after his long minority.[63] Under the Angevin kings, the Tosnys continued to marry well, but made only moderate gains as a result. Their taste for opportunism, rather than the patient work of estate-management, led them into further adventures, which brought material recompense,[64] although possibly at the expense of their political status. In feudal terms they were clearly a force to be reckoned with, but they seem never to have had any major political rôle, and it is probably no coincidence that although they rate a long entry in the *Complete Peerage*, they did not in fact obtain an earldom. Eventually, through failure of male heirs, their large English estates were conveyed to Guy de Beauchamp, earl of Warwick, by his marriage to Alice de Tosny, thus supplying the resources with which his own family might now embark on political adventures in the grand manner.[65]

The rise of the Beaumont earldom of Warwick provides a complementary analysis of factors which contributed to the rise of a great dynasty. In Normandy itself the senior line had achieved greatness a generation or more before 1066, but comparable houses sent over to England younger sons who laboured long and hard, and often in vain, to achieve greatness, while Henry de Beaumont had greatness thrust upon him. Recognition of his merits was not instantaneous—he did have to wait twenty years after his arrival before acquiring an earldom, yet many families waited for generations, and as we have seen, the Tosnys were still waiting when their direct male line was extinguished.

Henry's dynastic connections were, of course, one important reason for his elevation. When it eventually became fashionable to claim Norse ancestry, the Beaumonts liked to cite as their forebear a certain Torf, of dubious authenticity. On the fringes of historical memory, however, their earliest accredited ancestor was Thorold de Pontaudemer, who married a sister of the Duchess Gunnor, wife of Duke Richard I. Humphrey de Vieilles, the heir of this couple, added considerably to the family lands by appropriating estates of the abbey of Bernay, possibly with the connivance of Duke Robert I,[66] and by the mid-1030s the family, which took the surname Beaumont from property acquired by Humphrey's son Roger,[67] were locked in a bloodthirsty vendetta with their territorial rivals, the Tosnys.[68] At this point, however, the patterns begin to diverge, with the Beaumonts identifying their fortunes to a greater extent with those of the ducal house. Like the Tosnys, they were generally acknowledged as one of the great baronial dynasties of Duke William's adult years,[69] but unlike their rivals, they largely resisted the temptation to lapse into anachronistic feuding of a kind likely to provoke painful repercussions from above. The question should, of course, be raised as to whether Orderic's fuller knowledge of the Tosny family is partly the cause of the differing portraits he paints of these dynasties, yet the distinction between them seems by and large a fair one.

Roger de Beaumont, the head of the family in the mid-eleventh century, married Adeline, daughter of Waleran, count of Meulan, the strategic importance of whose lands was immense.[70] At the time of the Hastings campaign, Roger was one of those who stayed behind in the duchy, entrusted with its safe-keeping. His elder son, Robert, fought at Hastings,[71] although his younger son, Henry, is not known to have been present. However, when William I built Warwick Castle a year or so later, Henry was entrusted with its custody.[72] His promotion no doubt owed much to his wealthy, reliable and strategically placed kinsmen, although, since England was still in an unstable condition, even the grandest connections would have been useless without real natural abilities. Opportunities abounded for energetic and ambitious young men in newly-conquered England. Henry can barely have been twenty at the time, but perhaps had competition for the record as most junior castellan. His contemporary in Worcester Castle, Urse d'Abetot, was, as we shall see, scarcely any older. Urse did well for himself, but did not achieve Henry's great leap forward. The distinguishing factor cannot have been a differential in talent, since Urse's remarkable abilities are fully attested, but in family connections.

Henry's greatest asset was that his brother Robert succeeded their maternal grandfather as count of Meulan in the French Vexin, about 1081, and he was then ideally placed to be a great help, or a great hindrance, to Anglo-Norman interests. The brothers decided to support William Rufus against Robert Curthose, and in 1088 Henry was created earl of Warwick for services

rendered.[73] The earldom had no real military significance, but the creation of Henry's fief by the appropriation of several tenancies in chief within Warwickshire resulted in his holding a fairly compact block of lands,[74] with economic potential as well as some significance in regional politics—two advantages which the Tosny fief did not enjoy to the same extent. In 1094, on the death of Roger de Beaumont, Henry also acquired the Norman barony of Annebecq. With his brother, he was prompt to support Henry I against Robert Curthose, and was further rewarded with a grant of the Gower peninsular in South Wales.[75] The Beaumont brothers were important to successive kings because of their territorial resources, while their very usefulness to the crown generated more wealth for them—a fairly common cycle in this period.[76] Solid family teamwork was an asset not shared by the Tosnys in these crucial years, owing to the early death of the elder brother, and, in successive generations, the territorial insignificance of cadet branches.

Family wealth and solidarity continued to support the status of Henry's son, Earl Roger, who succeeded to the title in 1119, a year or so after his twin cousins Waleran and Robert became count of Meulan and earl of Leicester respectively. The textbook picture of this trio acting in concert throughout the political upheavals of the next thirty years and more is, by and large, a fair one. Roger does not get the limelight to the same extent as his cousins for two reasons. First, his own interests were now confined to England, since the barony of Annebecq had passed to his younger brother Robert 'de Neubourg'[77] and secondly because he was temperamentally better suited to stay in the shadows. Earl Roger was not felt by contemporaries to be making the most of his position, and the author of the *Gesta Stephani* pronounced him debauched and lacking in resolution.[78] Throughout most of Stephen's reign, Roger remained loyal to the king—apart, that is, from the almost obligatory acknowledgment of the empress in the early part of 1141.[79]

Events during the civil war underlined the lowered prestige of the earl. For one thing, he was obliged, on the advice of the king and the bishop of Winchester, as well as that of his own family, to marry off his daughter Agnes to the chamberlain Geoffrey de Clinton (II).[80] Geoffrey's family's fortunes had soared, and he was a man of some consequence, but very definitely 'new' by Beaumont standards,[81] while his curial connections were not the asset they might have been in more peaceable times. On military grounds, Roger perhaps expected to escape the worst of the fighting, ensconced as he was between his cousin Waleran, by now earl of Worcester, to the west, and his cousin the earl of Leicester to the east. In fact records from the early years of Henry II's reign indicate that Warwickshire had recently suffered very heavy devastation. The reasons for this are debatable, however, and there has been controversy over the significance of this evidence.[82]

Roger's military contribution to Stephen's cause was undistinguished. The episode for which he is best remembered is his collapse and sudden death at

Stephen's court on hearing that his wife had handed over Warwick Castle to Henry of Anjou.[83] The countess's recognition of the turn which events were taking perhaps served the earldom better than Roger could have foreseen. As it turned out, while the Beaumont earldoms of Warwick and Leicester survived intact, the earldom of Worcester was not inherited by Count Waleran's son.[84] No doubt this contrast owed much to the fact that the territorial interests of Earl William, Roger's heir, and Earl Robert were confined to England, so that their political potential, although considerable, had its limitations. Count Waleran's estates, however, had a disruptive potential on too wide a scale to be tolerated. By the middle of the twelfth century, accidents of politics and inheritance had disposed of many of the old cross-Channel estates, and it was, perhaps, the early death of Ralph de Tosny (IV) in 1162, following hard on that of his father Roger, which inhibited Henry II from enforcing a division of the Tosny estates, for the young heir was very much overshadowed by his loyal Beaumont kindred.

Stronger mechanisms of government, so inhibiting to the pretensions of the Tosnys and their like, were the means by which the *curiales* acquired wealth and status. It is an oversimplification to argue that as the Wheel of Fortune raised the *curiales* up, so it threw the magnates down, for, as we have been reminded, some magnates had the good sense to double as *curiales* themselves.[85] They had, after all, acquired magnate status in the first place by recognizing coming trends while there was time to take advantage of them. A cyclic movement of a kind did exist, however. The circulation of increasing amounts of money made it possible for rulers to recruit more *curiales*, who in turn made stronger government possible by raising more money.[86] It is debatable whether, in the first instance, money begat *curiales* or vice versa by the time our period opens, the wheel had already begun to turn. Eventually, of course, the success of the *curiales* was such that they became targets for the very operation which they had helped to set in motion,[87] and that was the point at which the balancing act at the top of the wheel became really difficult.

The *curiales* represented trained manpower in a different sense from the rank and file of the feudal host. The activities of the families discussed below demonstrate that in the final resort, even the *curiales* must be prepared to do battle to keep their gains, but essentially they were specialists in civilian government. As yet, the majority possessed little in the way of formal training, but like the more perceptive magnates, they put a high premium on prudence, *alias* useful intelligence. The application of reason to the problems of government was the way in which the *curiales* gained power, and vast new fields for the exercise of their abilities—and their ambitions—were opened up by the strengthening of government in Normandy and the subsequent establishment and maintenance of the cross-Channel *regnum*.[88]

There was a widely held belief that virtue was a quality exclusively found in nobles.[89] The vast majority of *curiales*, being non-noble, were therefore held

to be lacking in admirable qualities. The chroniclers repeatedly tell us that this was so, and despite the fact that the wealth of the chroniclers' monasteries was increasingly being siphoned off for the crown by these same men, we may reasonably agree that amiability, at least, was not a virtue for which *curiales* were celebrated. The problems of the Anglo-Norman kings, and the hostility to the activities of their servants, meant that the latter were inevitably tough men who used tough methods.[90] When it came to enjoying the fruits of office, this toughness had its advantages in dealing with territorial rivals and neighbours, but it had then to be augmented. In other words, the curialis in his new rôle as a landed proprietor had to acquire the noble's quality of virtue, for as we have seen, reputation and prestige were vital components of worldly success. In the latter part of the twelfth century, honour and generosity were deemed essential to the lord who was firmly established in his territory.[91] These qualities were normally lacking in a first-generation *curialis*, who said and did whatever best suited his interests on each occasion, oblivious of public opinion. It is ironic that when his arrogance was emulated by his descendants, it was taken to denote aristocratic bearing. Once the *curialis* had elbowed his way to the top, flattering clients, eager for his patronage,[92] attributed to him all the honour and generosity which could be desired.

The enjoyment of the king's patronage did not in itself bring recognition of noble virtues, as we see from the set-piece portrait of the brash *curialis*, which may owe something to sour grapes on the part of chroniclers from genteel families. The real problem for the successful *curialis*, determined to stabilize the territorial gains which had come his way, was not sniping of this kind, however, but how to be accepted in landed society. Endemic hostility towards 'new men' was not only caused by their increasing monopolization of patronage and their involvement in the creation and execution of unpopular policies. More important, so far as the social aspirations of the *curialis* were concerned, was that he was required to rely on personal influence rather than on feudal power during the formative stages of his career, and might fall from favour overnight. He was an undesirable territorial ally for a magnate, not only from the point of view of caste-exclusiveness, but for the more practical reason that if a son or daughter married into a 'new' family, the *curialis* might lose the king's favour; the lands involved in the marriage contract might be lost; and the 'old' family would lose influence by the loss of its friend at court. Established families had been new themselves in the early eleventh century, but time had proved them successful. Rising families were unwelcome as allies except in times of disturbance. Geoffrey de Clinton, as we have seen, and the young William Mauduit (III), as we shall see, made matches of this kind, with no overwhelming advantage to either. In peacetime conditions, curial families could negotiate such marriages only after they had become securely established, and not as a means towards achieving this end. Once the curial family had built up its landed power, aristocratic neighbours welcomed an alliance chiefly on that score. The *curialis* lived in the hopeful knowledge that successive kings frequently bestowed heiresses on their servants, partly as a cheap way of rewarding them, and partly in order to place the territorial assets of great families in reliable hands, but could never be certain that he himself would achieve stability in this way.

More surely, therefore, he hoped to consolidate his territorial gains with the help of colleagues who acted as justices, or through his tenure of a shrievalty or castellanship, which, as we shall see, played an important rôle in the rise of both the Beauchamp and the Mauduit families. Self-confidence was a further asset, intangible but real, which the *curialis* shared with the magnate. The rapid rise, first of the mid-eleventh century baronage, then of the *curiales* of succeeding generations, inspired a belief in boundless opportunities just waiting to be seized. Naturally enough, this created an opportunism, demonstrated in the charters which the Beauchamps and Mauduits obtained from the Empress, which was itself a major factor in generating further success.

The origins of the Mauduit family are something of a mystery. There is no evidence that they 'came over with the Conqueror', although William Mauduit (I), the first-known member of this curial dynasty, was active in the latter part of William I's reign. The family had some connection with Préaux,[93] and in the twelfth century held land in Ouville-sur-Dives, some kilometers to the east of this house, and also at Saint Martin du Bosc in the Vexin, besides property in Rouen itself.[94] It is also unclear when the surname Mauduit (or Malduit) first appears, since there are grounds for believing that William Mauduit, who appears under this name in the Domesday Survey, was also the William the chamberlain who attests charters of King William I, and, like contemporary treasury officials, he held land in Hampshire.[95]

Mauduit is a Normanization of *Maledoctus*, 'the dunce', probably an ironical nickname for someone who was in fact exceptionally numerate. That the surname was coined as a nickname at the Conqueror's court, perhaps as an analogy with the coining of Flambard as the cognomen of the chaplain Ranulf,[96] is suggested by a laisse of the Song of Roland:

> The king calls forth his treasurer Malduit:
> 'Have you made ready the tribute for Charles?'
> And he replies: 'Yes sire, in plenty too:
> Silver and gold—seven hundred camel-loads;
> And twenty hostages, noblest of men.'[97]

This poem, more or less in its present form, appears to have originated in the Anglo-Norman regnum in the latter part of the eleventh century, perhaps between 1080 and 1100, while the characters were collected by about 1050.[98] The Malduit of the poem is in the service of Marsile, king of the Muslims of Spain, and the use of the name of a contemporary Norman official in this way

might well have been intended to raise a laugh when the poem was read aloud in court circles.

William Mauduit (I) was perhaps a brother of the Gunfrid Mauduit living in Wiltshire in 1086.[99] If so, the surname, or nickname, was therefore first bestowed on a recent common ancestor, most likely their father, whose employment in the ducal court about the middle of the eleventh century inspired the poet to borrow his name for an official of King Marsile. Since William the chamberlain can appear without a surname, and Malduit appears in the poem as a name in its own right, this suggests that the real-life official was habitually addressed in this way, instead of by his Christian name. The nickname Mauduit, therefore, probably became accepted as a surname between about 1050 and 1080. From about 1100 onwards, when the earliest charters of the Mauduit family survive, the surname is regularly used. A cartulary copy of a writ of Henry II refers to 'Mauduit the chamberlain'[100] but this is more likely due to an omission on the part of the late fourteenth-century copyist than a whimsical literary jibe made by an Exchequer scribe about 1160.

In 1086, William Mauduit (I) held the little honour of Portchester in Hampshire, probably by virtue of his office of chamberlain and the need to have a reliable official in charge of Portchester castle, which was used as a base from which bullion was shipped to Normandy.[101] He also held half a fee of the abbot of Abingdon, in which tenancy he had recently succeeded a certain Benedict,[102] and it is arguable, though unproven, that William's wife Hawise was Benedict's daughter. William died about the end of William Rufus's reign,[103] and was succeeded in his office and his English lands by his son Robert, who was active in Normandy on financial duties in the reign of Henry I.[104] His younger son, William (II), acquired his father's Norman lands, or at any rate such of them as were hereditary, and not appurtenant to the chamberlainship.[105] Robert's office had considerable potential, as we know from the large sum which his successor fined for it,[106] hence, presumably, the decision to opt for the honour of Portchester. Our slight knowledge of the two Mauduit properties in Normandy depends on a few chance references. It may be that there were others, but it seems unlikely that the total Norman holdings can have been very great, since the family did not aspire to a territorial surname by the middle of the eleventh century.

Since the financial officers were key members of the royal bureaucracy, and could therefore hope for suitable recompense, Robert's expectations were promising. Unhappily, however, he was one of the officials who went down with the White Ship,[107] leaving an heiress, Constance, who, by 1128 at latest, was given in marriage to William de Pont de l'Arche, one of the most prominent *curiales* of the day. He acquired with his wife part of the honour of Portchester,[108] but William Mauduit (II) was given the rest of the Hampshire estates in the early 1120s.[109]

William Mauduit embarked on a curial career,[110] hence, presumably, his receipt of the Hampshire lands, and about 1131 he received a chamberlainship of his own, an unspecialized post of moderate recompense and no great dignity, as shown by his entry in the *Constitutio Domus Regis*.[111] Another landmark in his life occurred in 1131, for he then received in marriage Matilda, the daughter of Michael of Hanslope, together with some of the lands her father had held.[112] William, with dogged perseverance, now set about reconstituting the considerable position which Michael had earlier enjoyed in the east Midlands. The situation was complicated, in that Michael had acquired his fief by exercise of the royal prerogative, and was compelled to surrender his lands to Henry I at his death.[113] Michael was survived by a young son, Hugh,[114] probably illegitimate, in view of the lack of provision for him, although Michael's precarious tenurial position may argue otherwise. His predecessor in the honour of Hanslope had been Winemar the Fleming, whose own son Walter was virtually dispossessed to make way for Michael[115]—a small-scale analogy with the means by which the earldom of Warwick was created for Henry de Beaumont. The name Michael is quite rare in Norman sources of the period, and it might be argued that Michael of Hanslope was himself a Fleming. Certainly the name Flandrina occurs some generations later in the Mauduit family,[116] perhaps in residual memory of such ancestry. A *curialis* who was also a member of the vulnerable Flemish minority would be in a difficult position when it came to establishing a dynasty, particularly if he lacked influential connections. Whatever the facts of the case, Hugh of Hanslope took clerical orders, and by the early 1150s was in the service of Henry of Anjou. Hugh was still active at court in the earlier 1170s, and acquired modest properties in the Midlands. Throughout this time, he maintained a close connection with the Mauduit family,[117] and a man who may, on circumstantial grounds, have been his son appears later as a tenant on the Mauduit estates.[118]

The reconstruction of Michael's position took William Mauduit (II) over twenty years to complete, but by making a token appearance in the Empress's camp in 1141 and by joining her son's campaign in the summer of 1153,[119] he did much to expedite matters. William's ambitions were hampered by the fact that he was only a minor baron in a region where there was strong local competition. William Mauduit (III) declared that when his father acquired the fief, he found one and three-quarter fees there, and subsequently created a further two and a quarter, making a total of four and a half fees.[120] One is tempted to say that such a remarkable conclusion fully merits the cognomen Maledoctus, besides undermining the contention that arithmetical skills were essential to aspiring *curiales*,[121] yet it must be observed that the calculation occurs in the thirteenth-century transcripts of the *carta* returned in 1166, and perhaps the mistake crept in after the return left William's possession. Even so, the document underlines the point that the Mauduits could not hope to

enhance their position on feudal grounds alone. Happily, their support of the Angevin cause had resulted in the restoration of the soke of Barrowden in Rutland, and of the castellanship of Rockingham Castle.[122] This combination of delegated royal authority and franchisal rights enabled the Mauduits to accumulate land at the expense of the free peasantry of this fringe of the old Danelaw.[123]

Less successful were the first steps of members of the family on the ladder to aristocratic status, although the Peterborough Chronicler did describe William (II) as one of the local nobles from whom Abbot Martin had recovered lands which they seized in Stephen's reign.[124] Little in the way of permanent gain resulted from the marriage arranged between the young William (III) and a daughter of Simon de St Liz (II), earl of Huntingdon, at the end of Stephen's reign,[125] despite the differing political allegiances of the families. Arguably, of course the earl may have allowed the match in an attempt to keep the Mauduits out of the Angevin camp. When the legitimate St Liz line died out in 1184, the feudal position of William (III) was not strong enough for him to make a successful bid, in right of his wife, for even a share of her father's lands, let alone for the titles. The political advantages of recognizing the Scottish claimant far outweighed anything the Mauduits had to offer. It was only in John's reign that the match between William (IV) and a daughter of the deceased Waleran, earl of Warwick, set in motion the long chain of events which were to bring this earldom to the Mauduit family.

More immediate success came with William (II)'s acquisition of the hereditary Mauduit chamberlainship. In the latter part of Henry I's reign and most of Stephen's this office continued to be held by William de Pont de l'Arche. In the course of the latter reign, his position weakened, as typified, but not finalized, by his ill-treatment at the hands of his wife Constance and her lover, the renegade mercenary Robert Fitz Hildebrand.[126] Before this deplorable episode, however, Constance had borne children, including a son Robert, who was by hereditary right the successor to the chamberlainship and the remaining lands in Hampshire. William de Pont de l'Arche died shortly before 1150, and his heir had no real opportunity to obtain administrative experience before the end of the reign.[127]

In 1153, William Mauduit (II) successfully petitioned Henry of Anjou for this chamberlainship and its lands, together with confirmation of his own office.[128] Mauduit military support for the Angevin cause can only have been minimal, but William had gained much administrative experience in his earlier years, and the new regime was in need of his services. The chamberlainship carried with it the useful adjunct of friends in high places, demonstrated by their frequent attestations to Mauduit charters of the later twelfth century, and by the family's increasing predilection for litigation in the royal court, where they clearly expected to obtain a favourable hearing.[129] By the accession of Henry II, the Mauduits had not yet reached the top, but they were well on their way.

The rise of the Beauchamp family has some close parallels with that of the Mauduits, probably valid factors in the success of many curial dynasties. Local circumstances gave rise to some distinctive developments, although, as with the Mauduits, the Beauchamps owed the foundations of their power to the achievement of an earlier generation of *curiales*, in this case Urse d'Abetot, the notorious sheriff of Worcester, and his equally assertive brother, Robert Dispenser.

Their native village, Saint Jean d'Abbetot, on the escarpment above the lower Seine, possesses an impressive romanesque chancel and crypt in its parish church, and its tranquillity seems an unlikely setting for two of the most aggressive of the 'new men' of the Conquest era. The place-name is one of many in the Pays de Caux indicative of Norse settlement,[130] but the origin of the brothers themselves is uncertain. Early twelfth-century sources refer to a subsequent Robert d'Abbetot and his wife Lesza, tenants of the Tancarville family,[131] the centre of whose power lay a short distance up-river. Urse and Robert Dispenser, whether or not they were kinsmen of this later couple, were probably themselves tenants of the Tancarville family,[132] but seemingly owed their great good fortune to their own remarkable talents far more than to any bonds of patronage or kinship.

The celebrated plaque in Falaise castle notwithstanding, there is no conclusive evidence that either brother arrived in England in 1066. Within two or three years, however, Urse was installed in Worcestershire, supervising the building of Worcester Castle,[133] and was perhaps already sheriff, an office which he certainly held a few years later. In the late 1060s he was probably still in his early twenties, since his subsequent career lasted for forty years. Robert's activities are largely documented in royal charters of uncertain date, and it is not clear from these whether he arrived with his brother or slightly later. Although Urse is the better-known figure to most students of the period, Robert may have been the more prominent of the two on the national scene during the reign of William I. The Domesday Survey shows that the brothers held lands of approximately equal extent, although proportionately more of Robert's were tenancies in chief, and whereas Urse's estates were concentrated in the West Midlands, particularly in Worcestershire, Robert's stretched from his region to the North Sea.[134]

Robert is virtually always known by his cognomen, suggesting that he owed his fortune entirely to his curial rôle. According to Orderic Vitalis, it was Robert who bestowed the cognomen Flambard on the king's chaplain, Ranulf, expressing the opinion of the other *curiales* on his activities.[135] Robert joined his brother in appropriating estates of the great clerical landlords in Worcestershire, but although he was certainly married,[136] he evidently left no surviving legitimate son. He may, however, have been survived by a daughter, since about half his estates passed to the Marmion family, who maintained a long struggle against Urse's Beauchamp descendants to recover the remainder.[137] Such tenuous evidence as there is

suggests that the Abetot brothers cooperated closely to the end, but that when this came, Urse clearly envisaged himself as inheriting the fruits of their combined efforts.

Robert died in the course of William Rufus's reign.[138] By this time, Urse had emerged from his entrenched position in Worcestershire to become one of the aggressive group of 'new men' who administered the king's controversial policies,[139] and it was doubtless in return for services rendered that he was given some of Robert's lands. The king assented to the most outlying of these, in Lincolnshire, being exchanged with Robert de Lacy for property more conveniently located.[140]

Urse's own career was remarkable by any standards, and seems to have owed its success equally to his own determination and to the peculiar conditions prevailing in the west Midlands when he arrived there. Worcestershire was dominated by the great franchise of the bishopric of Worcester, the triple hundred of Oswaldslaw,[141] while Evesham Abbey held another of the hundreds. Both Bishop Wulfstan (1062–1095) and Abbot Ethelwig (1058–1077) cooperated with the new Norman regime and were entrusted with considerable secular authority. The abbot took advantage of this to acquire various properties by dubious means. When enquiries were made after his death into the legality of his title to these, Bishop Odo presided over the tribunal and redistributed the estates. Urse did noticeably well out of this process.[142] In addition, the Abetot brothers appropriated lands both from the estates of Worcester Cathedral priory and from those of Westminster Abbey in Worcestershire. Since the Westminster properties were so remote from the abbot's personal influence, there was little to be done except formalize the tenurial relationship, although Robert was induced on his deathbed to restore some of his ill-gotten gains.[143]

In the case of Worcester Cathedral priory, the gains made by the Abetot brothers remained in the family.[144] The real struggle waged here was whether the cathedral's dominance of the shire was to continue, or whether it must yield to the new feudal power. The contest was a long and hard one, reflected in the monastic chronicles of the region. At the outset, Worcester enjoyed the patronage of Ealdred, archbishop of York. When Urse encroached on the cathedral priory's precincts in building Worcester Castle, an act of symbolic as well as proprietorial importance, the archbishop rebuked him in a rhyming curse, a play on his name, according to William of Malmesbury.[145] Gerald of Wales put the jingle into the mouth of Bishop Wulfstan on the occasion when Urse allegedly attempted to have him removed from office. Wulfstan announced that he would resign his pastoral staff only to the king who had bestowed it on him, and worked a spectacular miracle, of the sword-in-the-stone genre, at the Confessor's tomb. William I was sufficiently impressed to confirm the bishop in office, but Urse, despite his inability to pluck out the staff, continued to assert his own authority against that of the bishop.[146]

Gerald's story may have gained something in the telling. There is, for instance, a distinct and probably deliberately symbolic parallel with the story in The Quest of the Holy Grail as to how the perfect knight Galahad acquired his invincible weapon.[147] Despite such literary embellishments, however, there is no reason to doubt that these stories have a factual basis, and that tensions between the formidable bishop and his well-matched territorial rival made the atmosphere in Worcestershire electrifying for nearly thirty years after the conquest of England. The three-cornered contest while Abbot Ethelwig lived doubtless rendered the situation explosive. The name Urse was increasingly found in later eleventh-century Normandy. It was a translation of 'the bear', the symbol in Norse culture of strength and ferocity,[148] and one wonders whether Urse and his contemporary namesakes, including an abbot of Jumièges,[149] originally received the appellation as a nickname bestowed after a precocious display of temperament. It was his forceful character which was Urse's chief aid in building up the position he unwittingly transmitted to his Beauchamp descendants. That they appreciated the means as well as the end is shown by their emblem of the bear and ragged staff, which possibly originated as his own device.

On one celebrated occasion, there was actually a successful collaboration between sheriff, bishop and abbot, together with Walter de Lacy of Weobley. During the rebellion of 1075, they were ordered to guard the Severn fords against the forces of Roger earl of Hereford and his allies. In addition to their duty to the king, there was a more immediate reason why they should work together, for Earl Roger, like his father William Fitz Osbern, had exercised palatine authority in Worcestershire as well as in Herefordshire and Gloucestershire. After Earl Roger himself, the four defenders were the most influential barons of the west Midlands. Whatever their mutual differences, they had a common interest in suppressing the further ambitions of their powerful neighbour.[150] That there had been earlier conflicts with the earl is indicated by his complaint against sheriffs being sent by the king into Herefordshire to hear judicial cases.[151] Any extension of royal authority in this region would almost inevitably strengthen Urse's own sphere of influence. When the rebellion failed, no new palatine earl replaced Roger, and Urse and his collaborators all became relatively more powerful in the region.[152]

Coexistence with the neighbouring Lacy family was evidently a reality, for Urse exchanged his only land in Herefordshire with Walter's son Roger,[153] presumably in order to strengthen his position nearer home. Following the suppression of the earl's rebellion, Urse was also free to resume his struggle with the bishop, and that this was not entirely one-sided is shown by the fact that Wulfstan became castellan of Worcester at one stage.[154] That Urse early intended to build up a hereditary power base by means of his official powers is indicated by his wife Adeliza's style of *vicecomitissa*,[155] also adopted by the wife of Roger de Pîtres, sheriff of Gloucester, at a slightly later date.[156]

On the national scene, Urse took an active part in the trial of William of St Calais, bishop of Durham,[157] and was one of Ranulf Flambard's close associates.[158] His personality made him an ideal choice as one whose function it was to tighten the grip of royal government on the realm, and his usefulness was such that he was still active in this respect in the early years of the next reign.[159]

When Urse died in the summer of 1108,[160] he was succeeded in his lands and office of sheriff by his son Roger.[161] He, however, did not enjoy his inheritance for long, since about 1110 he incurred the king's grave displeasure when he killed a royal officer, and his estates escheated to the crown. The chroniclers gloatingly considered the outcome to be the fulfilment of the archbishop's curse, with which had been coupled a prediction that Urse's descendants would not enjoy for long the position which he had built up.[162] Certainly Henry I's initial reaction was to separate the lands from the office of sheriff. This was allowed to stay within the family, and was conferred on Osbert d'Abetot,[163] possibly a younger brother of Urse, and at any rate not a legitimate son, in view of the subsequent fate of Roger's lands. Osbert served as sheriff for perhaps four or five years, and in the course of this period, Henry I conferred the lands of Roger d'Abetot, *alias* Roger of Worcester, on Walter de Beauchamp.[164]

Walter appeared at court early in Henry I's reign, but his origins are obscure.[165] He may have owed his place at court to Urse, but can have had few territorial expectations when marrying his daughter. The Worcester chronicler records that Urse's idea of providing a marriage portion for her was to seize yet another estate from the cathedral priory and bestow it on Emmeline, as she is believed to have been named.[166] Walter de Beauchamp was evidently no nonentity, for within a year or two of receiving Roger's estates, in itself a remarkable achievement, he persuaded Henry I that he was a suitable person to replace Osbert d'Abetot as sheriff of Worcester.[167] Osbert's descendants were tenants of the Beauchamps, while Roger d'Abetot faded from the scene. A Roger of Worcester appears as a tenant on one of Walter's Leicestershire manors in the 1130 Pipe Roll,[168] but it seems fanciful to suppose that this was the disinherited sheriff living out his later years as a dependant of his supplanter. In due course, Walter also obtained Robert Dispenser's office,[169] but did not reassemble the other powers enjoyed by the Abetot brothers, such as the castellanship of Worcester.

On Walter's death, about 1131, he was succeeded by his son William, who was very conscious of his kinship to Urse, as he made clear to the monks of Worcester.[170] In William's time and later, the relationship between the Beauchamps and the cathedral priory was decidedly ambivalent. Donations were made, and family burials took place there, even while the local power struggle continued. Evidently the family kept spiritual and territorial considerations strictly separate, an attitude which they shared with many contemporaries.[171] Acceptance of Christian doctrine and the disciplines of the Church was not necessarily considered to be in conflict with violent personal conduct.[172] Gregorian principles had not begun to permeate England when the contest between sheriff and bishop began. It should be understood as a purely territorial and jurisdictional dispute, from which no inferences can be drawn as to a lack of religious beliefs either on the part of Urse or of his Beauchamp successors.[173] The eagerness of the monks of Worcester for their patronage indicates that matters were regarded in this light on both sides.

William de Beauchamp, like so many of his contemporaries, had his big chance to recover lost rights in 1141, but unlike some of the others, he had something to offer in return, since the Empress needed him to checkmate the influence of Waleran de Beaumont, count of Meulan, who had been created earl of Worcester in 1138.[174] His strong exercise of comital authority threatened to curb the ambitions of William de Beauchamp, who was therefore an ideal counterweight to him.[175] Waleran himself went over to the Empress later in the year, however, and William was obliged to acknowledge his authority after all.[176] Even after Waleran's withdrawal to the Continent in 1142, he continued to send orders to William[177] whom he addressed in one such missive as *filio suo*.[178] In an ironical sense, there turned out to be more truth in this literary and patronizing conceit than Waleran imagined. During the breakdown in royal authority in Stephen's reign, the Beaumont earl Roger of Warwick had also revived the anachronistic claims of an earl to jurisdiction over his sheriff,[179] but there were new times coming. Count Waleran's earldom of Worcester disappeared, while William de Beauchamp was not only confirmed in his own shrievalty, but in addition held for several years at a stretch those of Gloucester, Herefordshire and Warwickshire, so that for a brief period in the 1160s he may almost be said to have inherited the mantle not only of Count Waleran, but even of William Fitz Osbern. Of course there was no question of his being granted palatine jurisdiction, but without effective local supervision, he was able to take full advantage of the wide scope open to him. With the increasing effectiveness of the royal bureaucracy, however, the day of reckoning was inevitable. It came in 1170, when the Inquest of Sheriffs brought to light some of William's more remarkable activities. His removal from office and death followed shortly afterwards. This is no tale of failure, however. The Beauchamps had rightly sensed that if they were to expand their influence, it must be by utilizing the expanding royal power. The later Beauchamps continued to enlarge their estates by un-orthodox exploitation of their office of sheriff, which was restored to William's son and remained in the family.[180]

In the years between 1066 and 1154, it was always possible for successful magnates and *curiales* to jump on Fortune's Wheel and stay balanced at the top, provided that they tempered the old heroic qualities with prudence. The

earls of Warwick, the Mauduits and the Beauchamps all stabilized their position by making use of the growing machinery of government. The Tosnys demonstrated by their anachronistic conduct that, although it might bring occasional windfalls, even in the Angevin era, their interests were not promoted as steadily as those of men who conformed to the new ways.

The comparative fortunes of the four families also suggest that on balance it was those who were forced to concentrate their interests in England who rose most rapidly. Analysis of the charters of the four families has revealed that, despite their great potential, the Tosny lands in England were only exploited in the thirteenth century, while the Mauduits made the most of their golden opportunity in the upper Welland valley only in John's reign, when they had been driven out of their small and scattered Norman holdings. The Warwickshire Beaumonts and the Beauchamps, obliged to concentrate their minds on comparatively compact areas in England, did so to wonderful effect.

Analysis of the policies of these, and comparable families, must be qualified by the recognition that our knowledge of even the best-documented dynasties is inevitably limited by their respective attitudes towards the keeping of records.[181] In addition, it was usually those families who, in their respective regions, were the first—or the last—to embark on unusual activities, who drew the attention of the chroniclers. This is demonstrable in that whereas the Abetots and Beauchamps provided abundant copy for the chroniclers of Worcestershire, when the Mauduits adopted virtually the same methods later in the twelfth century[182] they attracted little notice from Peterborough, the house most affected by their activities. When the mention of other families in local chronicles is minimal, the inference is not always that their activities were ineffectual. Two obvious alternatives are, firstly, that their policies might be commonplace among contemporaries and, secondly, that the chroniclers of their neighbouring religious houses may have lacked the literary talents to describe their conduct in meaningful terms.

In one obvious sense, every family which came to England after the Conquest rose as others fell, but the wheel continued to turn long after 1066. While others tumbled as it revolved, the magnates and *curiales* discussed above were, by various means, among those who kept their balance on the top.

Bishop's Lynn: The First Century of a New Town?

DOROTHY M. OWEN

The most recent writer on the history of medieval towns, in the introductory chapter of her interesting work, has explained as lucidly as one can hope for the reason why the student of the Norman Conquest cannot afford to ignore the history of its towns:

> The Normans continue to haunt the beginner in English urban history partly because of the undeniable topographical changes imposed by their castles and cathedrals, but partly, too, because their coincidence in time with the general flowering of urban life in medieval Europe has lulled many writers into confusing the two events in their words, if not in their thoughts. . . . The best hope of getting a little nearer to certainty on both When and Why lies in the informed excavation of individual towns and in studying all the material, archaeological, historical and linguistic with the closest possible attention to chronology.[1]

Professor Beresford's survey and gazetteer of new towns of the middle ages has drawn the attention of historians, topographers, and archaeologists to a phenomenon which he interprets as successive waves of new town foundations, beginning in the late eleventh century, and ending in the mid-fourteenth century.[2] This series of 'foundations' added innumerable names to the lists of English and French towns, and his conclusion seems to be that all were deliberate plantations in carefully selected locations, founded by some one man at a single point in time. It is true that local circumstances may have varied, but these, he feels, do not invalidate the general principle that there was a 'new town movement'. Maitland had, it is true, already given warning of the risks of generalization:

> Dark as the history of our villages may be, the history of the boroughs is darker yet; or rather, perhaps, the darkness seems blacker because we are to suppose that it conceals from our view changes more rapid and intricate than those that have happened in the open country. . . . We ought to protest that no general theory will tell the story of every and any particular town.[3]

It was with these pronouncements in mind that I began to examine the early history of King's Lynn, an ostensible 'new town' which sprang, if the earlier historians of the borough are to be credited, fully armed and fully grown, like Pallas Athene, from the head of Bishop Herbert de Losinga, about the year 1100, and which seems to meet all Professor Beresford's requirements for a new town: it was, or seemed to be, a deliberately planted, carefully planned 'instant' community. My interest in the town began with the collection of historical background information for an archaeological survey of the town, on which I have been engaged, with long interruptions, since 1964. You may well have seen the report on the archaeological survey, which was published in 1977 by the Society for Medieval Archaeology, and Vanessa Parker's earlier volume on the standing buildings of the town.[4] I hope soon to publish a volume of documents which will illustrate the topographical, social and economic development of the town; there will be detailed studies of some aspects of the subject, and this is one of them. Another will be Cecily Clark's examination of several early lists of personal names, in the manner she will demonstrate later in the programme for Battle.[5] Here, then, is the occasion which has caused me to scrutinize the earliest notices of the town; the more I have looked, the more complicated has the story become.

The basis of my whole story is SALT. As we know from Professor Darby's work on the Domesday geography of Eastern England, and from my husband's paper in a recent symposium, salt making was going on in the eleventh century on all the coasts of the Wash, as it was elsewhere on the eastern seaboard of the country.[6] The method used by the salters was essentially the same as that practised in the same areas since prehistoric times, on any gently sloping or flat coast where the sea water ran slowly up and down with the tides, and where considerable areas of sand were covered by water at full tide, except during neaps. A suitable location for salting must also have a number of open inlets up which the sea water might run inland beyond the high tide mark, and easy access to a source of fuel. Simply stated, the manufacture was based on the scraping together of heavily salted sand, often called mould, from below the high-tide mark, each salter having his own *greva*, or sand area, for this purpose. The heap of sand was put into a large container of wood or clay, and salt water from the adjoining watercourse was diverted to trickle down through it. This was then collected from the base of the container, after it had picked up more salt from the sand it had come through, and put into bowls, pans or lead vats in which it was boiled over peat or turf fires until the salt crystallized. The discarded sand was thrown behind the salting site on to vast heaps, which, as time went on, markedly raised the level of the land and pushed the high-tide mark, and the salters, nearer the sea.[7]

This creation of industrial waste heaps occurred from prehistoric times until about 1400 on all the coasts of the great basin known as the Wash. Domesday recorded one hundred and eighty active salterns in the region close to King's Lynn and the physical remains are still to be seen there in some parts, where vast mounds sixty or more feet in diameter, and often as much as twenty feet high, can be seen, in fields now a mile or more from the sea. Observation suggests that many existing farm-houses, some churches, and even the earliest surviving sea-banks, incorporate, or are built on saltern mounds, and the twelfth-century charters of North Norfolk religious houses provide evidence that the outlying settlements of North Lynn, South Clenchwarton and Terrington All Saints, were founded in land where active salting had only recently given place to pastoral and then to arable husbandry. It is my belief that Lynn was established on similar new land which had been literally raised from the sea by the long continued activities of the salters.

The area where this salting was carried on was obscure in nomenclature and indeterminate in location. The 'Lynn' or pool, seen as a triangular bay flanked by Lynn and West Lynn in Fig. 1, seems to have been the outfall for some of the rivers of the Norfolk marshland, notably for the Nar, which came from the southeast through Castle Acre and West Acre, and the Wiggenhall Eau from due south, which drained the narrow strip of marsh which in the twelfth century was divided among the three parishes of Wiggenhall. All the other rivers shown on this map flowed, until some time in the thirteenth century, north and west towards Wisbech.[8] There were large shallow areas on the borders of this pool, to the east, west, and south, and here salting was going on actively in 1086.

East of the Lynn, on ground which rose slightly but markedly above the salting level, lay the parishes of Gaywood, which was already held by the bishop of Thetford, who was soon to move his cathedral to Norwich, and Wootton (which in the twelfth century was divided into two parishes), held in 1086 by the Crown, but very soon to be granted to William d'Albini *pincerna*, who also succeeded, at the time of Odo of Bayeux's disgrace, to most of his other north Norfolk estates.

From the slightly higher ground (fifty to one hundred feet) behind Gaywood and Wootton there drained into the Lynn a number of small watercourses, some of which can be seen in the map in Fig. 2. At least three of these were considerable streams, all of which survived as open tidal inlets until the mid-nineteenth century, Millfleet to the south of St Margaret's church, Purfleet to the north, both now culverted and covered, and the Gaywood river, on the northern boundary between Gaywood and Wootton, which remains even now partly open. Salters had been active on all of these streams, and probably on many smaller inlets or fleets, which were drained in the later middle ages. Traces of salting remained, in the shape of a large mound called Rondhil, or Belasis, which could be seen in the mid-nineteenth century close to the site of the East Gate of the town, on the north bank of the Gaywood river, and my husband and I noted similar remains in Wootton marsh, which is now

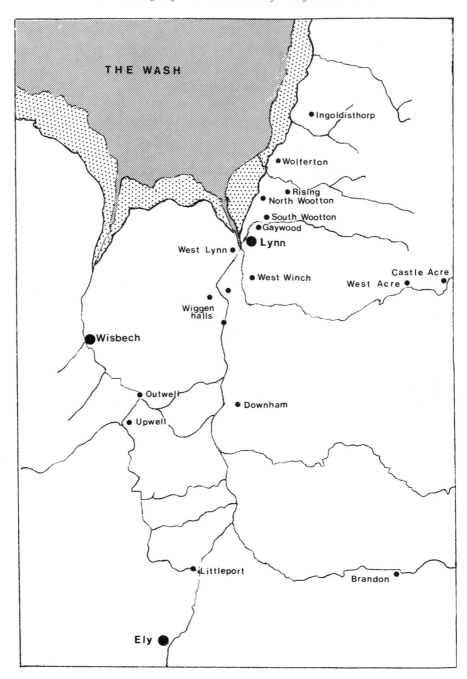

Figure 1. West Norfolk c. 1600

Figure 2. King's Lynn in 1589

an industrial estate, only three years ago. The earliest charters relating to land in the town convey salterns, with their *greve* or sand areas, in what would soon become the town territory, and it seems reasonably certain that Lynn first grew up on 'dead' saltern mounds between Millfleet and Purfleet. Some confirmation of this can be found, perhaps, in what I was told last year by an architect advising on the restoration of the west towers of St Margaret's church—that the 'natural' ground level below the towers was not flat sand as expected, but was decidedly hilly and irregular. In fact, the church was almost certainly built on one or more saltern mounds.

Why should traders wish to settle on, or even to visit the coasts of the Wash? It is true that Lopez and other scholars have told us that since the late tenth century the Germanic and Nordic peoples had been engaged in constant commercial and military expansion on the shores of the Baltic and the North Sea.[9] We know of communities of men of these nations in London and York, but between the Humber and the Thames, apart from Yarmouth, and perhaps Dunwich, there was no very considerable English port, either coastal or on a river. Nevertheless the Wash coasts must have been attracting traders for some time to buy salt, since the demand for this commodity for fish and meat curing was, it seems, inexhaustible.[10] No doubt traders landed on any beach where salt could be bought, during the summer season when production was at its height. Soon, probably, they were also buying wool, for at Domesday large flocks are recorded on the coastal marshes, newly reclaimed by salting, around the Wash.[11] The fens, too, were very slowly beginning to dry out, by a combination of draining and embankment, and although the major work would come later, in the twelfth century, enough arable was available for corn to be offered for sale, and thus by the late eleventh century there were a number of reasons why traders should wish to penetrate to the southern end of the Wash.[12] I am sure that similar factors led to the development of Boston, near the outfall of the Witham, and to Wainfleet, near the northern corner of the Wash.

It seems likely that at first the traders came to the beaches beside Wootton, Gaywood, South, East and North Lynn, indifferently, wherever salt and wool could be bought, but as their numbers, and the numbers of voyages, increased, and as they brought increasing quantities of goods for sale themselves, they had increasing need for a sheltered anchorage: this offered itself in the mouth of the Gaywood river between Wootton and Lynn itself, where in later years 'the port of Lynn' was located. Even at this early period, as the trade in salt and wool, and the demand for the furs, hawks, mill-stones, and general ships' stores brought by the traders increased, some form of protection for the merchant strangers, in the shape of organized markets and fairs, was plainly required, and it would be seen very early that the provider of such protection would be able to reap considerable revenue. The lord of the soil where a haven established itself would obviously try to establish a monopoly in this source of revenue, to the exclusion of neighbouring informal markets, on other men's soil, and certainly after the Conquest he would try to do so by acquiring a royal grant of markets and fairs. I think that this happened at Boston and Wainfleet in the late eleventh century, and I am sure that Gaywood marsh, or 'the Bishop's Lynn', grew at the expense of South Lynn and Wootton, and even of North and West Lynn.

A casual reading of Domesday betrays none of this, since trade and markets play little part in it.[13] The first considerable holding on the east side of the estuary to be named in the survey is an outlying portion of the large estate of Westacre, itself part of the larger holding of Necton, which was once held by Earl Harold, and in 1086 by Ralf de Tosny:

And in Lynn Ralf has five sokemen with eighty acres of land and three bordars and five salterns and two ploughs.

This is the future South Lynn, and to the north of it lay a second larger, and much more compact estate in the episcopal demesne of Gaywood:

Gaiwde was held by Ailmar the bishop TRE for a manor and for three ploughlands; now the bishop holds it in demesne. Then as now two ploughs on the demesne and one plough belonging to the men and sixteen villeins. Then twenty eight bordars, now twenty four. Then as now one serf, forty acres of meadow, woodland for twenty six swine, one mill and thirty two acres of land. Then thirty salterns, now twenty one. . . . Then it was worth thirteen pounds, now eighteen and ten shillings.

Northwards again is the royal holding of Wootton:

Wdetuna was held by Godwin a freeman TRE, then two ploughs on the demesne, afterwards and now one. Then twentyfour villeins, afterwards and now fifteen. . . . Then twenty salterns, afterwards and now fourteen. . . . Then it was worth four pounds, afterwards and now nine pounds.

The last big estate on the east side of the estuary is the former Snettisham holding of Stigand, which by 1086 was in the hands of Odo of Bayeux, and which had as an outlying dependency, Rising, where there would very soon be a castle, and which now had 12 salterns and a fishery along the Babingley river, which ran down through the marshes to the sea just to the north of Wootton.

On the western shores of the Lynn two holdings seem to be of some significance: the Bury St Edmund's manor of Islington, with its dependent territory on the Lynn which would become North Lynn:

to this manor belong six sokemen in Lena with twentysix acres of land, one plough and one saltern and Ralf Baniard's holding of Terrington:

> In Lun Ralf has fifty eight acres of meadow and three acres of land and two salt-
> erns . . .

which would later be known as West Lynn.

There are a number of thought-provoking points about these tantalizing entries. First of all the presence of salterns in quantity, especially on the eastern shore of the Wash suggests a considerable industry, which would certainly produce a surplus for sale. Then, too, the importance and character of the tenants-in-chief both before and after the Conquest suggest that some measure of exploitation of natural resources might be expected, especially from the King and the Bishop, and perhaps the increases in values of Gaywood, Wootton and Snettisham indicate that this was going on. At the same time the numbers of active salterns was declining in all these holdings between 1066 and 1086, and presumably leaving more dry land accessible to shipping. There were at the same time a number of local lords who might be expected to welcome and profit from the coming of ships and traders. Is it too fanciful to suggest that the rise in profits already mentioned represents tolls paid by traders who were already coming to the coasts, however informally, and that Castle Rising itself may have been founded in part to share in this local trade boom?

Bishop Herbert Losinga of Thetford decided to translate his cathedral from Thetford to Norwich, and to begin the construction of a cathedral priory at Norwich, about 1096. He now also granted to the monks he was installing there a church he had begun to build in the marsh of Gaywood 'at the request of all his sons around Lynn' in honour of St Margaret and St Mary Magdalen and of all holy virgins.[14] That is to say, he had begun to provide in his manor of Gaywood a second parochial church for the use of those living at its seaward end. This church was now to be served by a monk from the new house at Norwich, who was to impose penances and perform '*omne ministerium presbiteri*', that is to say, who was to be its parish priest. The parochial area of this new church, which was also given to the monks, was clearly described as all the Bishop's land between Purfleet and Millfleet, as far as the church of William son of Staingrim on the other side of Millfleet, that is to say the church of All Saints, South Lynn. The gift to Norwich also included a number of secular privileges within the new parish, where the monks were to have the soke over all those dwelling between the two fleets, the profits of the markets which are held on Saturdays, and of the fair which is held on the feast of St Margaret. In each of the latter cases it seems clear from the reading that the market and fair were already in existence, and not initiated by the grant in the charter. The final clauses of the charter mention a number of salterns in the area whose ownership is transferred to the monks, and a new mill just made by the monks in the Gaywood marsh, which may have been the tidal mill which gave its name to Millfleet. The gift of a fair at St Margaret's tide which was to last three days, was confirmed by Henry I to the Bishop and monks of Norwich in 1106, and this grant of the church to Norwich can reasonably be dated at about the same time, or even a little earlier.[15]

A number of other interesting points emerge from the charter, about the settlements on the eastern shores of the Lynn. The state of South Lynn, for example, is clarified, for it already has enough inhabitants to require a priest and a parish church, and it would soon be a suitable place for the monks of Ely to acquire a foothold. Nevertheless we know of no attempt by any lord to acquire market and fair rights in it, and if any unofficial or informal market began there it was very soon suppressed. In Lynn St Margaret, on the other hand, there was already a focus for trade and for habitation on the marsh between the two navigable fleets, but active salting was still going on, perhaps on the seaward side of the church, and probably outside the 'town' area on the Gaywood river. The settlers were numerous enough to need a church and to call for courts to hear their lawsuits, and enough traders came to visit the place to make it profitable to organize markets and a fair.

Traders visiting the area only for fairs are one thing, and no very big permanent settlement was needed to service them, but the meeting of a regular market, and the plying of ships and inland boats throughout the rest of the year called for something much bigger and more permanent. The evidence for the existence of such a large 'back-up' community in Lynn as early as the first decade of the twelfth century, seems to exist in another charter of Henry I, by which he confirmed to his *pincerna* William d'Albini the manor of Snettisham with the two and a half hundreds of Freebridge and Smithdon, with wreck and all appurtenances, presumably on the coasts of those hundreds, besides all the *misteria* of Lynn, with a mediety of the market, and toll and other customs, the port with its moorings for ships, *lofcop*, the way of the water and the passage, with all pleas . . . all this to be held with all free customs and liberties *infra burgum et extra* as it was given to him by William the King's brother in his lifetime.[16]

I might justifiably be suspicious about the authenticity of this charter. No original survives and the earliest known copy appears in an exemplification in the Patent Roll for 1329, which was made because the original was decayed. Besides, the text has some very curious features. What, for instance, are the *misteria* of Lynn? They cannot be craft gilds as the editors of the *Regesta* suggested, for Lynn at no time had very many such, and their occurrence at this early date seems unlikely.[17] Moreover, was there a *burgus* at this early period? Are we, in fact, looking at a 'doctored' thirteenth- or fourteenth-century version of a genuine charter of Henry I? I am fairly sure that a share in the tolls of Lynn was given by the King to Albini, for he or his immediate successor granted to Wymondham priory, early in its existence (it was founded in c. 1107), freedom from all toll in Lynn, which could not have been given if the tolls, or some share of them, had not been in his hands.[18] The Albini rights, moreover, are clearly recognized in King John's charter of 1204 to Bishop John de Gray:

> Salvis in perpetuum predicto J. Norwicensi episcopo et successoribus suis et Willelmo comiti Arundell et heredibus suis libertatibus et consuetudinibus quasi in predicta villa de Lenna antiquitus habuerunt[19]

Yet what basis was there for the original grant? Were the tolls somehow inherited in the reign of William Rufus from Odo of Bayeux, and did Odo get them from Stigand, who certainly had soke over some men in West Lynn and Rising? Are the tolls in some way associated with the hundred of Freebridge? I can make no good case to support either of these explanations, but I have, I hope, a solution to the problem in the Gaywood river. The grant includes 'the port of Lynn where the ships tie up', and from the thirteenth century the port was certainly known to be in the mouth of the Gaywood river, where there was a sheltered anchorage of reasonable size. There seems to be no valid objection to the wording of this part of the charter, or indeed to the '*transitum*' and '*pasagium*', which apparently represent the measurement of corn when it was transshipped for export.[20] Wootton formed the northern bank of the port at some points, and though it is not clear when Albini acquired that property from the Crown, it is reasonably likely that he had it before 1100. Why, then, should he not receive the tolls as lord of the northern bank of the port? It is conceivable, indeed, that some traders came to Wootton marshes to buy salt and wool, when others went to Gaywood, even before the Crown relinquished the manor, and that the grant of a half share of tolls and market rights was the price of surrender by Albini to the Bishop of Thetford of a competing market in his own territory.

A further development of the Lynn settlement suggests itself, if indeed the port was already beginning in the river mouth. Surely the south bank of the port, which is over half a mile from the nucleus by St Margaret's church, would attract some settlers, marshy and unattractive though it may have seemed. Perhaps this is the reason behind a charter granted by Henry I to Bishop Herbert's successor Everard (1129–1133), confirming to the Bishop all his customs and *bursa* (exchange?) and his market and toll, as freely as his predecessors held them.[21] Herbert had, after all, given the Saturday Market and fair, along with the church of St Margaret to his cathedral priory, and, so far as can be seen, Albini never claimed any share in those tolls. Can it therefore be possible that a second market had already begun on another site, before Herbert's death? The obvious place for it would be close to the port, and on, or near where the Tuesday Market place now stands. In fact, was the Tuesday Market functioning long before the Newland, in which it stands, was officially 'founded' by Everard's successor Bishop William Turbe? If a market had begun in this area, it seems probable that some settlement of a permanent nature was already developing there, if only to provide accommodation for the exchange, the toll-house and the storage of goods. A phrase in William Turbe's confirmation to the cathedral priory of all their possessions certainly indicates the existence of a road leading from St Margaret northward to the port. He includes in his grant the sandbank (that is, accreted sand) between the two bridges near to the market.[22] The northernmost of the two bridges was that which crossed Purfleet, and it obviously carried a road which ran towards the Tuesday Market, and which would scarcely have been made if no one lived or worked in that area. There seems little doubt that there were people in the Newland in the first two or three decades after the foundation of St Margaret. Probably they settled haphazard on any available dry mound; I can imagine that the houses, and the track which linked them, on the line of High Street and its northern extensions, were almost all founded on extinct salterns.

By the time Bishop Turbe granted to the monks of Norwich a chapel of St Nicholas which he had built 'in nova terra nostra quam de novo providimus', in a charter which Miss Dodwell has assigned to 1146–1150, the northern half of the site of Lynn was clearly well settled.[23] Turbe's charter is indeed not a foundation of a new town, but a recognition that land made available for settlement by the Bishop (probably by the construction of an east–west causeway on the line of Damgate, which would cross the already existing track leading from St Margaret to the port) was now sufficiently a community to require its own church. This church was built close to the focus of settlement on the northern corner of the territory, conveniently sited for the users of the port and the market. Perhaps the most significant point about Turbe's charter is the second half of its witness list: Warin *ostiarius*, Roger de Scales, William de Gernemuta, Radulfus son of Goche with his brothers Turchetel, Siric and Hugh, Outi and Ralph his brother, Ernald and Simon his son, William Chide and his sons Constantine and Deodatus, Seman the clerk, Wulmer Horn and his son John, Walter Godchepe, David de Bilneia, John Estreis, Elvard and his brother Archetel, Bond Rond, Richard son of Turolf and his brother Aschetil, Sunnolf, and Swein de Geiwud, Constantine son of Goderei, Robert son of Thein and his brother Robert, Hubert *grossus*, Eilmar the deacon and Robert his son, Miles *ruffus*. Almost all of these names recur in the cartularies of such Norfolk monasteries as Coxford, Castleacre, Dereham, Walsingham and Wymondham, as inhabitants of Lynn, making gifts of messuages, land and salterns within the Newland; they also figure in the list of men of Lynn which appears in the Pipe Roll of 1166.[24] What seems certain is that, by the time Turbe founded St Nicholas, these men were already settled in the Newland, and had acquired the property with which they were soon to endow the new religious houses of the county.

The list of Lynn men of 1167 includes in all one hundred and thirty-nine names, including a *mercarius*, a *marcandus* a *usurarius* (a nickname perhaps), three tanners, one fuller, one weaver, and several priests. They owe various sums which are placed among the 'pleas of Earl Geoffrey and Richard de Luci', and which seem to be connected with breaches of the Assize of Clarendon, for which Geoffrey and Richard were responsible. What they were fined for is not clear: breaches of the hundredal jurisdiction, a proto-gild merchant, a commune? At least Miss Clark, who is studying these and other Lynn names, is already prepared to say that the men in the list have rather old-fashioned names, and this strengthens my conviction that they are the seniors of the town. She may well be able in due course to tell us a good deal more about the racial origins of the Lynn settlers, but in the meantime, all I can do is to indicate that at least one of them is called Estreis, which is usually taken to mean North German, that a number seem to come from neighbouring parishes such as Wolferton, Wiggenhall, Heacham, Gaywood, and Well, but that there are also men whose surnames are Huntingdon, Lincoln, Stamford and London.

By the time these men were paying their amercements, the town could be regarded as fully developed, and it may be useful to look before we leave it, at the picture of the town presented by the cartularies which now become a useful source of topographical information. The main watercourses were bridged, the two market-places laid out. In the monks' soke a tidal mill had been constructed by Swartger on the Mill Fleet before 1166, a chapel dedicated to St James existed at the landward end of the same area as early as Turbe's charter concerning St Nicholas, and presumably the area between it and St Margaret had been settled by that time, on the street still called St James' Street. The High Street, or Briggate, which ran north towards Newland was already built up on both sides, and the building of houses on the north wall of St Margaret's churchyard had begun before 1200.

In the Newland, apart from building along the margins of the Tuesday Market and the High Street, the principal artery of the area became Damgate, which crossed a series of small fleets and subsidiary streams draining for the most part into the Gaywood river. There was an intense settlement of tanners and dyers along another fleet, which drained to Purfleet, and was named for an early settler on it, Hekwald the tanner, and the high ground near Gaywood river, where the eastward extension of Damgate bordered on an extinct saltern called Rondhil. There was a tidal mill here, which was fully active, and the Bishop had built, on the water front opposite St Nicholas, a great stone house where wine and other goods were stored for his household. Public quays and a crane seem to have been made in Newland and private staithes along some fleets, but ships also tied up in the port or even at the sandhills which bordered the Tuesday Market. There were two courts of pleas, Monday hall in the Saturday Market, for St Margaret's end and Steward's hall in the Tuesday Market for Newland. Even when the Bishop acquired from the monks the market and soke his predecessor had given them, the separate courts continued to function until 1540, although the toll-booth and tolls were never kept separate and the bishop's bailiff and the Albinis' officer worked from a single toll-booth in Newland. Until the bishop's charter and that of King John in 1204 the episcopal steward was the principal authority in the town and the townsmen remained anonymous. By this time however, Lynn had risen very high in the league table of English towns; no doubt its merchants had their unofficial gild merchant and it was ready to leap into public existence when the King permitted it to do so.[25]

I have been telling the story of the early years of a town which ostensibly sprang into life at the behest of a Norman bishop, but I hope that I have made my point that no town origin is quite like any other and that Lynn is by no means an instantaneous new town or a plantation such as Beresford would like us to believe it. On the contrary, it was due to the recognition by a shrewd landlord of settlers and traders who were already there, and to the adoption for toll purposes of markets and fairs which already existed. It had very little to do with land reclamation in the fens, as I am afraid Professor Beresford, following Professor Carus-Wilson, suggested, but it had a great deal to do with the availability of salt, and I do not think it can be blamed on the Norman Conquest.[26] There are good grounds for thinking that a number of other 'new' towns might be equally suspect and the time has come for a long, hard, *detailed* look at those foundations for which the Normans have often been given the credit—or the blame.

The Abbey of the Conquerors: Defensive Enfeoffment and Economic Development in Anglo-Norman England

ELEANOR SEARLE

In writing of Battle abbey, I in particular have characterized it as a royal *eigenkloster*, emphasizing that it was William I's private abbey, dependent upon him alone, and surrounded by a league of land immune from the jurisdiction of all other men.[1] And so, to a great extent, it was. But this can be overemphasized. No one in the world of Norman lordship was completely free from his community—not the Conqueror, not his magnates, however great. I should like therefore to look again at Battle abbey, as part both of its magnate-community, and the community of its district. I should like to argue that its foundation was the expected act of a good lord on behalf of his men, not of himself alone, that its location and liberties were a shrewdly thought-out part of the early feudal settlement, and that its history reveals with remarkable clarity the effectiveness and the long-term adaptability of Anglo-Norman lordship. I shall consider Battle abbey's experience, then, in the general context of the early Norman enfeoffments in England. It is not with the nature or definition of feudal enfeoffment I wish to deal, for I hope that after Professor Brown's masterly summary there need be no debate on that score, at least for many years.[2] But the dynamic of feudal enfeoffment leaves much still to be investigated. This is particularly so after Professor Milsom's reopening of old legal questions.[3] And debate still rages over whether feudal landlordship or human fertility should take pride of place among the determinants of social and economic change.[4]

The abbey of Battle, because of its foundation so soon after the Norman Conquest and because its twelfth-century chronicle is articulate about tenurial and economic problems, affords us a vivid picture of feudal tenures. Through the experience of Battle abbey it can be argued that Anglo-Norman tenurial ties so effectively induced economic development, were so dynamic, that even as early as the 1120s and '30s the feudal polity was in need of fundamental readjustment. The possessory assizes were that readjustment. It was not, I would suggest, the anarchy of Stephen's reign that made Henry II's legal reforms necessary. The rapidity of economic developments as a result of feudal tenures, as we shall see, made structural reforms a real need even under The Lion of Justice. One might indeed, from Battle's example, turn the usual causality around, and consider whether the anarchy of the mid-twelfth century resulted from a failure to achieve fundamental changes in land-holding when the power of the crown was still sufficiently intact to achieve them under Henry I.

As to the circumstances of Battle foundation, we must, I think, look with much scepticism at the element in the story that has Duke William vow on the battlefield and before the battle that, if he were to be victorious he would build an abbey upon the spot.[5] It could even be true, but it was the portion of the 'Norman myth' that was peculiar to the Battle monks. It could even have been part of their myth from the time the first monks were transferred from Marmoutier. Who knows what they were told? But we cannot accept even the likelihood of its truth. It is first heard of in a charter forged for a most significant occasion: to be presented for his confirmation to the young Norman duke who in December 1154 crossed the Channel to be crowned as Henry II at a Christmas court in Westminster, as his great predecessor had been crowned eighty-eight years before.[6] The occasion had its resonances—a kingdom won at last, and by its rightful heir, a Norman duke. The *clers lisants* at young Henry's Christmas festivities had a theme to elaborate, in tales of the earlier conquest to this William come again. Now one similarity between the dukes was their relative ignorance of England. This was an opportunity full of hope for those who wished a certain rearrangement in their situations. In an access of fraternal cooperation, and with the inspiration of *jongleur* myth-makers, Battle and Christ Church, Canterbury put their heads together to concoct a charter. It secured once for all, it was hoped, old liberties that Battle's modern-minded bishop was challenging, and brought Christ Church in by having the Conqueror swear to found an abbey and to make it as free as Christ Church.[7] The story of Battle's struggle for ecclesiastical exemption need not be retold, but it was under the pressure of that struggle that the story of Battle's foundation rapidly developed. In its earliest form it portrayed William already armed and on the battlefield, speaking to his barons and his knights to strengthen their hearts. He tells them that for the salvation of those who are about to die he will found an abbey.[8] Whether this would have appealed to the fighters, I leave to others; it did appeal to the monks of Battle. But it is perhaps significant that it never entered other chronicle-traditions. Once put down, this pre-battle vow-motif was exhuberently elaborated at Battle itself. The abbey became the talisman of the royal crown. For the duke's vow came to be the fairy-tale promise that had ensured his wish for victory and had brought him unscathed through perils to a throne: 'that which gave me the crown and through which my reign flourishes'.[9] Master Wace, telling the tale of the conquest, suggested a setting more in keeping with the numinous promise, and that setting was duly incorporated in the chronicle written at

Battle in the 1180s, completing the elaboration of the motif, and adding the further promise that the abbey's liberty would be no less great than the freedom with which the royal line would hold the realm.[10] And we all know what happens when the fairy-tale prince neglects to fulfill the whole of his promise. If the chronicler is to be believed, Richard de Luci, chief justiciar of England and the abbot's loyal brother, spoke of the abbey as a talisman of secure Norman landholding and inheritance, a nice rhetorical flourish from the man who would be so important in working out the possessory assizes.[11]

There is much, then, in the abbey's own account of its foundation that is self-serving and merely aesthetically pleasing. The monks wished their abbey to become the holy site of profitable Norman pilgrimage, as well as to secure the position of what one may call a 'royal peculiar'. It had nothing to make it a pilgrimage site, save ground made eerie by a miracle-working 'vow', some personal mementoes of the Conqueror, and such sight-seeing attractions as the dread 'Malfosse' of the battle, which the monks claimed to have located.[12]

And yet its claim to be the abbey of the conquerors, the talisman of the Norman settlement, may have something more to it than the insight into the Anglo-Norman imagination that it surely is. It is in fact not so far off the mark, I think. An abbey was, after all, founded, and it was called 'Battle', and there is no reason to doubt that it was located on the battlefield. Only the moment of William's vow need be adjusted. If we push it back to the 1070s, we solve several problems at once. William's behaviour before the battle is less bizarre, the monks' tale of his forgetting his promise after the battle becomes unnecessary (it is there only to explain the delay in allowing Marmoutier to send monks to the site), as does the problem of William's contribution to the Norman penances imposed by authority of the pope in the 1070s. Sometime in those years a penitentiary was issued for the rapine and bloodshed caused by the Norman invaders whom the Norman duke 'at his command' led against the English, and who had already been his men (*sui*), and who by duty (*ex debito*) owed him military aid.[13] The penitentiary therefore minces no words as to where the responsibility ultimately lay. The foundation of a great penitential abbey for his vassals, who had sinned out of loyalty to him, was surely an ostentatious act of good lordship.[14] To call it 'Battle' was perhaps a somewhat impenitent reminder that together they had fought and won great riches. In its very conception, Battle abbey was a feudal gesture, and the abbey of the conquerors as a group.

The abbey's location emphasizes the part it was to play in the group's aid, physically as well as spiritually. Not only does it occupy a Norman graveyard and a scene of victory, but equally important, it dominated the route of a successful invasion. It was placed here to help ensure that no one else might do the same. That is to say, whatever the penitential or commemorative character of the new abbey, it fitted shrewdly into the strategy of defence that determined the unusually early settlement of the south-east Channel coast. Just how early that Norman defensive settlement was, can be seen in the problem of creating the abbey's *banlieu*. When Battle abbey was given its lands, Norman knights were already enfeoffed here, and mightily disinclined to be un-enfeoffed for the benefit of the abbey of their salvation. They had had time to occupy their fiefs, and they disputed the settlement of monks upon their lands—it is a chief reason why one can know that the settlement of Battle abbey was relatively late.

The five great corridors to the Channel, the feudal rapes of Sussex, are too well known to require extensive description here.[15] It is sufficient only to recall a few significant features. These great corridors had been placed in the hands of William's most trusted magnates, the counts of Eu and Mortain, Roger de Montgomery, William de Warenne and William de Briouze. The lands of Anglo-Saxon lords had straggled across the county, ignoring the boundaries that marked the rapes. But whereas elsewhere in England old estates were to pass much as they had been to their new holders, along this coast and in its hinterland, these estates had been broken up, leaving each of the five great war leaders with lands only in a single rape. These lords thus controlled compact power bases, and they were left with no visible royal control over their exercise of power within their corridors. The king retained no demesne save Harold's manor of Bosham, and no royal sheriff acted here; each lord could speak of 'my county', and his own steward acted as sheriff.

The division of this 'Channel march' into these compact, independent lordships was an act of great feudal trust, and it was done with dispatch. Humphrey de Tilleul, it seems, was left in charge of the fort and coast of Hastings as William and the army moved on. But between 1067 and 1070, the divisions began to be made. Humphrey was replaced by the count of Eu, Arundel was assigned to Roger de Montgomery, Pevensey to the count of Mortain, and probably Lewes to Warenne.[16] For their part, they were expected to return their lord's trust and to accept adjustments. By 1073 a new corridor had been created out of the rapes of Arundel and Pevensey, and put into the hands of William de Briouze.[17] In the same way, and probably about the same time, the count of Eu was asked to accept the *banlieu* of Battle abbey as an independent rape within his rape of Hastings. The count, as far as we know, was amenable, but it took more than one sharp royal writ to him before he stopped his knights hunting and taking timber from the forest of the abbey, and it took the monks' cash, years of legal actions, and compromise before their near neighbours would relinquish claim to lands they had held before the foundation of Battle.[18]

If we look no further than the settlement of these knights we shall see what the Conqueror meant the count of Eu to accomplish here. Inland from the old English shore manors, the rape of Hastings was only lightly settled in 1066. There were but few manors back of the coastal plain, and those, small ones.

More characteristic was a dene or a peasant homestead, a virgate, sometimes tenurially attached to a parent manor from which it had been settled, but often isolated and independent in all senses. In assigning lands and tenants to his knights, the count of Eu had consistently disregarded the old English association of parent manor and outlier in the district. To each of his knights he seems to have assigned one or more 'parent' manors, a base for immediate support and supplies. In addition, each Norman fighter had a number of peasant outliers, scattered about the rape in such a way as to be associated with the manors of nearly all of his companion Normans. The vassals of the count were made interdependent by the intermingling of their strange estates. To their lord they owed castle-guard and the duty of making the castle bridges at Hastings. As we see their service in 1166, they did not normally owe service outside of Hastings rape. It was enough to defend the coast from Kent to the Pevensey levels, to keep the district under control, and to settle it safely, and in the meantime, to keep up a military—one can actually say 'colonial'— intelligence. For this, the intermingling of their holdings, and the resultant comings and goings of each knight throughout the rape, was essential. And from this need flowed the character of the court of the rape. It heard all pleas to life and limb, but more telling of its early character, in the fourteenth century still, fifty-two knights' fees owed suit to it—originally, clearly, the knights of Eu themselves—meeting every three weeks to report on 'all things which happen within the barony'.[19]

The early establishment of knights on this thinly settled district clearly gave a great impetus to immigration and development. Here, feudal lords preceded peasant settlers, and if the lords were to prosper, they would have to attract the peasants. Further, the intermingling of their holdings gave the impetus of competition to their efforts. Domesday Book shows us a landscape of scattered homesteads, paying rent to some Norman or other. What lay in between the homesteads, how rights of settlement and of lordship over the settlers were being decided, it does not, of course, tell us. Yet there lay the profit for the knights of Eu—the success of an individual lay not only in attracting immigrants, but in attracting them faster than his fellow knights and occupying the potential arable before it could be claimed by another. The difficulty of the monks in establishing their rights to land even within the boundary of their *banlieu*, and their difficulty in stopping the depredations of the peasants of the knights, tell us much about the competition.

It was onto this pattern of isolated, free peasant assarts, overlaid with the web of feudal enfeoffment and responsibility, then, that Battle abbey was set, like a 'go' stone on an only partially filled board. But it was meant to be free of the responsibilities and the dependences of the knights of Eu. It was set down, not in order to contribute to settlement and defence *through* the count, but to be his equal. Free of his court, free of his demands, the new abbey was a second, separate channel through which the resources of other counties might flow into this undeveloped region. Through the abbey, manors throughout the south, the south-midlands and the east sent their silver into the district, the very wildness of which made it a weak point in coastal defence.[20] The swiftness of settlement here must be understood in this light. By 1086 there were twenty-one *bordars*, clustering round the abbey; twenty years later the thriving town of at least 115 households analysed by Searle, and reanalysed by Clark in this conference, rang with the activities of craftsmen, builders and traders.[21] Peasant immigration and land clearance were as actively encouraged. In 1086 there were thirty-two tenanted virgates in the *banlieu*, but only one virgate of demesne, and two others waste. By the end of the first quarter of the twelfth century the monks' *banlieu* had much increased in value, mills had been built, orchards were established. Clearing was still actively going on: some 837 acres were peasant customary tenements, and a demesne of over 600 acres had come into existence. Clearly investment was bringing its returns. But the increased value of its local lands and the description of the abbey's demesne should direct our attention to an aspect of the feudal settlement in England that is easily overlooked. The abbey's tenants were free men, not villeins. Yet it is clear that rents had been raised, and it can be seen that nearly half the demesne had been created out of the engrossment of homesteads, like 'Oter's wist', which was now demesne.[22]

The economic potential of feudal tenure lay in a lord's power to vary his demands upon his men. Surely we must infer from the analysis of Professor Milsom that the essence of a feudal lord's control over his vassals and peasants alike lay in his own court being uncontrolled from above in the normal course of things. Within his court, inheritance and even security of tenure may be normal expectation, but surely the dynamic of feudal lordship is generated in the fact that the normal is not the inevitable.[23] The very necessities of coastal defence and communication among the ruling Normans meant that extraordinary demands would from time to time be made by the lords entrusted with these 'sea marches', and that inheritance could not be automatic. One of the abbey's Norman tenants was to provide it a rider 'as often as necessary'; one of the important serjeants of the count was to 'do what is bidden him'.[24] Under such tenurial arrangements the ends of the feudal settlement here were rapidly realized: no Herewards made the wealden forests dangerous for the conquerors; no invasions landed on these shores. Nor did the count hold the coast for nothing. He risked himself for profit, and his profit could increase with his demands, while his vassals were left to check him in the court of his great franchise. They in turn were in a position to vary their own demands upon the homesteaders who had been made over to them. The coming of Norman lordship forced an increase of productivity, just as it ensured a new degree of power for the king over his magnates, by leaving tenure insecure throughout society to an extent that had not been true before 1066. Increased demands for services, and expropriations, may have been bad lordship, but the power of uncontrolled lordship consisted precisely in the ability to be profitably bad and selectively generous.

The experience of Battle abbey happens to be particularly enlightening about this aspect of Norman lordship, in part because the district into which the monks were sent had no old weight of English tradition. But more important, tenure and profit were themes emphasized by the chronicler who told its story in the 1180s. He was a monk of Battle, and, I would argue, he was its advocate at the *curia regis* in land pleas, from the 1150s, for some twenty years. He is writing, quite specifically, to hand on to his successors evidence about the tenure of abbey lands, and the histories of lawsuits, some of them over land and not yet satisfactorily concluded.[25] His descriptions follow the pleading in the possessory assizes and in trials of right, clearly so that his successors in advocacy will know the abbey's claims concerning the past of the properties and the present state of the lawsuits. To have described the royal courts in operation precisely at the period when the possessory assizes were being worked out gives the Battle chronicle of course an extraordinary value. The chronicler moreover was an intelligent man, fully aware of the proprietary implications of those assizes, and fully in sympathy with them. In his chronicle we see the powers and problems of Anglo-Norman lordship through the eyes of a lord, and we can see just what it was in Henry II's assizes that should have appealed to a magnate.

Let me illustrate through an example. In the days of Abbot Ralph of Caen and of Henry, Count of Eu—that is, some time during the second decade of the twelfth century, the abbot of Battle determined to invest. He raised the capital by borrowing, in this case from the abbey relics, selling the chains of amulets which had hung from the necks of kings. With the money, he purchased, among other lands, land at Barnhorn, on the edge of the Pevensey levels. This was the holding of Ingleran 'beacon-rider', and the transaction was done with the consent of his lord, one of the count's knights, confirmed by the count, and for good measure, so it was later claimed, by Henry I. Tenurial security was thus assured by the knight and ultimately by the count, overseen by the king. The abbot did not stop, as we are often told lords did, with land purchase alone. He foresaw, the chronicler avers, that a great increase in profit would result from improvement. And so he made intensive investment as well, building a mill, constructing other buildings, and reclaiming marshland.[26] Just as in the early modern period, we are seeing an epoch in which investment was crucial to economic development. And a polity based upon feudal tenure was in a newly effective way channelling the capital for that investment into the hands of the magnates responsible for the control and defence of the realm. Great lords like the count and the abbot—and above all the king—through the uncertainty of their protection of their men's tenure, could direct varying amounts of their men's surplus into their own coffers. Intelligent lords neither kept it there nor spent it merely on pomp: they provided it for increased production. At Barnhorn the monks of Battle built the houses to which their labourers were encouraged to immigrate.

Battle's position as a lord with capital *and* an uncontrolled court meant that near to home, both rents and the growth of its demesne could proceed as an improving landlord would wish.[27] But on the coast, the abbot was only a lord with capital. There he was the man of an overlord. After Barnhorn had been improved, the 'lord of the estate', the knight from whose tenant it had been purchased, demanded increases in its money-service, until the abbey's hoped-for profit had been siphoned quite away. At length the monks would pay no more, and the land was repossessed by the lord. It was thereupon given out by him, with all the abbey's chattels there, to another.[28] Let us suppose that all this was done with the full formality of a seignorial court of the 1120s or '30s (it seems to have been done before Henry I's death, but the chronicler is naturally vague about the dates): there would have been a demand for service, a dispute over the amount owed, the vassal's refusal of the lord's demand, followed by hearings and debate among the vassals; distraint then, and at length confiscation and regrant. Of all of this we hear echoes, again and again, in the early plea rolls of the royal court; it cannot have been uncommon. This case is unusual only in that we can know the aspirations of one of the interested parties, and we hear his version of the motives of another. But how can we hope to know the many motives that might complexly influence the group of the lord's close vassals, who would constitute his court? What interest might some have had in the improved estate? The abbot was surely not one of them, though his predicament would be food for thought. His capital had bought him not only land, but, in the feudal polity of Anglo-Norman England, it bought him, with that land, membership in a group in which he was otherwise an outsider. He had improved what no one else in the group had the resources to improve. He had brought into existence vill, mill and demesne, where three peasant wists had paid rents before. And he had intended to keep the profit to himself—indeed to siphon it off to a corporation that produced no sons or daughters whose marriages would retain and redivide that profit within the group. The twelfth-century magnate, investing in manors beyond the reach of his own court, was a temptation to a local vassal group. The rich, one must admit, had a problem.

But the rich do tend to have solutions, *ad hoc* or long-term as the problem necessitates. The abbot of the 1130s had the connections and money to appeal. First he appealed to the knight's overlord, but the count's court was either ineffective or acted as the knight's patron. It did nothing. That the knight was being favoured is probable. Henry, Count of Eu was in a monastery in his later life—until his death in 1140. Hastings was supervised by his administrators, acting as agents of the king, but, it seems, virtually independent as long as they maintained order and obeyed commands of real interest to the king. Between c. 1120 and 1180, Drew of Pevensey and his son Simon held the count's courts as royal justiciars.[29] This put jurisdiction over land tenure in the hands of the count's most prominent subtenant, and fellow-vassal of the knight who was lord of Barnhorn. Appeal to the king proved equally fruitless. The chronicler, vague about times, but firm about his legal historiography, put it down to Henry I's death: '... across the channel King Henry had died, and (the monks) were unable to get any restoration of their rights. King Stephen succeeded and in his time justice seldom prevailed. He who was strongest prevailed. So for some time one yielded to anyone, as his right, what in fact he had stolen'.[30]

The principle of a lord as sole warrantor of his vassal's tenement includes necessarily the possibility that he will neither warrant nor give *escambium*. This is the 'disciplinary jurisdiction' of Professor Milsom's striking phrase, and it imposed a remarkably effective discipline throughout Anglo-Norman society. But by the mid-twelfth century, as Battle's experience indicates, that discipline had come into serious conflict with the investment plans of the accumulators and improvers who were a product of the feudal polity. To the young lawyer-monk who would become in age his abbey's chronicler, Stephen was a disaster because under his rule the conflict already inherent in the handling of land pleas was not only not solved, but actually worsened. Yet, weak as we must agree that Stephen's power was, *ad hoc* solutions were surely becoming daily more difficult. Royal patronage, in the form of writs of right for the benefit of the great and favoured, could hardly be expected to cope forever with the multiplicity of courts caused by the subenfeoffments that were in fact the investments of magnates. At least under Stephen's reign, the problem of tenure was so exacerbated that, to a lawyer like the Battle chronicler, both its dimensions and the need for a long-term solution became clear.

When Henry II was able, from the 1160s on, to offer, by means of the easily available possessory assizes, to supervise lordship—to make it work as it was supposed to work—the abbot of Battle and his lawyer-monk understood that power over tenure had been transferred from lords and their assembled vassals, to relatively disinterested courts and to advocates armed with evidence. With the evidence of old charters, the abbey proceeded briskly about the recovery of lands and advowsons lost during the reign of Stephen. Barnhorn was retrieved, despite a hostile lord and the count's still ineffective court.[31]

For such a lord as Battle abbey, it mattered less that some of its tenants would be protected from it, than that it could buy out freeholders, and that its purchases would now be safe from the continuing claims of family and other lords. Its policy of investment was rational, and other lords of the area did much the same, though generally with smaller resources. By the end of the twelfth century, one can see unmistakable signs of that specialization in cattle that has been characteristic of the district ever since.[32] Before long there are traces of an abbey-financed bark mill and tannery, serving specialized leather craftsmen in Battle workrooms, and supplying the demand of hide merchants at its semi-annual fairs.[33] Astonishingly, there is even evidence, and clear evidence at that, in the fourteenth-century accounts of its demesne, of the very 'convertible' (or 'up and down') husbandry we are accustomed to think came only with the profit-minded improvers of the sixteenth and seventeenth centuries.[34] It is not in doubt that that husbandry was indeed the foundation of the 'agricultural revolution'.[35] But in the Battle district, by the chance preservation of documents, we find convertible husbandry in a highly developed form several centuries before its supposed adoption as an agricultural innovation.

Improvement, innovation, specialization and industry: these are all aspects of an economy we think of as postmedieval, and indeed are certainly not generally characteristic of English estate management during the High Middle Ages. Yet in this district they were steps both rational and easy to accomplish without much direct involvement in management and marketing. The soils are far better suited to dairying, cattle, and horse-breeding than to arable. The widespread medieval forests meant oak bark, so necessary in the tanning process, which could, and was, taken over by tenant millers and tanners. The medieval demand for leather receives from us much less attention than that for wool, yet the demand must have been well-nigh insatiable. From this district, markets in London and Normandy were easily accessible. Surely it is important that by the end of the twelfth century burgess families of Battle made a practice of entering sons in Battle abbey, for the local flow of abbey capital mightily benefited burgess families. But perhaps the factor that most encouraged the precocious market-oriented specialization of the district was the isolation of the enclosed peasant fields, and that freedom of the local peasant tenures welcomed so early by the abbey. In this district it was difficult for a lord to choose the easy option, and take his profit from increasing rents and service-commutations. Here there was no scattering of strips in open fields to present difficulties to the accumulator, nor was there a peasant village community to discourage the kind of land market that would threaten the power of its social controls. Here a lord could buy, or drive, men off the land, and release the fields from their burden of corn.

At Battle then, it was not the depopulation and the consequent shattering of medieval land tenures that released imagination and capital for an agrarian 'leap forward'. Here a corporate feudal lord invested and innovated under the pressures of the rôle it was meant to play. Battle had been enfeoffed, not only to save the souls of the conquerors, but to guard their conquest: to reside, to provide hospitality (if necessary on a massive scale), to settle, control and defend. The counts of Eu had been much strengthened, supported, and no doubt spied upon, by the abbots of Battle, for their establishment necessarily resided in this place. The great lay tenants-in-chief here came and went with the vagaries of patronage and politics. The abbey remained.

Towards the end of its period of prosperity, it actually filled the emergency rôle implied in its placement here. I have elsewhere described the devastating raids, generally overlooked, directed against the south-eastern coastal districts during the fourteenth century.[36] Suffice it here to say that the handsome crenellations one sees today on the abbey wall were licensed in June 1338, and marked the beginning of a half-century of Battle abbey as leader of coastal defence.[37] From the 1330s until the Treaty of Brétigny in 1360, and from 1369 until the last years of the century, the abbots were the principal arrayers and levy-leaders of the coastal hundreds from Romney marsh to the Pevensey levels. In the summer of 1377, Abbot Hamo became a hero for his personal bravery in commanding the defence of Winchelsea, when in street-to-street fighting the French were for the first time beaten off.[38] Hamo's hauberk and his crossbow, mentioned in the abbey central accounts, are testimony to his activity, and those accounts make it clear enough that the revenues of manors in inland counties were now directed to the defence of the coast through the channel devised three hundred years earlier by William I and his war leaders. Battle abbey was the last of the Norman defence enfeoffments to remain in place and to fill a need here. It was the last time that those particular channels were used. The war had been the final blow in the series of economic reversals to Battle and to its place among the magnate-conquerors. By the end of the fourteenth century it had abandoned its rôle as innovator for that of *rentier*, and reduced its household to benefit its merely middling prosperity. But until then, the feudal settlement devised in the 1060s and 1070s served its purpose. It was no rigid yoke on the backs of men and land, to be thrown off but never to be changed. It was instead a polity of remarkable resilience and adaptability, and nothing can make this more clear than the rapid acceptance of the possessary assizes by the great lords.

The fate of the abbey that began as peculiarly associated with the conquerors and the maintenance of their conquest is as enlightening. For it had taken deep root here, and had slowly been absorbed into the community it had itself created. Those whom it defended at last were the minor men and women of the district—all others had retreated safely to their inland estates. The refugees, both from the communities along the shore, and those pitiable armies dumped ashore and forgotten, the monks housed, fed and clothed, as the accounts of their almoners bear witness. During the worst of the Peasants' Revolt, Abbot Hamo was not afraid to go off for a holiday at the abbey's little manor house at Maxfield, in the very years when the Earl of Arundel's castle at Lewes was stormed by men who hated him for, among other things, his refusal to come and fight in the defence of Lewes.[39] But as Abbot Hamo said to an episcopal visitor—and it may stand as a monument to the flexibility inherent in English feudalism and the unforeseen success of the Conqueror's essentially military strategy—'here at Battle our name might better be made anew to reflect us: non Bellum, sed Pax'.[40]

Notes

Once More: The Carmen de Hastingae Proelio   L. J. Engels

[1] Pertz, G. H., *Archiv der Gesellschaft für ältere deutsche Geschichtskunde* 7, 1839, 1006 seqq.

[2] *Hist. eccl.* 3.15 and 4.9; ed. Chibnall, ii. 184–6 and 214.

[3] Cf. Barlow (note 9), 38 seqq. and 63 seqq.; Morton-Muntz (*Carmen*), xxx seqq.

[4] *Monumenta historica Britannica or Materials for the history of Britain from the earliest period*, I, prepared by the late Henry Petrie assisted by John Sharpe, preface by Thomas Duffus Hardy, London 1848, 95 and 856, note a.

[5] *Descriptive Catalogue of Manuscripts relating to the history of Great Britain and Ireland*, R.S. 1862/1871, i, 671 seqq.

[6] 'Companions of the Conqueror', *The Genealogists' Magazine*, 9, 1944, 416–24; 'The Battle of Hastings and the Death of Harold', *The Complete Peerage*, XII, 1, London 1953, Appendix L.

[7] *Guillaume de Poitiers, Histoire de Guillaume le Conquérant*, éditée et traduite par Raymonde Foreville, Paris 1952, xxxv seqq. and passim in the notes on the text and translation.

[8] *The Battle of Hastings. England and Europe 1035–1066*, Lund 1964, 91 seqq.

[9] 'The Carmen de Hastingae Proelio', *Studies in International History. Essays Presented to W. Norton Medlicott*, edited by K. Bourne and D. C. Watt, London 1967, 35–67.

[10] *Wilhelm der Eroberer. Sein doppelter Herrschaftsantritt im Jahre 1066*, Sigmaringen 1977, 79 seqq. and passim.

[11] *Carmen*, xv–xxx and xxxv–lix.

[12] *Carmen*, xxx.

[13] White, 'Companions', p. 424.

[14] 'The Carmen de Hastingae Proelio', *EHR*, xciii, 1978, 241–61.

[15] Davis, 261.

[16] *Dichters over Willem de Veroveraar. Het Carmen de Hastingae proelio*, Groningen 1967.

[17] The lecture was given on 21 February 1967, 900 years after the beginning of Lent 1067. It will be clear that, although I exploited this coincidence, I did not make a very strong case that the *Carmen* was written for William's homecoming (cf. *Carmen*, xxviii seqq.; Jäschke, 87).

[18] The objection, for instance, that the *Carmen* does not answer to Orderic's description of Guy's poem (*Heraldum vituperans et condempnans, Guillelmum vero collaudans, Hist. eccl.* 3.15; ed. Chibnall, ii. 186), was raised as early as in 1840 (cf. *Carmen*, xvi, note 5) and one could give a picturesque survey of the diverging

learned opinions on this subject. I refrain from doing so, but I wish to draw attention to the fact that not only scholars who argue for Guy's authorship are inclined to reject the criticism (as Professor Davis, 244, suggests). Thomas D. Hardy, though raising objections to the attribution of the *Carmen* to Guy, wrote: 'The laudatory and vituperative character of the piece accords well with Ordericus's description of it' (*Descriptive Catalogue*, i. 672).

[19] Davis, 243 seqq.

[20] Cf. Schmitt, F. S., *S. Anselmi Cantuariensis archiepiscopi opera omnia*, iii, Stuttgart-Bad Camstatt 1968, 139 and 149–51; Barlow, F., *The Life of King Edward who rests at Westminster attributed to a monk of St Bertin*, London 1962, 102.

[21] Cf. Gibson, M., *Lanfranc of Bec*, Oxford 1978; Jäschke, 18 and 80.

[22] *De viris ill.* 156 (Witte, R., *Catalogus Sigeberti Gemblacensis monachi de viris illustribus*, Bern-Frankfurt a.M. 1974, 97 and 145).

[23] Corblet, J., 'Sur une inscription du XIᵉ siècle provenant de l'abbaye de Corbie', *Bull. de la Soc. des Antiquaires de Picardie*, ix, Paris-Amiens 1867, 79–94.

[24] Cf. Lair J., *Dudonis Sancti Quintini De moribus et actis primorum Normanniae ducum*, Paris-Caen-Rouen 1865, 115 seqq.

[25] Cf. Wilmart, A., 'L'Histoire Ecclésiastique composée par Hugues de Fleury et ses destinataires', *Revue Bénédictine* 50, 1938, 293–305.

[26] Orderic, v. 6, note 1.

[27] Cf. Dr Chibnall's notes on details added by Orderic (ii. 172 and 176–8).

[28] *Senlac*: Orderic ii. 172, 190; iii. 214; iv. 92; *Senlacium bellum*: ii. 180, 186, 356; iv. 138; v. 174; *Senlacium certamen*: ii. 266; iii. 304; *Senlacium proelium*: iii. 90.

[29] *Hist. eccl.* 6, 10: ed. Chibnall iii. 304.

[30] Davis, 245 seqq.

[31] Barlow, 40–62.

[32] Jäschke, 39 seqq. and passim.

[33] Davis, 247.

[34] Cf. Manitius, M., *Geschichte der lateinischen Literatur des Mittelalters*, iii, München 1931, 653: 'es zeugt nicht von irgendwelcher Gestaltungsfähigkeit, dass er im ersten Teile des Gedichts von Vs. 26–148 unausgesetzt Wilhelm anredet'.

[35] *Interemptus*: ed. Foreville, 58, 110, 192; *mortuus*: 10, 194, 202; *peremptus*: 200; *ossa*: 210; *cadaver*: 202; *carnes*: 210.

[36] Vv. 346, 402, 410, 418, 470, 570, 572, 573, 587, 589.

[37] Ed. Foreville, 24, 78, 98.

[38] Vv. 310, 384.

[39] *Gesta Guillelmi* 4, 82, 226, 238, 244, 262; *Carmen* vv. 5, 24, 43, 66, 113, 124, 162, 318, 319, 455 (twice), 548, 603.

[40] *Pontus*: 114, 162, 184; *aequor*: vv. 35, 69, 72, 94, 103; *fretum*: vv. 40, 202.

[41] Davis, 248–53 and 257. As to the demonstrative force of the list of persons (Davis, 252), one must take into account that the *Carmen* covers a shorter period than the other written sources it is compared with, and that a large proportion of the people mentioned by William of Poitiers appears only in enumerations (*Gesta Guillelmi* 2.1: p. 148 and 2.22: pp. 194–6), whereas the *Carmen* as a rule describes specific deeds of the persons it names. Moreover, the application of the criteria for insertion into the table can be queried; if, for instance, Harold's mother is to be

listed in spite of the absence of her name (no. 25), the same should go for Tostig (v. 130), Harold Hardrada (v. 174), Edgar Atheling (vv. 647 seqq. and 747) and queen Edith (vv. 627 seqq.).

[42] Cf. Raby, F. J., *A History of Secular Latin Poetry in the Middle Ages*, i, Oxford 1934, 360; Manitius (note 34), 653 seqq.; Engels, 9 seqq.

[43] Cf. Curtius, E. R., *Europäische Literatur und lateinisches Mittelalter*, Bern 1954[2], 449 seqq.; von Moos, P., '*Poeta* und *Historicus* im Mittelalter. Zum Mimesis-Problem am Beispiel einiger Urteile über Lucan', *Beiträge zur Geschichte der deutschen Sprache und Literatur* 98, 1976, 93-130.

[44] *Karolus Magnus et Leo papa*. Ein Paderborner Epos vom Jahre 799. Mit Beiträgen von H. Beumann, F. Brunhölzl, W. Winkelmann. Paderborn 1966, 64.

[45] Cf. Curtius, 138 seqq.; Arbusow, L., *Colores rhetorici*, Göttingen 1963[2], 102; Janson, T., *Latin Prose Prefaces. Studies in Literary Conventions*, Stockholm 1964, 146 seq.

[46] Cf. Lausberg, H., *Handbuch der literarischen Rhetorik*, München 1960, i. 377 seqq., and *Elemente der literarischen Rhetorik*, München 1971[4], 144 seqq.; Faral, E., *Les arts poétiques du XIIe et du XIIIe siècle. Recherches et documents sur la technique littéraire du moyen âge*, Paris 1962, 70 seqq.

[47] *Carmen*, xxxvi seqq.; cf. Giovanni Orlandi's review article (*Studi Medievali*, 3a serie, 13, 1972), 198 seqq.

[48] Cf. Petrie, 866, note d; *Carmen*, 116, note 1.

[49] Cf. Barlow, 67; *Carmen*, 130.

[50] *Carmen*, 117.

[51] Davis, 253 seqq. I wish to thank Mrs E. M. C. Hermans-van Houts (without whose assistance the following remarks on the manuscripts could not have been made) for the bibliographical information and for studying the codices *in situ* during a short visit to Brussels.

[52] Cf. *Carmen*, lix.

[53] See Appendix (Select Bibliography).

[54] Hervieux (see Appendix, Select Bibliography), lii. 182.

[55] *Carmen*, lx (inaccurately; see Appendix) and lxii; Jäschke, 17; Davis, 255.

[56] Hervieux, iii, 203.

[57] Cf. *Carmen*, 8, 12 and 28, note d.

[58] *Carmen*, lxxi.

[59] The most recent editors emendated the text preserved in A on about fifty places. In spite of this advance in comparison with previous editions, there remains some work to be done in the field of textual criticism. Orlandi (see note 47), who did not see the manuscript and based himself on the text printed by Morton and Muntz, proposed some fifteen emendations; a few of these turn out to be exactly the reading offered by A: v. 208 *uerba uerenda*, v. 328 *Vt uulpes*, v. 340 *Vulneribusque* (as Morton and Muntz give in their quotation of this verse on p. 87). Furthermore, I myself have doubts about, for instance, v. 58 *qua* (B reads *quo*), v. 183 *possit* (A *posset*), v. 278 *accitus* (*accitur*?), v. 445 *perspexit* (*prospexit*?), v. 764 *hinc* (*huic*?), whereas I suggest the reading *promtus* in v. 600 (for *partus*, cf. Orlandi, p. 210) and *Vi* in v. 658 (for *Vt*).

Battle c. 1110: An Anthroponymist Looks at an Anglo-Norman New Town

Cecily Clark

I have to acknowledge the help towards the cost of preparing and presenting this paper given by the British Academy Research Grant awarded to me in spring 1979.

[1] Reynolds, Susan, *An introduction to the history of English medieval towns*, Oxford 1977, ch. 4, esp. 66. Cf. Beresford, Maurice, *New towns of the Middle Ages: town plantation in England, Wales and Gascony*, London 1967, ch. 7, esp. 191–8, 299.

[2] Biddle, Martin, ed., *et al.*, *Winchester in the early Middle Ages: an edition and discussion of the Winton Domesday*, Winchester Studies i. Oxford 1976, with text on 33–141 (for the date of the earlier survey, see 410) and anthroponymical analysis by Olof von Feilitzen on 143–229 (see also review in *Archives* xiii, autumn 1977, 84–9); Urry, William, *Canterbury under the Angevin kings*, London 1967, with text on 221–444; Barley, M. W., *et al.*, eds., *Documents relating to the Manor and Soke of Newark-on-Trent*, Thoroton Society Record Series xvi, Nottingham 1956, with text on 1–15 and comments by Kenneth Cameron on xi–xv.

[3] See Appendix, pp. 33–41, for an annotated edition of these names, independently transcribed from BL Cotton ms. Domitian A II, fols. 16r–18r; also printed by Searle, Eleanor, ed., *The Chronicle of Battle Abbey*, Oxford 1980, 52–8 (I am deeply grateful to Dr Searle for allowing me access to her text in advance of publication; the divergences between her version and mine are mainly due to differing editorial conventions), and in [Brewer, J. S., ed.] *Chronicon Monasterii de Bello*, London 1846, 12–16. For the date, see Searle, Eleanor, *Lordship and community: Battle Abbey and its banlieu 1066–1538*, Toronto 1974, 69–70; also *eadem*, *Chronicle*, 52–3 nn. The qualification 'nearly all' the householders is made because, with plots large and with certain tenants holding several, there must have been sub-tenants whose names went unrecorded.

[4] See: 'People and languages in post-Conquest Canterbury', *Journal of Medieval History* ii, 1976, 1–33; 'Women's names in post-Conquest England: observations and speculations', *Speculum* liii, 1978, 223–51; 'Thoughts on the French connections of Middle-English nicknames', *Nomina* ii, 1978, 38–44; 'Quelques exemples de l'influence normanno-picarde sur l'anthroponymie cantorbérienne du XIIᵉ siècle', accepted for publication in *Revue internationale d'onomastique*.

[5] Cf. 'Clark's First Three Laws of Applied Anthroponymics', to appear in *Nomina* iii, 1979 (extract from a paper read in April 1979 at the Nottingham Conference of the Council for Name Studies in Great Britain and Ireland).

[6] Barrow, Geoffrey, 'The "Norman" settlement in Scotland', read at the first Battle Conference, but not printed in the *Proceedings*; the topic will be treated in his forthcoming Ford lectures.

[7] Smart, V. J., 'Moneyers of the late Anglo-Saxon coinage, 973–1016', *Commentationes de nummis sæculorum ix–xi in Suecia repertis*, pt. ii, Kungl. Vitterhets Historie och Antikvitets Akademiens Handlingar: Antikvariska Serien xix, Stockholm 1968, 191–276.

[8] See Michäelsson, Karl, 'L'anthroponymie et la statistique', *Quatrième congrès international des sciences onomastiques*, Uppsala 1954, 380–94; also O. Brattö, *Notes d'anthroponymie messine*, Göteborgs Universitets Årsskrift lxii/4, Göteborg 1956, 24–9.

[9] The numbers are those of the messuages concerned, see Appendix. The names, in the original all in the gen. because qualifying *mansura*, are normalized when quoted in the text.

[10] For a working bibliography relevant to the present study, see the list of special abbreviations prefixed to the Appendix, pp. 19–21. Fuller references will be found in the notes to the articles listed in nn. 4 and 5.

[11] See, for instance, B. Seltén, 'Some notes on Middle English by-names in independent use', *English Studies* xlvi, 1965, 168–81.

[12] I am grateful to John Insley for pointing this out.

[13] For a sceptical note about the currency of this name in England, see Smith. A. H., *The place-names of Gloucestershire*, 4 vols., E[nglish] P[lace-] N[ame] S[ociety] xxxviii–xli, Cambridge 1964–1965, i. 222; cf. the even more dubious cases discussed in Mawer, A., and Stenton, F. M., *The place-names of Bedfordshire and Huntingdonshire*, EPNS iii, Cambridge 1926, 264–5, in Smith, A. H., *The place-names of the North Riding of Yorkshire*, EPNS v, Cambridge 1928, 166, and in Cameron, K., *The place-names of Derbyshire*, 3 vols. continuously paginated, EPNS xxvii–xxix, Cambridge 1959, 284. For another possible occurrence of the rare name-element *Mæðel-*, see Gover, J. E. B., *et al.*, *The place-names of Wiltshire*, EPNS xvi, Cambridge 1939, 351 (*Mæðelhelm*); cf. also von Feilitzen, Olof, *The pre-Conquest personal names of Domesday Book*, Nomina Germanica iii, Uppsala 1937, *s.n. Madelgrim*.

[14] For *Godoinus*, see Morlet, M.-Th., *Les Noms de personne sur le territoire de l'ancienne Gaule du VIe au XIIe siècle*, 2 vols., Paris 1968–1970, i: *Les Noms issus du germanique continental et les créations gallo-germaniques*, 113, and von Feilitzen, *Winton Domesday*, 159. The form *Gisard* offers some difficulty, as, although a Continental-Germanic **Gis-hard* could have existed, the nearest form recorded seems to be the *Gisoard* of the *Polyptyque d'Irminon* (Morlet, *Les Noms . . . gallo-germaniques*, 110); for the modern surname *Gizard*, see Dauzat, A., *Dictionnaire étymologique des noms de famille et prénoms de France*, 2nd edn. rev. M.-Th. Morlet, Paris 1969, 294.

[15] See von Feilitzen, Olof, 'Planning a new *Old English Onomasticon*', in Voitl, Herbert, ed., *The study of the personal names of the British Isles: proceedings of a working conference at Erlangen*, Erlangen 1976, 16–39 and discussion 40–2; cf. Professor K. Cameron's obituary notice of Dr von Feilitzen in *The Times* for 27 July 1976.

[16] Cf., for instance, n. 13. See also Insley, John, 'Addenda to the survey of English place-names: personal names in field and minor names', *Journal of the English Place-Name Society* x, 1977–1978, 41–72. For Searle's *Onomasticon*, see the paper by von Feilitzen cited in n. 15.

[17] Reaney, P. H., *A dictionary of British surnames* [DBS], 2nd edn. rev. R. M. Wilson, London 1976. Cf. the comments by George Redmonds and Olof von Feilitzen in *Conference at Erlangen*, 78–80 and 83–4 respectively, and my own in Appendix, passim.

[18] See *The Peterborough Chronicle 1070–1154*, 2nd edn., Oxford 1970, esp. lxiii–lxv; also Strang, Barbara M. H., *A history of English*, London 1970, 284–9, 227–30 (the book is in reverse-chronological order).

[19] See: Storey, Christopher, ed., *La Vie de saint Alexis*, Geneva 1968, 46; Waters, E.

G. R., ed., *The Anglo-Norman Voyage of St. Brendan by Benedeit*, Oxford 1928, 171–2; Ekwall, Eilert, *Early London personal names*, Lund 1947, 195; and von Feilitzen, *Winton Domesday*, 225.

[20] See Rubin, S., *The phonology of the Middle English dialect of Sussex*, Lund Studies in English xxi, 1951. For certain caveats concerning evidence from the Lay Subsidy Rolls, see McClure, Peter, 'Lay Subsidy Rolls and Dialect Phonology', *Acta Bibliothecæ Regiæ Stockholmiensis* xvi (= *Otium et negotium: studies in onomatology and library science presented to Olof von Feilitzen*), 1973, 188–94.

[21] See Rubin, *Dialect*, 14, 224–7, and Mawer, A., and Stenton, F. M., *The place-names of Sussex*, 2 vols. continuously paginated, EPNS vi–vii, Cambridge 1929–1930, xxvii–xxix; also Ek, K.-G., *The development of OE ȳ and ēo in south-eastern Middle English*, Lund Studies in English xlii, 1972, map on 123 (ȳ > e).

[22] Beresford, *New towns*, 194–5.

[23] Searle, *Battle Abbey*, 71–6. Cf. the similar analysis in Biddle, *Winton Domesday*, 463–4, 474–6.

[24] Several of the Latin terms (such as 6 *corduanarius* and 10 *pionius*) are French ones only lightly disguised, and may indeed provide useful datings for French lexicography.

[25] On Battle's somewhat anomalous status, owing to its lack of a borough charter, see Searle, *Battle Abbey*, 79–88.

[26] See Searle, *Battle Abbey*, 299–303.

[27] Cf. 'Some early Canterbury surnames', *English Studies* lvii, 1976, 294–309, esp. 295.

[28] For a sceptical view of *noms d'origine*, see Beresford, *New towns*, 193–4. Richard McKinley has recently shown that some apparent *noms d'origine* must in fact have been mere nicknames (*The surnames of Oxfordshire*, London 1977, 203–6).

[29] For the surname *Haven*, *DBS* suggests derivation from the common noun; cf. the possibility mentioned on p. 31 that some settlers at Battle may have hailed from the ports of Pevensey, Hastings or Rye.

[30] See *Dictionnaire des communes* (listing eight possibilities) and Dauzat, A., and Rostaing, Ch., *Dictionnaire étymologique des noms de lieux en France*, Paris 1963, 162. One possibility is Cerisy-la-Forêt (*dép.* Manche), as some early records show *Cirisiacus* beside the commoner *Cerisiacus* (see Adigard des Gautries, Jean, 'Les noms de lieux de la Manche attestés entre 911 et 1066', *Annales de Normandie* i, 1951, 9–44, esp. 21; also Fauroux, M., ed., *Recueil des actes des ducs de Normandie de 911 à 1066*, Caen 1961, 194).

[31] Cf. Searle, *Battle Abbey*, 121, 272, 471.

[32] For *Gisard*, see n. 14. For *Colsuein* and *Fareman*, see n. 33. For the other forms, see Appendix *ad locos*. One form, 102 Ælfuine *Hachet*, remains entirely dubious, see Appendix.

[33] For *Colsuein* and *Fareman*, see von Feilitzen, *Winton Domesday*, 153, 157, and also, for instance, Gover, J. E. B., *et al.*, *The place-names of Devon*, 2 vols. continuously paginated, EPNS viii–ix, Cambridge 1931–1932, 687; cf. Fellows Jensen, G., *Scandinavian personal names in Lincolnshire and Yorkshire*, Copenhagen 1968, 179–80, 79–80. Only one DB instance of *Gest* is noted, in Wiltshire.

[34] At Newark in the 1170s Scandinavian forms account for some 60% of occurrences of insular names, and among the king's burgesses at Colchester *TRW* for some 10%

(*Domesday Book seu Liber Censualis Willelmi Primi Regis Angliae, &c.*, 4 vols., London 1783–1816, ii. 104r–106r). For pre-Cnutian Sussex, see Smart, 'Moneyers', 261 (no Scandinavian names at Hastings; one at Lewes).

35 The most marked south-eastern trait is the appearance of *e* for OE *ў̆*, as in 67 *Chebel*, 98 *Cheneward*, and 104 *Bodeherste* (see Rubin, *Dialect*, 83–120, cf. von Feilitzen, *Winton Domesday*, 223–4). The almost regular *e* for OE *ĕo* tells against south-western influence (10 *Dering*, 12 *Trewæ*, 31 *Hert*, 64 *Lefuine*, 69 *Leffelm*, 82 *Lefflet*, but 40 *Burnulf*); cf. von Feilitzen, *Winton Domesday*, 224. In the abbey itself south-eastern tendencies might have been reinforced by the drafting here in the 1090s of monks from Canterbury (see Searle, *Battle Abbey*, 28), but specifically Kentish spellings seem not to occur.

36 See von Feilitzen, *Winton Domesday*, 185 (table 7), also 184 (table 6).

37 For the dating, see n. 3. For the increasing popularity of 'Christian' names, see, for instance, Le Pesant, M., 'Les noms de personne à Evreux du XIIe au XIVe siècles', *Annales de Normandie* vi, 1956, 47–74, esp. 50–1.

38 See von Feilitzen, *Winton Domesday*, 189.

39 See Bridgeman, C. G. O., ed., 'The Burton Abbey twelfth-century surveys', *Collections for a History of Staffordshire edited by the William Salt Archaeological Society 1916*, London 1918, 209–310, esp. 212–47.

40 See Douglas, D. C., ed., *Feudal Documents from the abbey of Bury St. Edmunds*, London 1932, 25–44; for the date, see xlix, but cf. Galbraith, V. H., 'The making of Domesday Book', *EHR* lvii, 1942, 161–77, esp. 168 n. 1, where he suggests 'the early part of Henry I's reign'.

41 Rental B in Urry, *Canterbury*; also Urry, W., 'Saint Anselm and his cult at Canterbury', *Spicilegium Beccense* i, 1959, 571–93, esp. 585.

42 *The Great Roll of the Pipe for 12 Henry II, A.D. 1165–1166*, Pipe Roll Society ix, 1888, 21–9. Cf. my comments in 'First Three Laws'.*

43 For Lynn, see Dorothy Owen, 'Bishop's Lynn: the first century of a new town', below, and, in due course, the introduction to her forthcoming edition of the town's early records (superseding the brief remarks by Beresford, *New towns*, 467–8).

44 See 'Women's names', *passim*.

45 For Scandinavian forms among English women's names, see 'First Three Laws'.* The name *Gunnild*, borne by one of Harold Godwinesson's daughters, appears in Sussex *TRE* and is also one of the few Scandinavian personal names to have been identified in Sussex field-names (see von Feilitzen, *Pre-Conquest personal names*, 277, and Mawer and Stenton, *Sussex*, 564).

46 For Wealden assarters, see Searle, *Battle Abbey*, 46–8, and cf. Darby, H. C., and Campbell, E. M. J., *The Domesday geography of South-East England*, Cambridge 1962, 420–1, 477 *et seq*.

47 Cf. above n. 29, and see Darby and Campbell, *South-East England*, 438, 463, 469, 471–2, also Beresford, *New towns*, 494–6. For the general tendency of medieval towns to recruit from near at hand, see Reynolds, *English medieval towns*, 70, and cf. McKinley, *Surnames of Oxfordshire*, 105, and McClure, Peter, 'Patterns of migration in the late Middle Ages: the evidence of English place-name surnames', *Economic History Review*, 2nd ser. xxxii, 1979, 167–82.

48 See *Domesday Book*, i. 52r, 56r, 179r, 189r, 252r, 298r, and ii. 118r; also [Stevenson, W. H., ed.] *Records of the borough of Nottingham, &c.*, i: *1155–1399*, London and

Nottingham 1882, 116, 124–6 (*in burgo francisco*) and Platt, C., *Medieval Southampton*, London 1973, 7 (*French Street*). Cf. Le Patourel, John, *The Norman Empire*, Oxford 1976, 38–40; also 'French connections', 38–40.

[49] Searle, *Chronicle*.* Cf. *eadem, Battle Abbey*, 34–5.

[50] Searle, *Chronicle*.*

[51] Searle, *Chronicle*.*

[52] Searle, *Battle Abbey*, 61 n. 51; *eadem, Chronicle*.*

[53] Searle, *Battle Abbey*, 69 n. 2; *eadem, Chronicle*, 50.

[54] Although the absence of Normanno-Scandinavian names raises the question whether the link with Marmoutier may have attracted settlers from the Loire Valley, no special similarities of name seem to support this (cf., for instance, Laurain, E., ed., *Cartulaire manceau de Marmoutier*, 2 vols., Laval 1945).

[55] Searle, *Chronicle*.*

[56] Mawer and Stenton, *PN Sussex*, 496–7. For a Norman example, see Adigard des Gautries, J., 'Les noms de lieux de la Seine-Maritime attestés entre 911 et 1066', *Annales de Normandie* vi, 1956, 119–34 and 223–44, esp. 236.

[57] See: ms. Domitian A II, f. 10r; Searle, *Chronicle eadem, Battle Abbey*, 131, 146, 147; *eadem* and Ross, B., eds., *The cellarers' rolls of Battle Abbey 1275–1513*, Sussex Record Society lxv, Lewes 1967, 48.

[58] See Mawer and Stenton, *PN Sussex*, 498; also Searle, *Battle Abbey*, 121–2, 152. For the meanings of the term and a bibliography, see Tobler, A., and Lommatzsch, E., *Altfranzösisches Wörterbuch*, Berlin and later Wiesbaden, 1936–, *s.v. monjoie*. See also Rohlfs, G., '*Munjoie, ço est l'enseigne Carlun* (querelles d'une étymologie)', *Revue de linguistique romane* xxxviii, 1974, 444–52.

[59] See Beresford, *New towns*, 634; cf. Dauzat and Rostaing, *Dictionnaire*, 466–7 (examples include one in Manche).

* *Publisher's note:* Page references not available at date of going to press.

Some Developments in Military Architecture c. 1200: Le Coudray-Salbart

P. E. Curnow

[1] Renn, D. F., 'The Avranches Traverse at Dover Castle', *Archaeologia Cantiana*, XXXIV, 1969, 79–92.

[2] Cathcart King, D. J., 'Pembroke Castle', *Château Gaillard: Etudes de Castellologie médiévale*, viii, 1976, 159–69.

[3] Héliot, Pierre, 'Le château de Boulogne-sur-Mer et les châteaux politiques de plan polygonal', *Revue Archéologique*, 1947, i 41–59; Héliot, Pierre, 'La genèse des châteaux de plan quadrangulaire en France et en Angleterre', *Bulletin de la Société Nationale des Antiquaires de France*, 1965, 238–57. Both articles cite many examples, including those given in the present article; M. Héliot also discusses briefly many of the points raised here.

[4] Eydoux, Henri-Paul, 'Le Château du Coudray-Salbart', *Bulletin Monumental*, cxxv, 1967, 247–60.

[5] Héliot, 'Le château de Boulogne-sur-Mer'.

[6] Ridgway, M. H., and Cathcart King, D. J., 'Beeston Castle, Cheshire', *Journal of the Chester and North Wales Architectural Archaeological and Historical Society*, xvi, 1959, 1–23.

[7] Chartley, Staffs. Renn, D. F., *Norman Castles in Britain*, London 1968, Fig. 20.

[8] Thompson, M. W., 'The Origins of Bolingbroke Castle, Lincolnshire', *Medieval Archaeology, Journal of the Society for Medieval Archaeology*, x, 1966, 152–8.

[9] Ritter, Raymond, *Châteaux, donjons et places fortes: L'architecture militaire français*, Paris 1953.

[10] Héliot, 'Châteaux de plan quadrangulaire', 247.

[11] Ritter, 56.

[12] Héliot, 'Châteaux de plan quadrangulaire', 248–9.

[13] Vallery-Radot, Jean, 'La Tour Blanche d'Issoudun (Indre)', *Château Gaillard: Etudes de Castellologie européenne*, i, 1964, 149–60.

[14] Vallery-Radot, Jean, *Loches*, Paris 1954.

[15] Ralegh Radford, C. A., *Dover Castle*, London 1959.

[16] Chatelain, André, *Donjons Romans des pays d'ouest*, Paris 1973, 196–8.

[17] Coad, J. G., 'Excavation at Castle Acre, Norfolk', *Château Gaillard: Etudes de Castellologie médievale*, viii, 1976, 79–85.

[18] *An Inventory of Historical Monuments in the County of Dorset*, ii, London 1970, 64–5.

[19] Deschamps, Paul, 'Le château de Sâone, dans la Principaute d'Antioche', *Gazette des Beaux-Arts*, 1920, 329–64.

[20] Creswell, K. A. C., 'Fortification in Islam before A.D. 1250', *Proceedings British Academy*, xxxviii, 89–125.

[21] Creswell, 121–3, Fig. 15.

[22] Eydoux, 258 and footnote.

The Piety of the Anglo-Norman Knightly Class   C. Harper-Bill

[1] Douglas, D. C., *William the Conqueror*, London 1964, 91.

[2] Orderic, iii. 208.

[3] Orderic, ii. 154.

[4] Orderic, iii. 178.

[5] Du Boulay, F. R. H., *The Lordship of Canterbury*, London 1966, 36–43; Miller, E., *The Abbey and Bishopric of Ely*, Cambridge 1951, 65–74.

[6] Oderic, iv. 248.

[7] De Bouard, M., 'Sur les Origines de la Trêve de Dieu en Normandie', *Annales de Normandie*, ix, 1959, 169–89; Duby, G., 'Laity and the Peace of God', *The Chivalrous Society*, London 1977, 123–32.

[8] Cowdrey, H. E. J., 'Ermenfrid of Sion and the Penitential Ordinance following the Battle of Hastings', *Journal of Ecclesiastical History*, xx, 1969, 225–42. Cf. Searle, Eleanor, above p. 156.

[9] Southern, R. W., *St Anselm and his Biographer*, Cambridge 1963, 123 n. 1.

[10] Morris, C., *The Discovery of the Individual 1050–1200*, London 1972, 70–5.

[11] *Calendar of Documents preserved in France . . .* (hereafter *CDF*), ed. Round, J. H., London 1899, no. 724.

[12] Orderic, iii. 124–6.

[13] Orderic, ii. 120.

[14] Greenway, D. E., *Charters of the Honour of Mowbray*, London 1972, no. 4.

[15] Knowles, D., and Hadcock, R. N., *Medieval Religious Houses, England and Wales*, 2nd ed., London 1971, 196.

[16] Southern, *St Anselm*, 109.

[17] Cowdrey, H. E. J., *The Cluniacs and the Gregorian Reform*, Oxford 1970, 128–35.

[18] Orderic, iii. 164–6.

[19] Orderic, iii. 260–2.

[20] Orderic, ii. 10.

[21] *Recueil des actes des ducs de Normandie (911–1066)*, ed. Fauroux, Marie, *Mémoires de la Société des Antiquaires de Normandie*, xxxvi, Caen 1961, no. 208.

[22] Vernier, J. J., *Chartes de l'Abbaye de Jumièges*, Rouen 1916, no. 25, citing Matthew, v, 7; Luke, ix, 41; Prov., xi, 17.

[23] Goulburn, E. M., and Symonds, H., *The Life, Letters and Sermons of Bishop Herbert de Losinga*, London 1878, ii. 26, citing Eccles., iii, 33.

[24] *CDF*, no. 655.

[25] *Jumièges Cart.*, no. 37.

[26] *CDF*, no. 74.

[27] *CDF*, no. 1130.

[28] *CDF*, no. 1119.

[29] Orderic, ii. 96.

[30] Stenton, F. M., 'St Benet of Holme and the Norman Conquest', *EHR*, xxxvii, 1922, 225–35.

[31] BL, Cotton Appendix xxi (Suffolk Record Society, *Suffolk Charters*, iii and iv, forthcoming).

[32] Orderic, ii. 32–8.

[33] *Jumièges Cart.*, no. 56.

[34] *Jumièges Cart.*, no. 25.

[35] Orderic, ii. 154.

[36] *CDF*, no. 713.

[37] *CDF*, nos. 1213–4.

[38] *CDF*, no. 85. This point is made in a wider context by A. Murray, *Reason and Society in the Middle Ages*, Oxford 1978, 346 ff. The last four chapters of this book represent a fascinating discussion of the religious motivation of the nobility.

[39] Southern, R. W., and Schmitt, F. S., *Memorials of St Anselm*, London 1969, 68–9.

[40] Benton, J. F., *Self and Society in Medieval France—the Memoirs of Abbot Guibert of Nogent*, New York 1970, 54.

[41] Orderic, ii. 128.

[42] Orderic, ii. 84–6.

[43] *Vita Herluini*, in Robinson, J. A., *Gilbert Crispin, Abbot of Westminster*, Cambridge 1911, 94–5.

[44] *CDF*, no. 719.

[45] Fauroux, no. 108.

[46] Leclercq, J., 'La Vêture "ad succurrendum" d'après le moine Raoul', *Studia Anselmiana* xxxvii, 1955, 158–68.

[47] Orderic, ii. 178–82, 192–6.

[48] Orderic, ii. 124.

[49] Orderic, iii. 206.

[50] Fauroux, no. 46.

[51] Douglas, D. C., *The* Domesday Monachorum *of Christ Church Canterbury*, London 1944, 40; Orderic, iv. 302; v. 314.

[52] Orderic, ii. 14.

[53] Orderic, iii. 208.

[54] Orderic, iii. 202.

[55] Fauroux, no. 82.

[56] Orderic, ii. 132.

[57] Jessopp, A., and James, M. R., *The Life and Miracles of St William of Norwich by Thomas of Monmouth*, Cambridge 1896, 129.

[58] For a detailed discussion of payment for entry, see Lynch, J. H., *Simoniacal Entry into Religious Life from 1000–1260*, Ohio 1976, especially ch. 1 and 2.

[59] Musset, L., *Les Actes de Guillaume le Conquérant et de la Reine Matilde pour les Abbayes Caennaises*, Caen 1967, no. 18.

[60] *CDF*, no. 1171.

[61] *CDF*, no. 663.

[62] *CDF*, no. 320.

[63] Orderic, iii. 210.

[64] *Vita Herluini*, 87.

[65] For a fuller discussion, see Harper-Bill, C., 'Herluin Abbot of Bec and his Biographer', *Studies in Church History* xv, 1978, 15–25.

[66] For the wider context, see Murray, *Reason and Society*, ch. xv, especially pp. 374–82.

[67] Fauroux, nos. 88, 218.

[68] Orderic, iii. 334.

[69] For full discussion, see Baker, D., 'The Desert in the North', *Northern History* v, 1970, 4–6.

[70] For discussion of this and similar satire, see Leclercq, J., 'The Monastic Crisis of the Eleventh and Twelfth Centuries', in Hunt, N., *Cluniac Monasticism in the Central Middle Ages*, London 1971, 219–21.

[71] Benton, *Self and Society*, 54–7.

[72] Musset, L., 'Recherches sur les Pèlerins et les Pèlerinages en Normandie jusqu'à la Première Croisade', *Annales de Normandie* xii, 1962, 127–50.

[73] Orderic, ii. 56.

[74] Orderic, ii. 44.

[75] Orderic, ii. 68.

[76] Orderic, ii. 14.

[77] *CDF*, no. 85.

[78] *Jumièges Cart.*, no. 39.

[79] Orderic, iv. 308.

[80] Orderic, ii. 40, 46.

[81] Orderic, ii. 28, 76.

[82] Orderic, iii. 246, 254.

[83] *CDF*, no. 1167.

[84] *Vita Herluini*, 90–1.

[85] Fauroux, no, 113.

[86] *CDF*, no. 1045.

[87] *CDF*, no. 665.

[88] Southern, R. W., *The Life of St Anselm by Eadmer*, 2nd ed., Oxford 1972, 42–3.

[89] *Life of St Anselm*, 94–5.

[90] Leclercq, J., 'Profession Monastique, Baptême et Pénitence d'après Odon de Cantorbêry', *Studia Anselmiana* xxxi, 1953, 129–36.

[91] Orderic, iii. 216, 226; cf. ii. 262.

[92] Chenu, M. D., 'Monks, Canons and Laymen in search of the Apostolic Life', in *Nature, Man and Society in the Twelfth Century*, ed. Taylor and Little, Chicago 1968, 209.

[93] Orderic, iii. 144.

[94] *Vita Herluini*, 91, 93.

[95] Southern, *St Anselm*, 107–14.

[96] Rosenwein, B. H., 'Feudal War and Monastic Peace: Cluniac Liturgy as Ritual Aggression', *Viator* ii, 1971, 154.

[97] Robinson, I. S., 'Gregory VII and the Soldiers of Christ', *History* lviii, 1973, 178.

[98] Chenu, *Nature, Man and Society*, 227.

[99] Morris, C., '*Equestris Ordo:* Chivalry as a Vocation in the Twelfth Century', *Studies in Church History* xv, 1978, 87.

[100] *CDF*, no. 1235.

The Byzantine View of the Normans—Another Norman Myth?   Jos. Hermans

I am greatly indebted to Dr Ben Hijmans and Professor Allen Brown who were so kind as to correct my English text, to my wife Drs Liesbeth van Houts and Dr Wim Aerts who helped me with many useful remarks, and to East Sussex County Council and the British Academy who facilitated my contribution to the 2nd Battle Conference.

[1] Davis, R. H. C., *The Normans and their Myth*, London 1976.

[2] Davis, 16–17.

[3] Bréhier, Louis, *Le monde byzantin, II, Les institutions de l'empire byzantin*, Livre iii: 'Les grands services de l'état', Paris 1949, 1970, 179–342.

[4] Bréhier, 229–63, esp. 246.

[5] John Godfrey, 'The defeated Anglo-Saxons take service with the Eastern emperor', *Proceedings of the Battle Conference on Anglo-Norman Studies* i, 1978, ed. Brown, R. Allen, Ipswich 1979, 63–74. Blöndal, Sigfús, *The Varangians of Byzantium, An aspect of Byzantine military history*, translated, revised and rewritten by Benedikt S. Benedikz, Cambridge 1978.

[6] Davis, 87.

[7] Davis, 84.

Douglas, David C., *The Norman Fate 1100–1154*, London 1975; referred, however, to a royal charter speaking of 'our Norman ancestors'. Cf. Abulafia, David, 'The Normans and their impact on Europe', *Times Higher Education Supplement*, 19 March 1976, 18.

[8] Davis, 86.

[9] Deér, Joseph, *The Dynastic Porphyry Tombs of the Norman Period in Sicily*, Dumbarton Oaks Studies 5, Cambridge, Mass. 1959; Demus, Otto, *The Mosaics of Norman Sicily*, London 1950; Demus, Otto, *Byzantine Art and the West*, London 1970; Giunta, Francesco, *Bizantini e bizantinismo nella Sicilia normanna*, Nuova edizione, Palermo 1974; Kitzinger, Ernst, 'On the Portrait of Roger II in the Martorana', *Proporzioni*, 1950, 30 sqq.

[10] Davis, 100.

[11] Nicol, Donald M., 'The Byzantine View of Western Europe', *Greek, Roman and Byzantine Studies* 8, 1967, 315–39; quotations: George Pachymeres, *De Michaele Palaeologo*, ed. I. Bekker, Bonn 1835, 185 lines 15–16, 358 line 5. Nikephoros Gregoras, *Byzantina Historia*, ed. L. Schopen, ii, Bonn 1829, 689 lines 2–4.

[12] Eustathius of Thessalonike, *La Espugnazione di Tessalonica*, ed. St. Kyriakidis, Istituto Siciliano di Studi Bizantini e Neoellenici, Testi e Monumenti, Testi 5, Palermo 1961, 56 lines 27–8.

[13] *Espugnazione*, 52 line 25.

[14] *Dionysius Periegetes graece et latine cum vetustis commentariis et interpretationibus*, ed. Bernhardy, G., Geographi Graeci minores 1, Leipsic 1828 (reprint Hildesheim–New York 1974), I 22 line 285 and 23 line 304; on Eustathius and his commentaries now: Hunger, Herbert, *Die hochsprachliche profane Literatur der Byzantiner*, II. Band, Philologie e.o., Handbuch der Altertumswissenschaft XII,5,2, Munich 1978, 66–7.

[15] *Eustathii Commentarii* in the edition quoted in note 14, Vol. I, 140–1. An explicit identification of Φράγγοι with Γερμανοί can be found in Agathias (Agathiae Myrinaei *Historiarum Libri Quinque*, ed. Keydell, R., Corpus Fontium Historiae Byzantinae 5, Berlin 1967, 11 lines 1–2: ... τὸ γένος τῶν Φράγγων, εἶεν δ' ἂν οὗτοι οἱ πάλαι ὀνομαζόμενοι Γερμανοί). This information was taken from another sixth-century author, Procopius, who gave in his 'Gothic Wars' the same information: III, 3, 1; V, 11, 29; V, 12, 8; cf. *Historia Arcana*, 18, 17. Most probably Eustathius knew this text too.

[16] Nicol, 315.

[17] Dölger, Franz, 'Europas Gestaltung im Spiegel der fränkisch-byzantinischen Auseinandersetzung des 9. Jahrhunderts' in: Dölger, *Byzanz und die europäische Staatenwelt*, Ettal 1953, reprinted Darmstadt 1964, 282–369; Alexander, Paul J., 'The Strength of Empire and Capital as seen through Byzantine Eyes', *Speculum* 37, 1962, 339–57; Dvornik, Francis, *Early Christian and Byzantine Political Philosophy. Origins and Background*, 2 vols. Dumbarton Oaks Studies 10, Washington, D.C. 1966; Nicol, cited article; Ahrweiler, Hélène, *l'Idéologie politique de l'empire Byzantin*, Paris 1975.

[18] Nicol, 317.

[19] Lechner, Kilian, *Hellenen und Barbaren im Weltbild der Byzantiner*. Die alten

Bezeichnungen als Ausdruck eines neuen Kulturbewusstseins. Diss. Munich 1954, published 1955; Nicol, 317.

[20] Ioannis Cinnami, *Epitome rerum ab Ioanne et Alexio Comnenis gestarum*, ed. Meineke, A., Bonn 1836, 219–20; *Deeds of John and Manuel Comnenus by John Kinnamos*, translated by Brand, Charles M., New York 1976, 166–7. See for the comments on this passus: Dölger, Franz, 'Rom in der Gedankenwelt der Byzantiner' in Dölger, *Byzanz*, 98 f.; Alexander, Paul J., 'The Donation of Constantine at Byzantium and its Earliest Use against the Western Empire', *Zbornik Radova Vizantološkog Instituta* 8, 1963, 12–25.

[21] The most recent overall view with an enormous bibliography of all relevant literature is Ohnsorge, Werner, 'Abendland und Byzanz, I, Das abendländische Kaisertum', *Reallexikon der Byzantinistik* 1, Amsterdam 1969, 126–69.

[22] We must however realize that especially in the Army and Civil Service very often Latin titles were retained. To give but one example: in Cecaumenus' *Strategicon et incerti scriptoris de officiis regiis libellus*, ed. B. Wassiliewsky-V. Jernstedt, St Petersburg 1896, we meet both a κόμης τῶν Φράγγων (30 line 11) and a κόμης δρουγγάριος (103 line 1). For these titles see e.g. Bréhier, *Institutions*, index s.v. 'comtes'. (The new edition by G. G. Litavrin, Moscow 1972, was not accessible to us.)

[23] Perhaps the best-known incident about the claim on the Roman character of Western *imperium* is the legacy of Liutprand of Cremona in 968 to ask for a Byzantine princess as a bride for Otto II. On this topic literature can be found in Ohnsorge (see note 21). About Constantinople as New Rome: Fenster, Erwin, *Laudes Constantinopolitanae*, Miscellanea Byzantina Monacensia 9, Munich 1968.

[24] Mango, Cyril, *Byzantine Literature as a Distorting Mirror*, An Inaugural Lecture, Oxford 1975, esp. 4–6.

[25] Mango, *passim*; Aerts, Wim J., *Anna's Mirror, Attic(istic) or Attiquarian? A philological Commentary on the first Chapters of Anna Comnena's Introduction to the Alexiad*, XVth International Congress of Byzantine Studies, Rapport in the Section 'Langue, Littérature, Philologie, 1. Courants archaisants et populaires dans la langue et la littérature (1071–1261)', Athens 1976. The suggestion made by Dr Wirth at the same congress to make a division in three groups, 'Trigraphie', seems not very useful to us (Wirth, Peter, *Die sprachliche Situation in dem umrissenen Zeitalter. Renaissance des Attizismus. Herausbildung der neugriechischen Volkssprache*, Athens 1976, 6 ff.: 'Diglossie und Trigraphie').

[26] Mango, 16–17.

[27] The list of *historians* tries to be complete. It includes all writers mentioned in the introductory chapters on sources in Ostrogorsky, George, *History of the Byzantine State*, translated by Hussey, Joan, Oxford 1968, 316–19 (A.D. 1025–1081), 351–6 (1081–1204), as well as in Hunger I, 'Viertes Kapitel: Geschichtsschreibung', 372–441 (from Psellos to Nicetas Choniates). I did not include all the minor writing to be found in Karayannopoulos, I. E., Πηγαὶ τῆς Βυζαντίνης Ἱστορίας ('Sources for the Byzantine History'), Thessalonike 1971, 264–316. I left out Joel, *Chronographia*, ed. Bekker, I., Bonn 1836, though mentioned in Ostrogorsky, since this author (early XIIIth century) has no independent historical value, and, even more important, no Normans occur in this world chronicle which extends to the Latin conquest of 1204. For this paper I deliberately left out any Western sources,

though from 'fairy tales' and other minor texts one could take tall stories (like those known at Monte Cassino, as Dr Graham Loud from Leeds informed us).

At the conference several scholars urged me to add to my footnotes a list of translations of the Greek texts quoted. Most of the texts were printed in Migne, *Patrologia Graeca*, where a Latin translation was added. Modern editions sometimes do have a translation, which I have indicated between brackets [ ].

²⁸ Georgius Cedrenus, Ioannis Scylitzae *opera*; ed. Bekker, I., II, Bonn 1839, 43–638 [Latin]; Ioannis Scylitzae *Synopsis historiarum*, ed. Thurn, J., Corpus Fontium Historiae Byzantinae (= *CFHB*) 5, Berlin–New York 1973.

²⁹ Ἡ συνέχεια τῆς χρονογραφίας τοῦ Ἰωάννου Σκυλίτση (*Ioannes Skylitzes Continuatus*), ed. E. Th. Tsolakes, Ἑταιρεία. Μακεδονικῶν Σπουδῶν, Ἵδρυμα Μελετῶν Χερσονήσου τοῦ Αἵμου 105, Thessaloniki 1968; see for detailed information now: Hunger, *Hochsprachliche Literatur*, I, Geschichtsschreibung, 389–92.

³⁰ Two vols. (cf. note 28), Bonn 1838–1839; Hunger I, 393.

³¹ Michel Psellos, *Chronographie, où Histoire d'un siècle de Byzance (976–1077)*, ed. Renauld, E., Paris 1926–1928 [French; English: Fourteen Byzantine Rulers. The *Chronographia of Michael Psellus*. Translated . . . E. R. Sewter, Harmondsworth 1966]. This edition was based on the only known ms., but since recently a new manuscript was discovered there will be a partial re-edition (the new codex from Sinai does not contain the complete text) by the Groningen Psellos Study Group: W. J. Aerts *et al.* (eds.), to be published in *Byzantinoslavica* 41, 1980; Hunger I, 372–83.

³² Michaelis Attaliotae *Historia*, ed. Bekker, I., Bonn 1853 [Latin]; Hunger I, 382–9.

³³ Nicephori Bryennii *Historiarum libri quattuor*, ed. Gautier, P., CFHB 9, Brussels 1975 [French]; Hunger I, 394–400.

³⁴ Anne Comnène, *Alexiade*, ed. Leib, B., Paris 1937, 1943, 1945, Index: P. Gautier, Paris 1976 [French; English: The Alexiad of Anna Comnène transl. . . . E. R. Sewter, Harmondsworth 1969]; Hunger I, 400–09.

³⁵ Ioannis Zonarae *Epitome historiarum* I, II: ed. Pinder, M., Bonn 1841, 1844; III: ed. Th. Büttner-Wobst, Bonn 1897 [Latin]; Hunger I, 416–19.

³⁶ Constantini Manassis, *Breviarium Historiae Metricum*, ed. Bekker, I., Bonn 1839 [Latin]; Hunger I, 419–22.

³⁷ Michaelis Glycae *Annales*, ed. Bekker, I., Bonn 1836 [Latin]; Hunger I, 422–6.

³⁸ See for edition and translation note 20; Hunger I, 409–16.

³⁹ Edition (including an Italian translation) mentioned in note 12; Hunger I, 426–9.

⁴⁰ Nicetae Choniatae *Historia*, ed. van Dieten, J. A. J., CFHB 11, 1.2., Berlin–New York 1975 [German: Grabler, Franz (in three volumes): Die Krone der Komnenen; Abenteurer auf dem Kaiserthron; Kreuzfahrer erobern Konstantinopel, Byzantinische Geschichtsschreiber 7, 8, 9, Graz-Vienna-Cologne 1958]; Hunger I, 429–41. Nicetas and his elder brother Michael have been known since the *editio princeps* of the διήγησις (Basilea 1557) as 'Acominatus'. Since this pretended surname has no manuscript basis at all, one ought to avoid it. A synopsis of the origin of this ghostword can be found in our article: 'Le nom Akominatos. Considérations codicologiques sur un "Mot-fantôme"', *Scriptorium* 30, 1976, 241–8.

⁴¹ See for edition note 22, for translation note 60; Hunger I, 162 for a survey of

modern ideas whether both texts were written by one and the same author.

[42] *Prodromus*: Theodoros Prodromos, *Historische Gedichte*, ed. Hörandner, W., Wiener Byzantinistische Studien 11, Vienna 1974; *Tzetzes*: Ioannis Tzetzae *Historiae*, ed. Leone, P. A. M., Pubblicazioni dell' Istituto di Filologia Classica 1, Naples 1968.

[43] Michael Acominatus Choniates, *Τὰ Σωζόμενα*, ed. Sp. Lampros, Athens 1879–1880 (reprint Groningen 1968); Nicetae Choniatae *Orationes et Epistulae*, ed. van Dieten, J. L., CFHB 3, Berlin–New York 1972 [German: Kaisertaten und Menschenschicksale im Spiegel der schönen Rede. Reden und Briefe des Niketas Choniates, übersetzt, eingeleitet und erklärt von Franz Grabler, Byzantinische Geschichtsschreiber 11, Graz-Vienna-Cologne 1966].

[44] Michel Italikos, *Lettres et Discours*, ed. Gautier, P., Archives de l'Orient Chrétien 14, Paris 1972; Georges et Dèmètrios Tornikès, *Lettres et Discours*, ed. Darrouzès, J., Le Monde Byzantin, Paris 1970 [French]; for Michael and Nicetas Choniates see the editions mentioned in note 43.

[45] Most of these remarks can be proven with literature indicated in Ostrogorsky or Hunger (see our notes 28–44).

[46] Cf. Tinnefeld, Franz, *Kategorien der Kaiserkritik in der byzantinischen Historiographie von Prokop bis Niketas Choniates*, Munich 1971, 153 ff.

[47] Van Dieten, Jan Louis, *Niketas Choniates. Erläuterungen zu den Reden und Briefen nebst einer Biographie*, Berlin–New York 1971.

[48] Cecaumenus, 95 line 8.

[49] Was Prodromus the same as Ptochoprodromus, and if so, are all these poems really written by him? See for instance the introduction in Hörandner's edition.

[50] Davis, 89.

[51] Buckler, Georgina, *Anna Comnena, A Study*, Oxford 1929 (reprinted 1968), 446.

[52] Anna Comnena, I, 37 line 33; I, 37 lines 38, 25, 38 line 20.

[53] Psellus, II, 97 (Michael VI; XXIV, 23).

[54] Psellus, II, 169, 170 (Romanus IV; XXXIX, 3 and 5).

[55] Cecaumenus, 35 line 4, resp. 67 line 3.

[56] Cecaumenus, 30.10; 30.16; 30.18; 35.10; 35.12; 95.28.

[57] Cecaumenus, 96 lines 9–10; lines 14–15; a confusion like this can be found in Eustathius; cf. note 15.

[58] See Lemerle, Paul, 'Prolégomènes à une édition critique et commentée des "Conseils et Recits" de Kekauménos', *Mémoires Académie Royale de Belgique, Classe des Lettres et des Sciences Morales et Politiques* 54, 1960, 1–120; esp. 41 ff., 58.

[59] Cecaumenus, 97 lines 1 ff.; see index s.v., p. 105.

[60] Cecaumenus, 97, 5 ff.; cf. Beck, Hans-Georg, *Vademecum des byzantinischen Aristokraten*, Das sogenannte Strategikon des Kekaumenos, Byzantinische Geschichtsschreiber 5, Graz-Vienna-Cologne 1964², 163, notes 11 and 12 and Lemerle, 62–4.

[61] Riasanovsky, Alexander V., 'The Varangian Question', *I Normanni e la loro espansione in Europa nell'alto Medioevo*, 18–24 aprile 1968, Settimane di studio del Centro Italiano di Studi sull'Alto Medioevo 16, Spoleto 1969, 171–204; discussion: 553–69.

[62] Riasanovsky, 184; he quotes the study of Shakhmatov, Aleksei Aleksandrovich,

Drevneishiya sud'by Russkago plemeni, Izdanie Russkago Istoricheskago Zhurnala, St Petersburg 1919. (Reprinted: Russian Reprint Series 40, The Hague 1967, 47.) None of these authors use Cecaumenus.

[63] Cecaumenus, 30 line 5.

[64] Cecaumenus, 95 line 28.

[65] Cecaumenus, 97 line 17 f.; cf. Lemerle, 62.

[66] Anna, II, 210–11; III, 38; Buckler, 449–50.

[67] Anna, III, 23–5; for Normans as horsemen see the chapter on military affairs in Buckler, 353 ff. and 442 note 4.

[68] See Buckler, 451 note 1.

[69] Anna, I, 37 lines 4–5. I quote the translation by E. R. A. Sewter, *The Alexiad of Anna Comnena,* Harmondsworth 1969, 53.

[70] See the index on Anna s.v.

[71] Two descriptions: Anna, I, 37 f. and II, 59 f.; Buckler, 451 gives all notes to the text.

[72] Davis, 71.

[73] Anna, I, 38 lines 19–27; Sewter, 54.

[74] See for this pretender: Buckler, 448, 452.

[75] Anna, I, 37 lines 15–18.

[76] Cf. Buckler, 452–5.

[77] Buckler, 451.

[78] Anna, I, 166–7.

[79] Resp' Zonaras III, 714 lines 5–6; 734, 18.

[80] Bryennius 213, lines 19–21; the like can be read in Scylitzes Continuatus, 167 lines 4–5: τὸν τὴν Λογγιβαρζίαν κατέχοντα Φράγκον, Ῥουμπέρτον καλούμενον.

[81] Chalandon, Ferdinand, *Histoire de la domination Normande en Italie et en Sicile* I, Paris 1907 (reprint: New York 1969), 42 ff.; see also: Galasso, Guiseppe, 'Social and Political Developments in the Eleventh and Twelfth Centuries', *The Normans in Sicily and Southern Italy,* Lincei Lectures 1974, Oxford 1977, 47–63, esp. 55 ff.

[82] Chalandon, 58 note 2 discusses the question mark which Gay (Jules, *l'Italie méridionale et l'empire Byzantine depuis l'avènement de Basile Ier jusqu'à la prise de Bari par les Normands (867–1071),* Paris 1904 (reprint: New York s.d.), p. 415–16) put at the identification of Normans with the Φράγγοι that occur in a charter of the victorious Byzantine general Bojoannes. See also Von Falkenhausen, Vera, *Untersuchungen über die byzantinische Herrschaft in Süditalien vom 9. bis 11. Jahrhundert,* Schriften zur Geistesgeschichte des östlichen Europas 1, Wiesbaden 1967.

[83] Cedrenus, 740–44, 755B–757C and Zonaras, 594 and 621 ff. speak only about Arabs, Anna mentions rebellious 'Italians' (cf. Buckler, 443).

[84] Cedrenus II, 545 lines 11–12.

[85] Ostrogorsky, 332–3.

[86] Bryennius 269 line 11 explicitly speaks about Franks brought by the famous (ἐκείνος) Maniaces; cf. Scylitzes Continuatus, 167, Anna Comnena, II, 117.

[87] Bryennius, 135 line 5; cf. Attaleiates, 122–4; Scylitzes Continuatus, 134.

[88] Psellus, II, 169–70.

[89] Psellus, II, 170 line 1 writes that he is writing about Crispin at the moment the latter died; Bryennius 147, 24.

[90] Bryennius 149, 6.

[91] Bryennius 167 ff.; 179 line 12: as a pretext he had the pretender John Doukas proclaimed emperor.

[92] Buckler, 450.

[93] Bryennius 181; see for a general view of Roussel: Hoffmann, Jürgen, *Rudimente von Territorialstaaten im byzantinischen Reich (1071–1210)*, Miscellanea Byzantina Monacensia 17, Munich 1974, 13–20, 80–82.

[94] Anna, III, 123 last line, 124 line 2; Buckler, 440–41; 473–4.

[95] See Anna's description of Bohemund, 122 line 20–124.2; cf. Buckler, 473–4.

[96] E.g. Cecaumenus, 33.7, 33.15, 35.5, 59.7, 65.12, 70.32, but Symeon, emperor of the Bulgarians is called a τυράννος too (32.39).

[97] Cecaumenus (38, 29 f.) divides the world into true believers and others; the latter being Arabs and the like. Anna tells explicitly—as we saw in note 76—that Robert was doing lawless deeds by fighting against Christians. Bryennius tells about Roussel (185, 3) who did barbarous things but did not kill some enemies, 'since all of them were Christians'.

[98] Cf. Buckler, 458.

[99] Buckler, 475–7.

[100] Marquis de la Force, 'Les conseillers latins du basileus Alexis Comnène', *Byzantion* 11, 1936, 153–65.

[101] Anna, III, 124–5.

[102] Beck, Hans-Georg, 'Byzanz und der Westen im 12. Jahrhundert', *Vorträge und Forschungen* 12, Constance 1969, 227–41, esp. 234.

[103] ἅπαντες καὶ τῶν ἵππων ἀποβαίνοντες ταῖς ἐκείνου (=Bryennius) χερσί τὰς χεῖρας ἐμβάλλοντες, ὡς δὴ πάτριος νόμος τούτοις ἐστί, πίστεις ἐδίδουν ... Bryennius 275, 16. Almost the same text is quoted in the Alexiad, I, 24 line 22.

[104] The last chapter of Book XIII of the Alexiad is filled with the treaty between the Romans and the Normans. See also Buckler, 474 ff.

[105] Beck, 234.

[106] Cinnamus distinguished three defeats of the Sicilians (p. 101).

[107] Mathieu, Marguérite, 'La Sicile Normande dans la poésie Byzantine', *Bolletino Centro di Studi Filologici e Linguistici Siciliani* 2, 1954, 52–84.

[108] Σικελῶν ῥήξ: cf. Mathieu, 54; τυράννος: ed. Miller, v. 64, cf. Mathieu, 72; *Syracusans*: Mathieu, 69, 75; δράκων Σικελίας: Prodromus (Hörandner), poem XXX, v. 200, p. 354;—δράκοντα πλωτόν; 'dragon of the water': ed. Miller, RHC Gr. II, 280, cf. Mathieu, 71; —δράκοντα τῆς θαλάσσης τὸν μέγαν: ed. Mathieu, 57–8, v. 703.

[109] τοῦ δυτικοῦ ... δράκοντος; Dölger, Franz, *Regesten der Kaiserurkunden des oströmischen Reiches* II, 1025–1204, Munich 1925 (reprinted Hildesheim 1976), Regest 1327; *Jus Graecoromanum*, ed. Zepos, J. & P., I–VIII, Athens 1931 (reprinted Aalen 1962), I, 376.

[110] Ed. Miller, *Annuaire de l'Association pour l'encouragement des études grecques* 1883, 57; cf. Mathieu, 65.

[111] Ed. Hörandner, XXX, v. 407, p. 360; cf. Mathieu, 70.

[112] Mathieu, 82.

[113] The best study on this period is Brand, Charles M., *Byzantium confronts the West 1180–1204*, Cambridge, Mass., 1968. A good instance of such a celebration and the use of the word tyrant is the Λόγος ἐγκωμιαστικός written by Michael Choniates

PARTIAL FAMILY TREE OF NORMAN RULERS IN ITALY

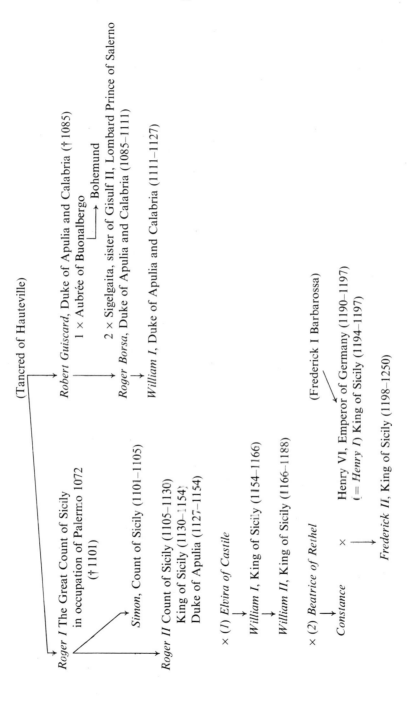

(Tancred of Hauteville)

Robert Guiscard, Duke of Apulia and Calabria († 1085)

1 × Aubrée de Buonalbergo

└→ Bohemund

2 × Sigelgaita, sister of Gisulf II, Lombard Prince of Salerno

Roger Borsa, Duke of Apulia and Calabria (1085–1111)

William I, Duke of Apulia and Calabria (1111–1127)

Roger I The Great Count of Sicily
in occupation of Palermo 1072
(† 1101)

Simon, Count of Sicily (1101–1105)

Roger II Count of Sicily (1105–1130)
King of Sicily (1130–1154)
Duke of Apulia (1127–1154)

× (1) *Elvira of Castile*

William I, King of Sicily (1154–1166)

William II, King of Sicily (1166–1188)

× (2) *Beatrice of Rethel*

Constance ×

(Frederick I Barbarossa)

Henry VI, Emperor of Germany (1190–1197)
(= *Henry I*) King of Sicily (1194–1197)

Frederick II, King of Sicily (1198–1250)

for emperor Isaac Angelus (probably 1187). 'A double *Tyrannis* is removed' (I, 209 line 15), the first is Andronicus (I, 217, 26 ff.), the second is the dangerous revolution of general Alexius Branas (end 1186) (I, 246, 5 ff.). The Norman threat, σικελικὴ χάρυβδις (I, 210, 22) has been turned off, their knights and footsoldiers have been defeated as well as their navy (I, 245, 12 ff.).

[114] About the reading of shorter version or no reading at all (the text is of substantial length) see Hunger, I, 428.

[115] Eustathius, 56 line 11 to 62 line 28; about Roger and William 58, lines 4–11.

[116] Eustathius, 34 lines 11–20, esp. line 20: ἐκεῖθεν γὰρ ἡμῖν καθήκει τὰ πάροντα κακά.

[117] Eustathius, 10 line 9 to 12 line 5.

[118] Eustathius, 154–8; cf. Brand, 160–75.

[119] Eustathius, 146–8.

[120] Eustathius, 152, 4–5.

[121] Eustathius, 130, 1.

[122] Anna, I, 141 line 28 to 142 line 3; Leib gives the name of this ambassador: Urson (142, note 1).

[123] καὶ τὰς ἀρχὰς προύβαλλεν ἐς ἐξώνησιν, ὡς τὰς ὀπώρας οἱ ἀγοραῖοι, 444 lines 6–7.

[124] Cf. Brand, 140, 148, 189 ff.

[125] Nicetas first had the intention to end his work at 1204, 'since it was not right to write on battles the Romans could not win', and he ends with an elaborate description of the capture of Constantinople and an appeal to trust in God (572 line 79 to 582 line 46).

[126] See the excellent study of Brand.

[127] Kindlimann, Sibyll, *Die Eroberung von Konstantinopel als politische Forderung des Westens im Hochmittelalter*. Studien zur Entwicklung der Idee eines lateinischen Kaiserreichs in Byzanz, Zürich 1969. A survey of the ideas about the Fourth Crusade: Queller, Donald E., and Stratton, Susan Jane, 'A Century of Controversy on the Fourth Crusade', *Studies in Medieval and Renaissance History* 6, 1969, 235–77. A reader: Queller, Donald E., *The Latin Conquest of Constantinople*, London–Sydney–Toronto 1971.

[128] Ebels-Hoving, Bunna, *Byzantium in Westerse Ogen*, 1096–1204, Assen 1971.

[129] Tornikès, 343 lines 1–5.

* After this paper was completed, I was able to read for the first time Bernardinello, Silvio, 'Sicilia e Normanni in Teodoro Prodromo', in: *Byzantino-Sicula II, Miscellanea di scritti in memoria di Giuseppe Rossi Taibbi*, = Ist. Sic. di Studi Biz. e Neogreci, Quaderni, 8 =, Palermo, 1975, 51–72. It adds some valuable information, but does not change my view on the Normans.

Henry I and the Anglo-Norman Magnates   C. Warren Hollister

[1] Hollister, C. Warren and Thomas K. Keefe, 'The making of the Angevin Empire', *Journal of British Studies* xii, no. ii, 1973, 4–11. The leading 'Norman' rebel on both these occasions, Amaury de Montfort, was at once count of Evreux in Normandy, a major vassal of the king of France, and uncle of the count of Anjou.

[2] Orderic, vi. 472. Similarly, Suger pictures Normandy at Louis VI's invasion in 1118

as a land 'fruitful from a long peace': *Vie de Louis VI le Gros*, ed. Henri Waquet, Paris 1964, 186; the Norman monk Robert of Torigny describes the period from 1124 through 1135 as one of total peace throughout the duchy: Jumièges, 296; and William of Malmesbury credits Henry with giving Normandy 'a peace such as no age remembers, such as his father himself . . . was never able to effect': *De gestis regum*, ii. 476.

3 Stenton, Sir Frank, *The first century of English feudalism*, 2nd ed., Oxford 1961, 257: from Stenton's Ford Lectures of 1929, first published, under the above title, in 1932. Stenton concludes his analysis of English feudalism by contrasting Henry I, whose magnates were suppressed, with Henry II, whose magnates cooperated willingly with the crown.

4 Southern, Sir Richard, *Medieval humanism and other studies*, Oxford 1970, 218, 231; Brooke, Christopher, *London 800–1216: the shaping of a city*, London 1975, 317.

5 Mason, Emma, 'William Rufus: myth and reality', *Journal of Medieval History* iii, 1977, 15.

6 Corbett, William J., in *Cambridge medieval history*, v. 1926, 508–11. I am drawing here from Hollister, C. Warren, 'Magnates and "curiales" in early Norman England', *Viator* vii, 1977, 63–81.

7 Hollister, 'Magnates and "curiales"', 65 (Table A), with some corrections. The ten wealthiest lay landholders in 1087 (with the value of their tenancies-in-chief expressed in pounds per year) are Odo of Bayeux (3000), Robert of Mortain (2100), Roger of Montgomery (2100), William I of Warenne (1165), Alan of Richmond (1100 + waste), Hugh earl of Chester (800), Richard of Clare (780), Geoffrey of Coutances (780), Geoffrey de Mandeville (780), and Eustace II of Boulogne (770). The ten most frequent lay attestors (excluding William I's wife and sons) are Roger of Montgomery (40), Odo of Bayeux (34), Geoffrey of Coutances (33½—the half being either William I or II), Robert count of Mortain (23), Robert count of Meulan (23), Roger of Beaumont (21), Alan of Richmond (21), Eudo *Dapifer* (16), Hugh earl of Chester (15½), and Richard of Clare (14).

8 I am again drawing from Hollister, 'Magnates and "curiales"', 63–81.

9 Hollister, 'Magnates and "curiales"', 69 (Table B): Robert of Mowbray (2 attestations for Rufus), Hugh of Montgomery (2), Philip of Montgomery (0), Gilbert of Clare (4), William of Eu (0), Roger of Lacy (0), Odo of Champagne (1), Stephen of Aumale (0).

10 Corbett's Class A begins at £750: Corbett, 510–11. For the list of Rufus's major attestors see Hollister, 'Magnates and "curiales"', 76 (Table D).

11 Southern, 231.

12 See Hollister, C. Warren, 'The taming of a turbulent earl: Henry I and William of Warenne', *Réflexions historiques* iii, 1976, 85.

13 Hollister, C. Warren, 'The Anglo-Norman civil war: 1101', *EHR* lxxxviii, 1973, 315–34.

14 Hollister, 'Magnates and "curiales"', 77–80.

15 The figure of 140 is a corrected total, slightly higher than the figures provided in my *EHR* and *Viator* articles. It is based on the following list of Henry's supporters and their attestations for William II: Hugh of Chester (8), Richard of Redvers (1), Robert fitz Hamon (21), Hamo II *Dapifer* (9), Eudo *Dapifer* (37), Henry of

Warwick (8), Robert of Meulan (16), Roger Bigod *dapifer* (28), Urse of Abitôt (12).

[16] Hollister, 'Magnates and "curiales"', 78–79. My figures are £7875 for Curthose's nine, £2620 for Henry's nine.

[17] See Mason, J. F. A., 'Roger de Montgomery and his sons (1067–1102)', *TRHS*, 5th ser., xiii, 1963, 1–28.

[18] Orderic, vi, 30.

[19] Hollister, C. Warren, 'Henry I and Robert Malet', *Viator* iv, 1973, 116–17. He attested nineteen of Henry's surviving charters between 1100 and 1105.

[20] Kaplan, Jonathan D., 'The Pipe Roll of 1130, an English translation and statistical analysis', unpublished Ph.D. dissertation, University of California, Santa Barbara 1971, 203.

[21] For example, Walter Giffard earl of Buckingham, Robert of Ferrers, and Henry count of Eu rarely attest royal charters; Walter Giffard has no danegeld exemptions, and the exemptions for Robert of Ferrers and Henry of Eu are trivial. Stephen of Blois' exemptions drop, inexplicably, from £134 in 1129 to £66 in 1130: *The Pipe Roll of 31 Henry I*, ed. Joseph Hunter, London 1929, *passim*.

[22] The Pipe Roll of 1130 records danegeld exemptions on Roger's lands in excess of £150, indicating at least 1500 demesne hides or, very roughly, £1500 a year. I have classified Roger as a magnate rather than a prelate because the bulk of his landed wealth was clearly non-episcopal: the total value of the bishop of Salisbury's Domesday manors, demesne and enfeoffed, was £580 a year. Cf. William of Malmesbury, *Historia Novella*, ed. K. R. Potter, London 1955, 31: Stephen arrests Roger not as a bishop but as a royal servant and castellan, much as William I had arrested Odo not as bishop of Bayeux but as earl of Kent.

[23] Douglas, David, *William the Conqueror*, London 1964, 89, and more generally 83–104; Le Patourel, John, *Norman Barons*, The Historical Association, Hastings and Bexhill Branch 1966, 3–25; Musset, Lucien, 'L'aristocracie normande au xie siècle', in *La noblesse au moyen âge, xie–xve siècles. Essais à la memoire de Robert Boutruche*, ed. Contamine, Philippe, Paris 1976, 88–94.

[24] The eight Class A magnates in 1125–1135 are Stephen of Richmond, Ranulf earl of Chester, Robert earl of Leicester, William of Warenne, Richard of Clare, Roger earl of Warwick, Hugh Bigod, and Brian fitz Count. Geoffrey of Clinton, with a demesne exemption of £59, may well have enjoyed almost comparable wealth; although Southern regarded him as a middle-rank landholder, the exemption suggests that his demesne alone may have been worth some £600 a year. Corbett's Class A begins at £750, but the figure includes both demesne and enfeoffed manors.

[25] Stephen of Richmond, Ranulf of Chester, Robert of Leicester, William of Warenne, Richard of Clare, Roger of Warwick, and Hugh Bigod.

[26] All but Stephen of Richmond, Richard of Clare and Roger of Warwick.

[27] Sanders, I. J., *English Baronies*, Oxford 1960, 110, 129, 138. Of the twelve Class B barons, at least seven were either *curiales* of Henry I or deeply beholden to him.

[28] Orderic, vi. 234–36; 'Chronica monasterii de Hida', in *Liber monasterii de Hyda*, ed. Edward Edwards, RS 1866, 316–17. See 'De libertate Beccensis monasterii', in *Annales ordinis sancti Benedicti*, ed. Jean Mabillon, Paris 1703–1739, v. 604, placing Roger fitz Richard at Henry's side at the siege of Brionne in 1124. On the honors of Netherwent and Little Dunmow see Sanders, 110–11, 129.

[29] Orderic, vi. 238.

[30] *Liber eliensis*, ed. E. O. Blake, Camden series, iii. 92, London 1962, 226–7.

[31] Hollister, C. Warren, 'The strange death of William Rufus', *Speculum* xlviii, 1973, 646–51; see 647 for the Clare-Giffard genealogy.

[32] This discussion is based on Hollister, 'Taming of a turbulent earl'.

[33] Orderic, vi. 164; by 1150, however, Saint-Saens was back in the hands of Elias's descendants.

[34] *Liber monasterii de Hyda*, 316–17.

[35] Orderic, vi. 222, 304.

[36] Hollister, C. Warren, 'The misfortunes of the Mandevilles', *History* lviii, 1973, 21–4.

[37] The honour of Eudo *Dapifer* escheated at about this time under similar circumstances.

[38] Orderic, vi. 84, 88, 222–4.

[39] *Complete peerage*, iii. 166; vii. 668, 745.

[40] On the vast estates the earls of Chester might have controlled had they made good all their claims, see Jolliffe, J. E. A. *The constitutional history of medieval England*, 4th ed., London 1961, 172. Ranulf seems to have held for a time the lands between Ribble and Mersey that Henry had seized in 1102 from Robert of Bellême's brother, Roger the Poitevin: White, Graeme, 'King Stephen, Duke Henry and Ranulf de Gernons, earl of Chester', *EHR* xci, 1976, 558.

[41] Eleven attestations in the eight years between his advancement in 1121 and his death in 1129: *Regesta regum anglo-normannorum*, ed. H. W. C. Davis *et al.*, Oxford, 1913–1969, ii, nos. 1243–1602 *passim*.

[42] Simeon of Durham, *Opera omnia*, ed. Thomas Arnold, RS, ii. 1885, 267–8.

[43] *P. R. 31 Henry I*, 110. Young Ranulf received danegeld exemptions on 210 demesne hides in addition to his Chester lands, which owed no geld.

[44] Keefe, Thomas K., 'Feudal surveys and the assessment of knight service under Henry II and his sons', unpublished Ph.D. dissertation, University of California, Santa Barbara, 1978, 189–241: William de Mandeville, for example, was assessed £183 over twenty-two years in scutages, aids, pleas, and fines, but paid only £1 of this sum into the exchequer; the remainder was eventually pardoned.

[45] Stenton, 222, from *P.R. 31 Henry I*, 103.

[46] Orderic, v. 298; cf. Worcester, ii. 57.

[47] Sanders, 46–7; *Complete peerage*, ix. 575–9.

[48] Fox, Levi, 'The honour and earldom of Leicester: origin and descent, 1066–1399', *EHR* liv, 1939, 385–8; Mason, J. F. A., *William the First and the Sussex rapes*, The Historical Association, Hastings and Bexhill Branch 1966, 20.

[49] In 1172; no earlier enfeoffment data exist for the Beaumont earldom of Leicester.

[50] See Walker, Barbara M., 'King Henry I's "old men"', *Journal of British Studies*, viii, no. i, 1968, 3–5; Le Patourel, 12–15.

[51] White, G. H., 'The career of Waleran, count of Meulan and earl of Worcester (1104–66)', *TRHS*, 4th ser., xvii, 1934, 19–48.

[52] *P. R. 31 Henry I*, 13–16 and *passim*.

[53] *Regesta*, ii. nos. 1607, 1688–90, 1693, 1699, 1702, 1711. Waleran was at Henry's deathbed in 1135 and was one of five *comites* who bore the king's body from Lyons-la-Forêt to Rouen.

[54] Southern, 220.

[55] On Robert of Gloucester see *Earldom of Gloucester Charters*, ed. Robert B. Patterson, Oxford 1973, 3.

[56] Davis, R. H. C., *King Stephen, 1135–1154*, London 1967, 7–9.

[57] Southern, 213.

[58] William I's third 'super-magnate' was likewise connected, though remotely, with the ducal family: *Complete peerage*, xi. 682–3.

[59] De Aragon, Gena, 'The growth of secure inheritance in Norman England', unpublished paper, University of California, Santa Barbara, 1978.

[60] On this and what follows see Hollister, C. Warren, 'The Anglo-Norman succession debate of 1126: prelude to Stephen's Anarchy', *Journal of Medieval History*, i, no. i, 1975, 19–41; bad typesetting and proofreading made a shambles of the genealogical chart on 20–1.

[61] See Hollister and Keefe, 'Making of the Angevin Empire', 16.

[62] King, Edmund, 'King Stephen and the Anglo-Norman aristocracy', *History* lix, 1974, 192.

[63] Orderic, v. 296.

Anglo-Norman as a Spoken Language   M. D. Legge

[1] Woodbine, George E, *Four Thirteenth-Century Law Tracts*, Yale and Oxford, 1910.

[2] Woodbine, *Speculum* xviii, 1943, 395–436.

[3] Rothwell, William, 'The teaching of French in Medieval England,' *Modern Language Review* lxiii, 1968, 37–46; 'The rôle of French in 13th Century England', *Bulletin of the John Rylands Library* lviii, 1976, 445–66; 'A quelle Epoque a-t'on cessé de parler français en Angleterre?' *Mélanges Ch. Camproux* ii, Montpellier, 1978, p. 1075–89.

[4] Guernes de Pont-Sainte-Maxence, *La Vie de Saint Thomas Becket*, ed. Walberg, E., Paris 1936, 1.6165.

[5] Legge, M. D. *Anglo-Norman Literature and its Background*, Oxford 1971, 63, 64.

[6] Philippe de Beaumanoir, *Oeuvres Poétiques*, ii. Ed. Suchier, H., Société des anciens Textes français, 1885.

[7] Montaiglon A. et Raymaud G., *Fabliaux*, Paris 1877. 4–9.

[8] Ritchie, R-L. G., *The Normans in England before Edward the Confessor*, Exeter 1948.

[9] Rothwell, *Bulletin* 448.

[10] *L'Histoire de Guillaume le Maréchal*, ed. P-Meyer, i. ll. 744–6, Soc. de l'hist. de France, 1891.

[11] Quoted Bateson, M., *Mediaeval England*, London 1905, 175.

[12] Giraldus Cambrensis, *Opera*, R.S.i. 1861, 21a.

[13] North, Roger, *Lives of the Norths*, i. 4972, F24.

[14] Froissart, Jehan, ed. Kervyn de Lettenhove xv, Brussels 1891, 115.

[15] Lancaster, Henry of, *Le Livre de Seyntz Medicines*, ed. Arnould, E. G. Anglo-Norman Text Society, ii, Oxford, 1940.

[16] Clark, Cecily, 'Women's names in Post-Conquest England', *Speculum* liii, 1978, 223–51.

[17] NcNeill, F. Manion, *Iona*, London and Glasgow 1959, 60.

[18] *Die Anglonormanische Boeve de Haumtone*, ed. Stimming, Albert, Halle 1899, ll.326–36.

[19] Wilson, R. M., 'English and French in England, 1100–1300', *Histag* xxviii, 1943, pp. 37–60.

[20] Wilson, 53.

[21] Fordun, John of, *Cronica Gentis Scottorum*, ed. Skere, W. F., Edinburgh 1871, i. 326, 314.

[22] Wilson, 53.

[23] Giraldus Cambrensis, 218.

[24] Froissart, xv, 167, xvi, 147.

[25] Walsingham, Thomas, *Chronicles*, R.S. 1843, ii. 273.

[26] P.R.O., *Chancery Warrants*, I, 1350, No. 4B.

[27] *Le Traité de Walter de Bibbesworth sur la Langue française*, ed. Owen, Annie, Paris 1929. Cf. Baugh, Albert C. 'The Date of Walter of Bibbesworth's Traité' *Festschrift fur Walter Fischer*, Heidelberg 1959, 21–33.

[28] Ed. Wright, W. A., Roxburghe Club, 1909.

[29] *The Anglo-Norman Element in our Vocabulary*, Manchester 1944, 10.

[30] I. 33.

[31] Wilson, 'English and French', 49.

[32] Higden, Ranulf, *Polychronicon*, R.S. ii. 160.

[33] *Li cumpoz Philippe de Tham*, ed, Mall, E., Strasbourg 1873.

[34] *Orthographia Gallica*, ed. Sturzingen, J., Heilbonn 1884.

[35] Arnold, I. D. O., 'Thomas Sampson and the *Orthographia Gallica*', *Medium AEvum* vi, 1937, 193–210.

[36] Legge, M. D., 'William of Kingsmill', *Studies presented to M. K. Pope*, Manchester 1939, 141–6.

[37] Pope, M. K., 'The Tractatus Orthographiae of T. H. Parisii Studentis', *Modern Language Review* v, 1910, 185–93.

[38] Gibson, S. *Statuta Antiqua*, Oxford 1931, 171.

[39] Higden, *Polychronicon*, 160–1.

[40] Higden, *Polychronicon*, 161.

[41] Gessler, J. *La Manière de Langage*, Brussels, Paris, Louvain, 1934.

[42] Lambley, K., *The French Language in England*, Manchester 1920, 40.

[43] *The Chronicle of Jocelin of Brakelond*, ed. Butler, H. E., Medieval Classics, 1940, 40. 128, 129.

[44] *Magna Vita Sancti Huganis*, ed. Douie, D. L. and Farmer H., Medieval Classics, ii. 1962, 7, 117.

[45] *Les Contes Moralisés de Nicole Bozon*, ed. Toulmin Smith, L. and Meyer, P., Société des anciens textes français, 1889.

[46] Heton, Sir Thomas Gray of, *Scalacronica*, ed. Stevenson, Y., Maitland Club, 1836.

[47] *The Oak Book of Southampton*, ed. Studer, P. Southampton Record Society, 1910, 1911.

[48] *Register of Daniel Rough*, ed. Murray, K. M. E., Kent Records xvi, 1945.

[49] Goebl, H., *Die Normandische Urkundensprache*, Vienna 1970.

[50] Woodbine, *Speculum*, 431.

[51] *Year Books of 1 and 2 Edward II*, edited Maitland, F. W., Selden Society xvii, 1903, xiii, xvi, 29.

Magnates, Curiales and the Wheel of Fortune   Emma Mason

[1] I am grateful to Professor David Ross for his advice on literary matters, and to Penelope and Andrew Wallis for assistance in visiting sites in Normandy.

[2] As in the case of the chamberlain William Mauduit. *ASC*, tr. Whitelock, D. with Douglas, D. C. and Tucker, S. I. London 1961, 200.

[3] Murray, Alexander, *Reason and Society in the middle ages*, Oxford 1978, 100.

[4] Orderic, vi. 242.

[5] Pickering, F. P., *Literature and art in the middle ages*, London 1970, 185–6, 196; plate 1b, facing 202.

[6] Le Patourel, John, *Norman Barons*, Hastings and Bexhill 1966, 21.

[7] Murray, 126–7, 136.

[8] Douglas, David, 'The "Song of Roland" and the Norman conquest of England', *French Studies* xvi, 1960, 110.

[9] Davis, R. H. C., *The Normans and their myth*, London 1976, 12, 23; Douglas, David, 'The rise of Normandy', *Proceedings of the British Academy* xxxiii, 1947, 120.

[10] Davis, 54.

[11] *The Deeds of the Franks*, ed. and tr. Hill, Rosalind, London 1962, 61.

[12] Davis, R. H. C., 'The Carmen de Hastingae Proelio', *EHR* xciii, 1978, 261.

[13] *Carmen*, 36, 38. The significance of the burial is discussed by the editors, xliii–xlv, but against this should be set the opinion of Davis, 'Carmen de Hastingae', 261, that the poem is not a contemporary record, but a literary work dating from the third or fourth decade of the twelfth century.

[14] Le Patourel, John, *The Norman Empire*, Oxford 1976, 254n–55n.

[15] Douglas, David, *William the Conqueror*, London 1964, 283.

[16] Le Patourel, *Norman Empire*, 191.

[17] Douglas, *William the Conqueror*, 90.

[18] Murray, 336–7.

[19] Mason, Emma, 'Timeo barones et dona ferentes', *Studies in Church History* xv, Oxford 1978, 61–75.

[20] Mason, 'Timeo barones', 75.

[21] *The Song of Roland*, tr. Owen, D. D. R., London 1972, laisse 141, lines 1880–82.

[22] Mason, 'Timeo barones', 73–4.

[23] *The Complete Peerage*, ed. Cokayne, G. E., Gibbs, V., and others, 13 vols. in 14, London 1910–1959, xii (i). 757–74 (Tosny), and xii (ii). 357–67 (Warwick).

[24] Douglas, *William the Conqueror*, 92.

[25] Orderic, ii. 140, 218–20.

[26] Douglas, *William the Conqueror*, 269.

[27] Douglas, 'The rise of Normandy', 115, 127.

[28] Douglas, 'The rise of Normandy', 116, 128.

[29] Orderic, ii. 10; Douglas, 'Song of Roland', 110.

[30] Orderic, iii. 124; v. 26, 268.

[31] Douglas, 'Song of Roland', 110.

[32] Orderic, ii. 40.

[33] Douglas, 'Song of Roland', 111.

[34] *Song of Roland*, laisse 12, line 174; laisse 14, line 208.

[35] Klein, Karen, *The partisan voice*, The Hague 1971, 146.

[36] Klein, 146, 152.

[37] Douglas, 'Song of Roland', 110.

[38] Orderic, iv. 212.

[39] *Njal's Saga*, tr. Magnusson, Magnus, and Pálsson, Hermann, Harmondsworth 1960, 97–119.

[40] Orderic, iii. 128; iv. 212–4.

[41] *The Vinland Sagas*, tr. Magnusson, Magnus, and Pálsson, Hermann, Harmondsworth 1965, 37–8.

[42] Orderic, iii. 124, 126; *Calendar of documents preserved in France*, ed. Round, J. H., London 1899, no. 625.

[43] Matthew, Donald, *The Norman monasteries and their English possessions*, Oxford 1962, 32, 139.

[44] Mason, Emma, 'English tithe income of Norman religious houses', *BIHR* xlviii, 1975, 91–4.

[45] Mason, 'Timeo barones', 61–75.

[46] Loyn, H. R., *The Norman conquest*, London 1965, 35.

[47] Orderic, ii. 90, 104–6.

[48] Orderic, ii. 140.

[49] Orderic, ii. 140, 218–20.

[50] *Njal's Saga*, 347–8.

[51] *Domesday Book*, i. folios 62v, 138, 168, 176, 183 r–v; ii. folios 91, 235.

[52] Stenton, F. M., *The first century of English feudalism 1066–1166*, 2nd edn., Oxford 1961, 64.

[53] Stenton, 64, 192, 281.

[54] Orderic, vi. 54.

[55] *The red book of the Exchequer*, ed. Hall, H., 3 vols., RS, London 1896, ii. 642. An inquest held in 1264 revealed 52 fees in England, but there were probably more than this: *Calendar of inquisitions post mortem*, i. no. 588.

[56] *The Beauchamp cartulary*, ed. Mason, Emma, Pipe Roll Society, ns, xliii, 1980, no. 360.

[57] Lega-Weekes, E., 'Neighbours of North Wyke', ii, *Report and trans. of the Devonshire Association* xxxiv, 1902, 589–90.

[58] Orderic, iv. 216–8.

[59] Orderic, iii. 128.

[60] Orderic, vi. 524–5; *Book of Fees*, i. 134.

[61] Orderic, vi. 444–6, 456–8, 462–4, 474, 480, 484.

[62] Orderic, vi. 524.

[63] *Beauchamp cartulary*, nos. 367, 370.

[64] *Beauchamp cartulary*, nos. 360, 373.

[65] Mason, Emma, 'The resources of the earldom of Warwick in the thirteenth century', *Midland History* iii, 1975, 74.

[66] Douglas, *William the Conqueror*, 86; Le Patourel, *Norman Barons*, 12–13.

[67] Le Patourel, *Norman Barons*, 13.

[68] Orderic, ii. 40.

[69] Orderic, ii. 140.

[70] Le Patourel, *Norman Barons*, 13–14.

[71] Douglas, *William the Conqueror*, 87; Orderic ii. 218–20.

[72] Orderic, ii. 218.

[73] Le Patourel, *Norman Barons*, 14–15.

[74] *VCH Warwickshire*, i. 277–8. 310–25, 332–5.

[75] Le Patourel, *Norman Barons*, 15.

[76] Murray, 86.

[77] Le Patourel, *Norman Barons*, 15–16.

[78] *Gesta Stephani*, ed. and tr. Potter, K. R., new intr. by Davis, R. H. C., Oxford 1976, 116–8.

[79] *Regesta Regum Anglo-Normannorum*, iii. ed. Cronne, H. A., and Davis, R. H. C., Oxford 1968, no. 597.

[80] *Beauchamp cartulary*, no. 285.

[81] Southern, R. W., 'The place of Henry I in English history', *Proceedings of the British Academy* xlviii, 1962, 136–40.

[82] *Historia Novella*, xxv; Poole, A. L., *From Domesday Book to Magna Carta*, Oxford 1951, 151–3.

[83] *Gesta Stephani*, 234.

[84] White, G. H., 'The career of Waleran, count of Meulan and earl of Worcester (1104–66)', *TRHS* 4th ser. xvii, 1934, 43.

[85] Hollister, C. Warren, 'Henry I and Robert Malet', *Viator* 4, 1973, 121; and 'Magnates and "curiales" in early Norman England', *Viator* 8, 1977, 80–81.

[86] Murray, 83–4.

[87] Mason, Emma, 'The Mauduits and their chamberlainship of the Exchequer', *BIHR* xlix, 1976, 15.

[88] Murray, 120–22, 124, 136–7.

[89] Murray, 272.

[90] Mason, Emma, 'William Rufus: myth and reality', *Journal of medieval history* iii, 1977, 18.

[91] Klein, 147.

[92] Lally, J. E., 'Secular patronage at the court of King Henry II', *BIHR* xlix, 1976, 159–84.

[93] *Calendar of documents preserved in France*, nos. 322, 332.

[94] *Beauchamp cartulary*, nos. 160, 167, 180–82. A certain Malconductus of Anglesqueville (Seine Inférieure) attests, about 1080, a charter for Fécamp. His connection, if any, with the Mauduit family, is unclear.

[95] Tout, T. F., *Chapters in the administrative history of medieval England*, i.

Manchester 1928, 75; Round, J. H., *The commune of London*, Westminster 1899, 81–5.

[96] Orderic, iv. 172.

[97] *The Song of Roland*, laisse 51, lines 642–6.

[98] Douglas, 'The Song of Roland', 100.

[99] *VCH Wiltshire*, ii. 157.

[100] *Beauchamp cartulary*, no. 173.

[101] Poole, R. L., *The Exchequer in the twelfth century*, London 1912, 35.

[102] *VCH Berkshire*, i. 338; *Chronicon monasterii de Abingdon*, ed. Stevenson, J., 2 vols., RS, London 1858, ii. 5, 135.

[103] *Beauchamp cartulary*, no. 159.

[104] *The great roll of the pipe for the thirty first year of the reign of Henry I*, ed. Hunter, J., London 1833, 37.

[105] *Pipe roll 31 Henry I*, 38; *Beauchamp cartulary*, no. 167.

[106] *Pipe roll 31 Henry I*, 37.

[107] Orderic, vi. 304; *Symeonis monachi opera omnia*, ed. Arnold, T., 2 vols., RS, London 1882–1885, ii. 259.

[108] Mason, 'The Mauduits and their chamberlainship', 2–3.

[109] *Beauchamp cartulary*, nos. 161–3.

[110] *Pipe roll 31 Henry I*, 134.

[111] *Dialogus de Scaccario and Constitutio Domus Regis*, ed. Johnson, C., London 1950, 133.

[112] *Beauchamp cartulary*, no. 164.

[113] *Beauchamp cartulary*, no. 164.

[114] Mason, 'The Mauduits and their chamberlainship', 17.

[115] *VCH Buckinghamshire*, i. 272; *VCH Northamptonshire*, i. 341–2, 354, 358, 374–6.

[116] *Pipe roll 12 John*, 192.

[117] *Regesta* iii. nos. 44, 492, 495–6; *Pipe roll 5 Henry II*, 52; *Pipe roll 6 Henry II*, 37; *Cartae Antiquae rolls 11–20*, ed. Davies, J. C., Pipe Roll Society, ns xxxiii, London 1960, no. 411.

[118] *Beauchamp cartulary*, no. 219.

[119] *Beauchamp cartulary*, nos. 166–7, 176.

[120] *Red book of the Exchequer*, i. 313–4; *Liber Niger Scaccarii*, ed. Hearne, T., London 1774, 191–2.

[121] Murray, 206, 209.

[122] *Beauchamp cartulary*, nos. 166–7.

[123] Mason, 'The Mauduits and their chamberlainship', 5.

[124] *ASC*, 200.

[125] *Beauchamp cartulary*, no. 177.

[126] *Gesta Stephani*, 150–52.

[127] Mason, 'The Mauduits and their chamberlainship', 2–3. There is detailed discussion of these matters by Emma Mason, 'The king, the chamberlain and Southwick priory', *BIHR*, liii, 1980.

[128] *Beauchamp cartulary*, no. 167.

[129] Mason, 'The Mauduits and their chamberlainship', 10–11.

[130] Davis, 24.

[131] *Calendar of documents preserved in France*, no. 568.

[1] Reynolds, Susan, *Introduction to the history of the English medieval town*, Oxford 1977, 42.

[2] Beresford, M., *New towns of the middle ages*, London 1967, 61–2, 216.

[3] Maitland, F. W., *Domesday book and beyond*, London 1960 reprint, 213.

[4] Clarke, Helen and Carter, A., *Excavations in King's Lynn, 1963–70*, Society for Medieval Archaeology, monograph 7, London 1977; Parker, Vanessa, *The making of King's Lynn*, London and Chichester 1971.

[5] Above pp. 21 ff.

[6] Darby, H. C., *The Domesday geography of eastern England*, Cambridge 1952, 134–6; Owen, A. E. B., 'Medieval saltmaking and the coastline in Cambridgeshire and north-west Norfolk', in K. De Brisay, *Salt, the study of an ancient industry*, Colchester 1975.

[7] Baker, F. T., Hallam, S. J., Rudkin, E. H., Owen, D. M., Hallam, H. E., 'Iron-age, Romano-British, and medieval salt industry in Lincolnshire', *Reports and Papers of the Lincolnshire architectural and archaeological society*, ns viii, 1960.

[8] Darby, H. C., *The medieval fenland*, Cambridge 1940, 94–8.

[9] Lopez, R. S., *The Commercial revolution of the middle ages, 950–1350*, Cambridge 1976, 56–84, 113; Sawyer, P. H., 'The wealth of England in the eleventh century' TRHS, 5th ser., xv, 145–64.

[10] On the medieval need for salt see especially, Bridbury, A. R., *England and the salt trade in the later middle ages*, Oxford 1955.

[11] Darby, *Domesday geography*, 144–5.

[12] Hallam, H. E., *New lands of Elloe*, Leicester 1954.

[13] *VCH Norfolk*, ii. 54, 68, 114, 130, 161.

[14] Dodwell, B., *The charters of Norwich cathedral priory*, Pipe Roll Society, ns xl, 1974, no. 107.

[15] Dodwell, no. 17, where the suggested date is 1107 × 1116; Johnson, C. and Cronne, H. A., *Regesta regum Anglo-Normannorum*, ii. Oxford 1956, 762, date this as ?1106.

[16] Johnson and Cronne, 911 and p. 322.

[17] Professor Eleanor Searle has suggested to me that the word *misteria* might be used for tithing pledge groups.

[18] BL ms. Cotton Titus C viii, fol. 20v.

[19] Blomefield, F., ed. Parkin, C., *An essay towards a topographical history of Norfolk*, Norwich 1805–10, viii. 486.

[20] Assize roll 6–14 Edward I, m. 87v, cited in *Norfolk antiquarian miscellany* iii, Norwich 1887, 603–18.

[21] Johnson and Cronne, 1853.

[22] Dodwell, no. 123.

[23] Dodwell, no. 124.

[24] *The great roll of the pipe . . . 1166–1167*, Pipe Roll Society xi, 1889, 20–31. BL ms. additional 47784, nos. 411, 416; ms. Harley 2110, fols. 80 and 80v; ms. additional 46353, no. xxiv; ms. Cotton Titus C viii, fols. 53v, 100v.

[25] This section is based on a number of detailed topographical charters among the archives of the Dean and Chapter of Norwich, and in the cartularies of Ely,

Dereham, Blackborough, Coxford, Castleacre, Walsingham, and Wymondham, and on surviving pleas rolls from the two courts, all of which I hope to include in my projected volume of documents.

[26] Beresford, 336; Carus-Wilson, E. M., 'The medieval trade of the ports of the Wash', *Medieval Archaeology* vi–vii, 1962–3, 183–4.

The Abbey of the Conquerors: Defensive Enfeoffment and Economic Development in Anglo-Norman England   Eleanor M. Searle

[1] See Searle, Eleanor, *Lordship and Community, Battle Abbey and its Banlieu 1066–1538*, Pontifical Institute of Medieval Studies, Toronto 1974, esp. 21–36.

[2] Brown, R. Allen, *Origins of English Feudalism*, George Allen and Unwin, London 1973.

[3] Milsom, S. F. C., *The Legal Framework of English Feudalism*, Cambridge 1976.

[4] Brenner, Robert, 'Agrarian Class Structure and Economic Development in Pre-Industrial Europe': *Past and Present*, no. 70 (1976), 30–75. For the Symposium that followed, see *Past and Present*, no. 78, pp. 24–55, no. 79, pp. 55–69, no. 80, pp. 3–65.

[5] *The Chronicle of Battle Abbey*, ed. Searle, Eleanor, Oxford Medieval Texts, Clarendon Press, Oxford 1980, 36, 66.

[6] Searle, Eleanor, 'Battle Abbey and Exemption: the Forged Charters', *EHR*, lxxxiii, 1968, 454–6. The charter, BL Harleian Ch. 83 A 12, is printed there, 469–70.

[7] Saltman, A., *Theobald Archbishop of Canterbury*, London 1956, 56–64, has the account of the monks' quarrel with their archbishop. An attempt to make both Battle and Christ Church exempt can be seen in the comparison drawn between them in the charter cited in n. 6 above.

[8] *Chron.*, 66 and charter cited: 'ad eorum corda roboranda'.

[9] Searle, 'Forged Charters', 473: 'illa que mihi coronam tribuit et per quam viget decet nostri regiminis'.

[10] *Chron.*, 36. Wace, ll. 7499–530.

[11] *Chron.*, 178–82.

[12] *Chron.*, 38.

[13] See Morton, Catherine, 'Pope Alexander and the Norman Conquest', *Latomus*, xxxiv, 1975. The Penitentiary is printed there, 381–2. See also Brooke, C. N. L., 'Archbishop Lanfranc, the English Bishops and the Council of London of 1075', *Studia Gratiana*, xii, 1967, 36–60.

[14] The monks were quite clear about their duty: they were a 'cenobium, quo Dei servi congregarentur pro omnium illorumque nominatim qui in eodem bello occumberent salute ... qui locus refugii et auxilii omnibus esset, quatinus iugi bonorum operum instantia commissa illic effusi cruoris redimeretur'. *Chron.*, 66.

[15] See J. H. Round's essay in *VCH. Sussex* i. esp. 354. See also Mason, J. F. A., 'The Rapes of Sussex and the Norman Conquest', *Sussex Archaeological Coll.*, 1964, 68–93 and refs. there.

[16] Mason, 'Rapes of Sussex', 76–7.

[17] The new rape followed the valley of the Adur, and was thus squeezed between Arundel and Pevensey rapes.

[18] Searle, *Lordship*, 201–5; *Chron.*, 118, 128.

[19] For settlement and the court of the rape, see Searle, *Lordship*, 50–4, 201–3, and refs. there.

[20] For Battle's manors, see Searle, *Lordship*, Appendix 1, 447.

[21] *Chron.*, 52–8. For an analysis of these, see Searle, *Lordship*, 69–88, and Appendix 12, 465–6, and Clark, Cecily, above.

[22] For the twelfth-century demesne, see *Chron.*, 60–4; Searle, *Lordship*, 55–9. I exclude the abbey park from both estimates.

[23] Milsom, esp. chaps. 1, 2.

[24] *Chron.*, 60. *Red Book of the Exchequer* (RS) ii. 624.

[25] *Chron.*, 32.

[26] *Chron.*, 118, 210.

[27] For the services due in the early twelfth century and the mid-thirteenth, see Searle, *Lordship*, 59–61, 167–74.

[28] *Chron.*, 212–18.

[29] Searle, *Lordship*, 210 and nn. 47, 48.

[30] *Chron.*, 212.

[31] *Chron.*, 212–18.

[32] Searle, *Lordship*, 63–8.

[33] Searle, *Lordship*, 299–303.

[34] Searle, *Lordship*, 272–86.

[35] Chambers, J. D., and Mingay, G. E., *The Agricultural Revolution 1750–1880*, New York 1966, 4. Kerridge, E., *The Agricultural Revolution*, London 1967, esp. 181–221.

[36] Searle, E., and Burghart, J., 'The Defense of England and the Peasants' Revolt', *Viator* iii, 1972, 365–88. For Battle's rôle in coastal defence, see Searle, *Lordship*, 338–46, and for another coastal abbey, cf. Hockey, S. F., *Quarr Abbey and its Lands 1132–1631*, Leicester 1970, 131–55.

[37] *Calendar of Patent Rolls 1338–40*, 92.

[38] Thomas of Walsingham, *Historia Anglicana* (RS), 341–2.

[39] The Huntington Library, Battle Abbey Collection, Almoners' Accounts, 1381–2. The abbot was said to have gone 'circa recreandum'. For Arundel, see *Cal. Pat. Rolls 1381–5*, 259.

[40] BL ms. Harley 3586.

Index

SHL
WITHDRAWN
UNIV